Southeast Asia in the 1990s

Authoritarianism, democracy and capitalism

Edited by
Kevin Hewison
Richard Robison
Garry Rodan

ALLEN & UNWIN

© Kevin Hewison, Richard Robison, Garry Rodan, 1993
This book is copyright under the Berne Convention.
No reproduction without permission. All rights reserved.

First published 1993
Allen & Unwin Pty Ltd
9 Atchison Street, St Leonards, NSW 2065 Australia

National Library of Australia
Cataloguing-in-Publication entry:

Southeast Asia in the 1990s: authoritarianism, democracy and capitalism.

Includes bibliographies.
ISBN 1 86373 230 6.

1. Asia, Southeastern—Politics and government—1945– . 2. Asia,
Southeastern—Economic policy. I. Hewison, Kevin J. II. Robison,
Richard, 1943– . III. Rodan, Garry.

320.959

Set in 10/12 Times by DOCUPRO, Sydney
Printed by Chong Moh Offset Printers, Singapore

10 9 8 7 6 5 4 3 2 1

Contents

Acknowledgments

The editors wish to express their gratitude to all of those who have contributed to the completion of this collection. Beth Leslie assisted with the copy-editing of all papers and made many useful suggestions. She also assisted in the preparation of the data sheets appearing at the beginning of each country study. The maps were drawn by the staff of the Educational Services and Teaching Resources Unit at Murdoch University. Murdoch University's Asia Research Centre provided assistance for the editors and was supportive in seeing the book through its final stages to completion. In addition, the Politics Programme at Murdoch University provided considerable encouragement.

Contributors

Melanie Beresford studied politics and economics at the Universities of Adelaide and Cambridge, and is presently a Senior Lecturer at the University of Wollongong. In addition to being a member of the editorial board of *Journal of Contemporary Asia*, she has authored and co-authored a number of publications including *Manual of Political Economy* (Karrel), *Vietnam: Politics, Economics and Society* (Frances Pinter), and *National Unification and Economic Development in Vietnam* (Macmillan). She has also written for a number of academic journals including *Journal of Contemporary Asia* and *Contemporary Southeast Asia*.

Harold Crouch is a Senior Fellow in the Department of Political and Social Change, Research School of Pacific Studies, Australian National University. Prior to taking up this appointment he was at the National University of Malaysia. He is the author of numerous publications on Southeast Asian politics, and especially Indonesia and Malaysia. Among his best known works are *The Army and Politics in Indonesia* (Cornell University Press) and *Domestic Political Structures and Regional Co-operation* (Institute of Southeast Asian Studies). He is a frequent contributor to academic journals.

Geoffrey C. Gunn, who completed his PhD at Monash University, is now a Senior Lecturer in Southeast Asian History at Universiti Brunei Darussalam. Prior to taking up this appointment he taught at universities in Libya, Singapore and Australia. He is the author of *Political Struggles in Laos (1930-1954)* (DK Books), *Rebellion in Laos: Peasant and Politics in a Colonial Backwater* (Westview), and co-author of *Cambodia Watching Downunder* (IAS). He has also had articles published in academic journals including *Journal of the Siam Society, Journal of Contemporary Asia* and *Asian Survey*.

Kevin Hewison is a Lecturer in Politics at Murdoch University and a Fellow of the Asia Research Centre. With a PhD from Murdoch University, he has held positions at universities in Australia, Papua New Guinea, and Thailand and has been a consultant to a number of agencies in Thailand and the Lao PDR. His publications include *Bankers and Bureaucrats* (Yale), *Power and Politics in Thailand* (Journal of Contemporary Asia Publishers), (with Seri Phongphit) *Village Life in Thailand: Culture and Transition in the Northeast* (Mooban Press), and the edited collection *Southeast Asia in the 1980s*. He has published in academic journals, including *Journal of Contemporary Asia, Asian Survey, Australian Outlook, Bulletin of Concerned Asian Scholars, Revue Tiers Monde*, and *Southeast Asian Journal of Social Science*.

Jane Hutchison is an Associate Lecturer in Politics in the School of Social Sciences at Murdoch University, where she is completing her PhD on the labour process in the Philippine garments industry. She has written for the *Journal of Contemporary Asia*.

Richard Robison received his PhD from Sydney University in 1979. He is now Professor of Southeast Asian Studies and Deputy Director of the Asian Research Centre at Murdoch University. He has written and edited several books including *Indonesia: The Rise of Capital* (Allen & Unwin), *Power and Economy in Suharto's Indonesia* (Journal of Contemporary Asia Press), *Southeast Asia* (Routledge & Kegan Paul) and *Southeast Asia in the 1980s* (Allen & Unwin). In addition he is a regular contributor to journals including *Journal of Contemporary Asia, Australian Outlook, Revue Tiers Monde, World Politics* and *Bulletin of Concerned Asian Scholars*.

Garry Rodan completed his PhD in 1986 at Murdoch University, where he is a Lecturer in Politics in the School of Social Sciences, and a Fellow of the Asia Research Centre. He is the author of *The Political Economy of Singapore's Industrialization* (Macmillan and St Martin's Press), and editor of the forthcoming *Singapore Changes Guard* (Longman Cheshire). He has also published articles in various journals, including *Bulletin of Concerned Asian Scholars, Politics* and *Australian Outlook*, as well as chapters in a range of books on the politics of economic development in Southeast Asia and Australia.

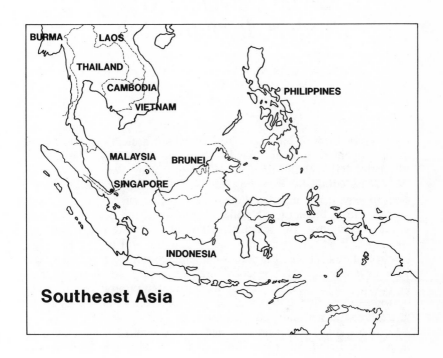

BURMA LAOS

THAILAND

CAMBODIA

VIETNAM

PHILIPPINES

MALAYSIA BRUNEI

SINGAPORE

INDONESIA

Southeast Asia

1 Introduction: Changing forms of state power in Southeast Asia
Kevin Hewison, Garry Rodan, Richard Robison

Any original book, but especially an edited collection, takes time to put together, and this one has been no exception. The editors originally felt that the time was right to update *Southeast Asia in the 1980s*, edited by Robison, Hewison and Higgott (1987). However, it was soon decided that a new collection would be more useful, with a focus on the political aspects of the Southeast Asian political economy. The reasons for this choice were many, but two stand out. First, the pace of social, economic and political change has been rapid, almost breakneck in some countries in recent years, so a new assessment was considered necessary. Most significant, however, was the second reason, the substantial progress being made by forces identified as 'democratic', not only in Southeast Asia, but in Eastern Europe and Latin America.

Certainly more representative institutions seemed to be emerging in many parts of Southeast Asia: in the Philippines, Marcos was gone, and vigorous (some would say vociferous) debate characterised politics there; Thailand was moving toward a more representative political system, and 1988 saw the first elected prime minister since 1976; in Singapore, Lee Kuan Yew finally retired from the prime ministership, handing over to the second generation of leaders; there was a succession and openness debate in Indonesia; and there were impending elections in Indonesia, the Philippines and Singapore. Even the more insulated Indochinese nations were being influenced by the breakdown of Stalinism in Eastern Europe, and being forced to at least consider political change.

While many saw these changes as being positive influences, it must be recognised that challenges to authoritarianism are not always successful. This was emphatically illustrated in the crushing of China's democracy movement and in Burma where the manic military regime refused to acknowledge the election victory of the civilian opposition. In both cases authoritarian rule was confirmed

2

in a brutal and decisive manner. Nor does the unravelling of authoritarian regimes necessarily lead to a democratic solution; the experience of eastern Europe has clearly shown that such developments have re-awakened anti-democratic nationalist movements and neofascist sentiments.

The organising theme which emerged from these observations was to ask whether there was a shift taking place from authoritarianism to democratic forms in Southeast Asia. This began with a survey of the various theoretical concerns involved in the issues of authoritarianism, democracy and the nature of transitions from one to the other. Then, these themes were to be examined in the context of various Southeast Asian nation-states. Of course these theoretical issues are not new ones in political studies, but recent discussions of democracy and authoritarianism have gained much impetus from a renewed theoretical interest. As Held (1991: 876) has noted, this renewed theoretical attention has been marked by a striking convergence of perspective among theorists interested in democracy, as

> . . . non-Marxists have come to appreciate the limitations placed on
> democratic life . . . [and] Marxist work has undertaken a reappraisal
> of liberal representative institutions and affirmed that state activity
> has to be partly understood in relation to the dynamics of electoral
> processes, changing patterns of interest constellations, and the
> competitive pressures of groups. . .

Recent corporatist theory may also be seen as falling into this category of convergence (cf. Cawson 1986). In Southeast Asian studies, research influenced by neo-pluralism and corporatism, including Anek (1992) and MacIntyre (1990a,b), have suggested useful avenues for new inquiry on the relationship between business and government in Southeast Asia. However, when it comes to the question of the transition to democratic or parliamentary forms, these studies suggest that because business people play greater and more direct roles in the political sphere, democratic reform is more likely. Unfortunately this is a crudely instrumentalist position, and offers few insights into the democratisation question.

Of more significance in approaching questions related to passage from authoritarianism and the rise of democratic forms, especially in industrialising nations, has been the *Transitions* debate (cf. O'Donnell & Schmitter, 1986a,b; O'Donnell, Schmitter & Whitehead 1986). In Chapter 2 the editors examine some of the themes that have emerged from this recent literature, and link it to earlier debates within modernisation and dependency theory.

The often unacknowledged question lurking behind the debate is whether changing socio-economic conditions, including shifts to high levels of capital accumulation and the development of a strong capitalist class, bring about structural tensions within authoritarian regimes which may lead to a democratic transition. A related question is whether these authoritarian structures, which have often involved hijacking of the state apparatus by its officials, are contradictory to the economic 'free market' and the political needs of increasingly complex social systems. In other words, the question is whether parliamentary democracy is the 'natural' or best political framework for the bourgeoisie and capitalism.

In Chapter 2 the editors address a number of issues which re-emerge in each of the country studies. Specifically, the editors reject the notion that authoritarian regimes are transformed through voluntarist processes of compromise and negotiation and the increasing institutionalisation of political rights, or that success or failure in the democratisation enterprise is a factor of strategies, tactics, leadership qualities or even accidents and coincidences (cf. O'Donnell & Schmitter 1986b). Such an approach is a rejection of any general theory of social or economic determination of political outcomes, replacing it with an approach that is more behaviouralist. We do not reject real and consequential factors such as accidents, leaders and the 'Machiavellian' dimensions of political action, and we can agree that social structural factors are not, of themselves, sufficient to explain or predict the nature of political transitions. However, we strongly argue that social structural factors establish the environment in which politics operates, and establishes sets of constraints and pressures that shape political outcomes.

At the same time the editors reject normative positions on capital–state relations which, for example, might imply that the emergence of business as a powerful interest group is to be expected. Rather, it is suggested that there is no clear historical highway, but a network of paths, some of them cul-de-sacs, which classes, regimes and governments must navigate.

In attempting to bring some clarity to a confusing discussion, the authors of each of the chapters have endeavoured to distinguish between the concepts of state, regime and government. While each author has tended to modify their usage, some useful distinctions may be drawn here.

The **state**, as understood by the editors, is an amalgam of social, political, ideological and economic elements organised in a particular manner. In this sense the state is not so much a set of functions or a group of actors, as an expression of power. This accords with Jessop's (1983: 273) understanding, when he argues that 'the state is not a real subject that exercises power, [but that] state power certainly exists. . .' and is central to political struggle. He goes on to argue that state power is a set of complex social relationships that are dynamic, but at all times shaping the use of the state apparatus. By **state apparatus** we mean the real, existing institutional forms of state power, namely the coercive, judicial and bureaucratic arms of the state. Because these forms exist within a context of social relations, it is misleading to view the state or its apparatus as neutral.

The state and its apparatus can be differentiated from the **regime**, which can be said to be a particular type of organisation of the state apparatus which may take a variety of forms: liberal democracy, democratic corporatism, oligarchic democracy or dictatorship, fascism, authoritarian corporatism, totalitarianism of various types and so on. **Government** is regarded here as being the legislative and executive branches of the state apparatus and those officials, parties or individuals who control them.

In the sense of these definitions, it can be seen that governments may rise and fall, as in the cases of Italy and Thailand, while the state and regime remain relatively stable. It may also be, as Petras (1989: 27) proposes, that in order to maintain the state and the social order, a regime must be changed. The acquiescence of the Chilean bourgeoisie in the takeover of Pinochet may be seen as an example of this, as may democratisation in South Korea under Roh Tae Woo.

It is important to note, however, that neither the state nor its apparatus are the only centres of power within society. Clearly and unambiguously, class relations involve a broad exercise of political and social power, with the state being one of the major arenas for this.

Another important question is what is meant by democracy. It is argued by some (Keyfitz 1988) that democracy is a culturally relative term and indeed there is no regime that does not in some way describe itself as democratic. However, to accept this cultural relativist position is to deny any universal meaning to the word and, in the process, to indemnify the most scurrilous of dictatorships and to undermine the legitimacy of democratic and reformist oppositions. Another problem with the concept is that the formal structures of democracy—parties, parliaments and elections—may guarantee nothing. Even the most repressive of regimes have these. As Petras (1989) notes, peasants and workers may suffer more under civilian parliamentary regimes than under some authoritarian regimes.

In this way, Hewison (1992) has recently argued that Thailand's rapid industrialisation does not imply that bourgeois parliamentary forms will necessarily emerge and, if they do, that they will be a boon for all. Indeed, some of the signs for the future are not encouraging. Take, for example, the odd alliances between business people, gangsters and state officials (cf. *Far Eastern Economic Review* 18 April 1991). Money has become central to electoral politics and the pattern of seeking financial support from business

has meant that so-called 'influential persons' (gangsters) have been
politically legitimised. Thus, the capitalist and middle classes may
not institute parliamentary forms that are necessarily more representative for the majority.

To avoid these problems we choose to regard democracy in terms
of certain objectives and guarantees. First, legal guarantees of
'citizens' to participate in the formulation of policies. Second, the
institutionalisation of specific political freedoms including freedom
of speech, association and judicial rights, as well as representative
control over the executive and the bureaucracy. Third, political
contestation is considered legitimate and is legally supported.
Finally, political democracy is also seen to encompass popular
accountability. From our point of view, democracy is not, as in the
pluralist model, a case of the triumph of 'civil society' over the
state, or a situation where a neutral state aggregates and adjudicates
the demands of competing interest groups in a society where all
may compete on an equal footing. Rather, it is a political accommodation, but one that nevertheless reflects and essentially under-
pins the prevailing hierarchies of power embodied in the social
order.

It should also be pointed out that we do not propose that the
bourgeoisie, the 'middle class' and democracy go together naturally
in all historical situations. Political revolutions that turn out to
favour the interests of these classes have not always involved them
as the primary agents of transition (Hobsbawm 1990; Mooers 1991;
Callinicos 1989). Miliband (1989: 32–3) argues that in many of
Europe's capitalist societies the bourgeoisie had to fight for political
power, first against entrenched aristocracies, and then against
organised labour. This has led to a partnership between state power
and corporate power, meaning that the capitalist class *is not, by
nature*, a force for broad participatory democracy, suggesting that
many regime types and state forms may emerge in capitalist societies.

In the case of state-dominated societies, like many of those of
Southeast Asia, significant elements of the capitalist and 'middle'
classes actively support authoritarian regimes because their social
position, their access to resources and their protection from other
social forces require the coercive power of the state. Democracy,
we suggest, requires a degree of social and ideological hegemony
on the part of dominant social forces that makes redundant coercive
state power in its most naked form. Hence, what may be suggested
is that parliamentary systems provide the greatest flexibility for
capitalists.

Of course, in the chapters that follow, not all authors agree with
every point the editors make here and in Chapter 2, and there is a

degree of healthy heterogeneity in theoretical approach. Not only this, but the political situation of each of the countries is dynamic and anything but homogeneous. Thus, in completing their chapters, the contributors have faced many frustrations. Not only has the assortment of political and economic situations posed a variety of difficult issues and produced diversities in response to the questions posed by the editors, but political change has been rapid since the authors began their chapters. For example, there have been elections in Thailand (and a coup and dramatic street demonstrations), Indonesia, the Philippines, and Singapore. Still, each author has managed to address the important theoretical questions concerning democracy and authoritarianism for their country study.

In Chapter 3, Richard Robison examines the tensions that have emerged in Indonesia as the state confronts the difficulties of maintaining its *dirigiste* and authoritarian structures in the face of international market forces and the coming presidential succession. Singapore's authoritarianism in the context of parliamentary forms is the subject of Garry Rodan's Chapter 4. Quite another situation is presented in Chapter 5, where Geoffrey Gunn examines the world's richest nations with one of the last absolute monarchies, Brunei. Chapter 6, where Harold Crouch examines Malaysia, suggests that significant economic growth can have a rather ambiguous outcome, creating some pressures for democratisation and others for authoritarianism. Thailand's rocky road toward more democratic forms is the subject of Chapter 7, where Kevin Hewison uses the 1991 coup as a focus for discussing the emergence of political forces opposed to military authoritarianism. The problems of transition from authoritarian forms under Marcos to a parliamentary system in the Philippines is the subject of Jane Hutchison's Chapter 8. Finally, Vietnam's passage away from 'bureaucratic centralism', representing a marked political contrast, is discussed by Melanie Beresford in Chapter 9.

References

Anek Laothamatas 1992, *Business Associations and the New Political Economy of Thailand. From Bureaucratic Polity to Liberal Corporatism*, Institute of Southeast Asian Studies, Singapore

Callinicos, Alex 1989, 'Bourgeois Revolutions and Historical Materialism', *International Socialism*, no. 43

Cawson, Alan 1986, *Corporatism and Political Theory*, Basil Blackwell, Oxford

Held, David 1991, 'The Possibilities of Democracy', *Theory and Society*, vol. 20, no. 4, pp. 875–89

Hewison, Kevin 1992, 'On becoming a NIC: 'New' social forces in Thailand',

Paper presented to the Conference of the Asian Studies Association of Australia, July

Hobsbawm, Eric 1990, *Echoes of the Marseillaise*, Verso, London

Jessop, Bob 1983, 'Capitalism and Democracy: The Best Possible Shell?' *States and Societies*, New York University Press, New York

Keyfitz, Nathan 1988, 'The Asian Road to Democracy', *Transactions: Social Science and Modern Society*, vol. 26, no. 1, pp. 71–6

MacIntyre, Andrew 1990a, *Business and Politics in Indonesia*, Allen & Unwin, Sydney

—— 1990b, *Business–Government Relations in Industrialising East Asia: South Korea and Thailand*, Australia–Asia Papers No. 53, Griffith University, Nathan

Miliband, Ralph 1989, *Divided Societies. Class Struggle in Contemporary Capitalism*, Oxford University Press, Oxford

Mooers, Collin 1991, *The Making of Bourgeois Europe*, Verso, London

O'Donnell, Guillermo & Schmitter, Philippe C. (eds) 1986a, *Transitions from Authoritarian Rule: Tentative Conclusions about Uncertain Democracies*, The Johns Hopkins University Press, Baltimore

—— 1986b, 'Tentative Conclusions about Uncertain Democracies', in Guillermo O'Donnel & Philippe C. Schmitter eds (1986a) The Johns Hopkins University Press, Baltimore

O'Donnell, Guillermo, Schmitter, Philippe C. & Whitehead, Laurence (eds) 1986, *Transitions from Authoritarian Rule: Comparative Perspectives*,

Petras, James 1989, 'State, Regime and the Democratization Muddle', *Journal of Contemporary Asia*, vol. 19, no. 1, pp. 26–32

Robison, Richard, Hewison, Kevin & Higgott, Richard (eds) 1987, *Southeast Asia in the 1980s: The Politics of Economic Crisis*, Allen & Unwin, Sydney

2 Political power in industrialising capitalist societies: Theoretical approaches
Richard Robison, Kevin Hewison, Garry Rodan

Following World War II decolonisation in Asia saw initial enthusiasm for Western parliamentary forms. The Philippines, newly independent, engaged in a vigorous electoral process, while in Thailand elections were again in the offing after years of military rule. While decolonisation was proving more difficult in Indochina, Malaya, Indonesia and Singapore, there were widely held hopes that 'democrats' would emerge within the independence movements.

Political theory at this time also suggested considerable scope for democracy in Asia and the rest of the developing world (e.g. Geertz 1963). It was not long before this enthusiasm for democratic forms was shaken, however. In Thailand the military returned to power; in Burma a one-party state was established; Communists were making gains in Indochina and on the Malay peninsula; and Indonesia was involved in a bloody war of independence. Indeed, the situation in much of the emerging post-colonial world seemed quite chaotic, and democratic government did not appear to hold a solution. Indeed, authoritarianism soon emerged as a common political arrangement.

These shifts caused some significant reassessments of theories positing a basic contradiction between political authoritarianism and the forward march of societies towards modernity. Conservative theorists like Huntington (1968) and pluralists like Riggs (1966), both greatly influenced by structural functionalism, argued that authoritarianism may be a necessary or inevitable stage on the road to modernity.

Later, and from a quite different theoretical perspective, radical dependency theorists, drawing on the Monopoly Capital school of American Marxism, also rejected any link between democracy and development in developing countries. In fact, they suggested that capitalism brought underdevelopment to the periphery, while the metropoles demanded strong authoritarian governments in order to maintain the process of surplus extraction. For those writers, revolution and a transformation to socialism was the only solution to dependency and poverty (cf. Frank 1969; Amin 1974).

Throughout the 1960s and 1970s military regimes appeared *de rigueur* throughout the Third World, and where civilian regimes emerged to replace authoritarianism, they did not persist. For example, in Chile, Salvadore Allende's left-wing government was crushed in 1973, while in Thailand, three years later, the military returned, with blood on its hands, to re-establish authoritarian rule. Meanwhile, Marcos established his own form of authoritarianism in the Philippines, and Lee Kuan Yew's Singapore evidenced increasing repressiveness.

For theorists of all bents, democracy ceased to be of great significance in their writings. Indeed there appeared to be considerable agreement that some form of authoritarianism was inevitable or perhaps even necessary to the processes of development (or underdevelopment) taking place in the capitalist Third World. This view held sway for some time, and few theorists spent much time considering the prospects for parliamentary forms in the Third World.

By the mid-eighties, however, the political tide seemed to be turning. There had been a dramatic retreat from authoritarianism in the Third World and Southern Europe, and more dramatically, authoritarian state socialist regimes—too complex to discuss in this chapter—began to crumble. In Asia, parliamentary systems appeared to be gaining strength in Thailand, South Korea, Taiwan and even in Indonesia, even though the military remained important players in each country. In Laos, political controls were loosened, while most spectacularly, the people of the Philippines had ousted the corrupt Marcos clan.

These events brought a revival of theoretical interest in the relationships between political authoritarianism, democracy and capitalism. The often unacknowledged issue behind this renewed interest was the adoption of increasingly neo-classical approaches to economic reform and the relationship between this 'free market' environment and democratic forms (Almond 1991). Even the World Bank has become interested in how it might support good 'governance' and economic development (Brautigam 1991). However, the main political question which seems at the heart of the re-emerged debate is whether changing economic and social conditions, including shifts to high levels of capital accumulation and the development of a strong bourgeoisie, bring about structural tensions within authoritarian regimes which may lead to a democratic transition. A related question is whether these authoritarian structures, which have often involved hijacking of the state apparatus by its officials, are contradictory to the economic 'free market' and the political needs of increasingly complex social systems. In other words, the question is again raised as to whether parliamentary democracy is the 'natural' or best political shell for the capitalist system and the bourgeoisie as, for example, Anderson (1990) has recently suggested for Thailand. Across the theoretical spectrum the prevailing explanation for the rise and fall of authoritarianism is that this form of state power is specific to particular phases in social and economic development.

For those working out of the intellectual amalgam of structural functionalism and Weberianism which constitutes North American behavioural social science, authoritarian states are regarded as providing the integrative cement and organisational force in a period when 'rational' values and modes of behaviour are still in a process of formation. Within this perspective it is implicit that authoritarianism will evaporate as civil society is able to manage its own affairs, as rational modes of behaviour and thought are generalised throughout society and as powerful institutions emerge within civil society. For those working out of intellectual traditions that place more emphasis on systems of production and their social relations, authoritarianism is widely regarded as a form of state power endemic to capitalist societies prior to the emergence of a cohesive and hegemonic bourgeoisie.

These interpretations have been criticised from a number of perspectives. First, by conservatives who have recently challenged the assumed natural partnership of representative democracy and economic liberalism on the grounds that the former allows constraint of market forces by 'special interest groups'. The implication of this is that certain forms of authoritarianism may indeed be essential for the long-term survival of market capitalism. A second challenge is contained in the proposition that forms of state power, authoritarianism or democracy, are not related to stages of economic or social development but to an enduring cultural framework that transcends the material organisation of societies and economies. Hence, in specific cultural traditions, authoritarianism will be the natural political form as that society passes from feudalism to capitalism, and in turn to more advanced forms of capitalist industrialisation. Third, there is the proposition that the nature of political regimes is shaped by dynamics quite separate from those that operate in the spheres of society, economy or culture.

In this chapter we intend to review these issues in the light of the earlier debates and their re-emergence. In doing so we will concentrate on three basic theoretical lines—modernisation theory, dependency theory, and post-dependency empiricism—prior to suggesting elements of a wider ranging social structural explanation. This requires a reassessment of the way in which previous theories have attempted to explain state power in the process of social and political transformation.

Modernisation, rationality and political order

Predicated on a blend of Parsonian structural functionalism and cultural behaviouralism, modernisation theorists of the fifties and sixties assumed an essentially linear process of social and political change as society became more complex and increasingly legal–rational in outlook and practice. In this context authoritarian regimes were regarded as traditional residues; patrimonial, despotic, particularist and corrupt practices were inevitably to be replaced as modernisation proceeded and liberal–democratic forms took root (cf. Almond & Coleman 1960; Higgott 1983 chs 2–3). Political struggle was essentially a question of the bearers of modern values (the middle class or bourgeoisie) overcoming traditional elites and their old values and replacing them in political power positions.

The difficulties with this approach soon became obvious, and have been outlined in a number of critical assessments, including Higgott (1983: chs 3–4) and Taylor (1979: ch. 3). However, only two of these difficulties will be examined here.

First, the assumption that Weber's category of legal–rational authority constitutes a democratic form is not warranted. Weber (cited in Haralambos 1980: 284) himself argued that while this kind of authority appeared superior to both the charismatic and traditional forms, he warned that only a strong parliamentary system could prevent society being overtaken by private and public bureaucratic (legal–rational) juggernauts. Second, the relationship between the middle class and democracy, while central to the analysis, is not adequately theorised. These analysts have tended to coalesce the bourgeoisie (entrepreneurs) and salaried and professional people who are brought together by their shared values, which are assumed to be rational and democratic. Clearly, though, this group can be no more than a coalition of groups or classes with quite different interests. Certainly, this middle class or elements of it, have supported a whole range of political arrangements including authoritarian regimes. As Burris (1986) and Goldthorpe and others (1969) have suggested, it is necessary to recognise fundamental contradictions between capital-owning and salaried classes.

These problems were brought into stark relief as democratic experiments collapsed throughout the Third World, even where the theorised conditions for democratic transition had appeared to be present. It was Huntington (1968) who found a path out of this dilemma. While accepting the basic values and behavioural assumptions of modernisation theory, Huntington argued that the tasks of managing integration, economic growth and political order could best be achieved by an authoritarian regime. In suggesting this, he broke the previous analytical nexus between authoritarianism and tradition, democracy and modernity.

For Huntington, a conservative, rapid social, political or economic change raised the spectre of revolution—societies out of balance presented opportunities for change outside of the normal bounds of organic growth within any society. If any society was to be saved from chaos and disorder, political power needed to be institutionalised. The military can play a leading role in this for it is the 'advance guard' of modern values, and it may hold power prior to the 'middle class' establishing its political hegemony.

In this context authoritarianism becomes a functional response to social disintegration and economic malaise. The political dynamics involved are systemic, with integration necessarily triumphing over disintegration, and authoritarian rule being the appropriate instrument of integration. It does this by developing institutions capable of integrating civil society into the political process *without* falling into revolution and by providing the conditions for investment and rapid industrialisation. In other words, authoritarianism creates the basis for capitalism and, *in the long term,* for democratic institutions. The authoritarian regime fulfils its historical mission by eventually integrating all social groups into the increasingly democratic process and relinquishing its role to a rational elite of the middle class.

A decade and a half later, however, Huntington (1984: 199) found himself explaining the persistence of authoritarian regimes even in situations where his earlier writings suggested that a transition to democratic forms would have been expected. Huntington maintains his earlier insistence that the 'middle class' is central to the transition, but argues that social determinism must be avoided. That is, even though the prerequisites might be present for a democratic transition, other political dynamics are at work also, so that authoritarianism may be maintained.

While Huntington still foresees situations where authoritarianism becomes dysfunctional for political order, his general approach is to reject his earlier view that authoritarian rule is transitional. This change was apparently in response to two issues. First, the persistence of authoritarian regimes in East Asia despite the emergence of strong middle classes and rapidly rising living standards. Second, within American Conservatism a thesis emerged suggesting that there was a basic contradiction between rapid economic growth and democratic forms of government (cf. Olson 1982). Huntington

(1987: 21) suggests that middle classes may be willing to sacrifice political interests for the benefits of high economic growth, arguing that there is often a choice between:

> . . . a populist 'vicious circle' involving expanded political participation, more socio-economic equality, slower economic growth and intensifying class conflict leading to a military coup and a participation 'implosion' and . . . a technocratic 'vicious circle' often starting with a military coup, and involving suppression of political participation, rapid economic growth, and increased socio-economic inequality, leading to a mounting popular discontent and a participation 'explosion' against the regime.

Of more interest in Huntington's revised thesis is his introduction of a decisive cultural factor to explain why countries with the prerequisites for a democratic transition will take different paths. He argues that the transition is only possible given an appropriate political history and within a values system and cultural environment that is conducive to democracy. For example, West European Protestantism allowed for compromise and equality and is conducive to democratic transformation, whereas Islam and Confucianism were more hierarchical and intolerant and so provide obstacles to transformation. Culture thus attains the status of a decisive and independent factor in the transition process, thereby overturning much of his earlier comparative and functional analysis. Authoritarianism is therefore explained in tautological fashion by pointing to the authoritarian nature of the culture of a particular country (Huntington 1984 :216). This approach also tends to have little regard for history, seeing a culture as an unchanging factor in any social system.

The problems with cultural determinism have been discussed elsewhere for the cases of Thailand and Indonesia (cf. Hewison 1989a: ch. 3; Keesing 1991) but Cotton's (1989) paper on authoritarianism in Korea demonstrates that, even with an awareness of the range of factors at play, these factors are extremely difficult to effectively integrate when analytical primacy is given to culture.

Cotton (1989: 248–9) considers that there are two sets of factors at work in the transformation of Korean authoritarianism: a socio-economic set and a cultural set. The socio-economic factors, in the form of trade imbalances and technological maturity, are generating pressures for a move from state-led industrialisation to a more internationally responsive economy. This implies a state more concerned for the management of the conditions for capital accumulation within the framework set by international market forces. On the other hand, the cultural factors are represented as Confucian traditions of obedience and hierarchy which act to ensure that authoritarianism remains the dominant element of the political system.

While these factors are not necessarily irreconcilable as in Johnson's (1987) 'soft authoritarianism', they do provide quite different, even conflicting, interpretations. For example, the cultural perspective suggests that the contending forces, defined by values and behaviour, are traditional Confucian elites facing a more secular and rational middle class. In contrast, the socio-economic perspective produces a picture of a complex coalition of military bureaucrats, corporate capitalists and middle classes, driven by vested interests which cut swathes through the tradition–Confucian/modern–secular divide. Such contradictions are difficult to reconcile. However, Cotton does not openly confront this difficulty, instead placing emphasis on supposedly hostile cultural factors which make transition a doubtful proposition. This is only likely to be overcome through the humility, patience and statesmanship of political leaders willing to compromise and change social attitudes (Cotton 1989: 259).

The most serious flaw in the culturalist approach is the incapacity to explain tensions in authoritarian regimes, a failing that has its basis in structural functionalism. Within this perspective, the various classes become interest groups, with no theory of the state to explain the content of their interests or their mediation to differentiate between the classes, or to explain political action. In the end they are little more than categories with little to distinguish their political position and power. Ultimately, then, from this perspective it is only cultural factors that can plausibly explain the differences between societies even though as Huntington (1987: 22–3) himself notes,

> Just exactly how culture is responsible for the political and economic differences one is attempting to explain is often left extraordinarily vague. Cultural explanations are thus often imprecise or tautological, or both, at the extreme coming down to a more sophisticated rendering of 'the French are like that!'

Yet this kind of explanation is the refuge of theorists who attempt to categorise societies as 'democratic' or 'authoritarian' without acknowledging either the wide variations within each cultural tradition or historical change within culture.

If Huntington's return has not taken him beyond culturalist tautologies, the re-emergence of modernisation theory in response to transitions in the Third World and Eastern Europe seems to complete a theoretical circle. Indeed, some of the same theorists who wrote in the 1950s and 1960s have reappeared in the recent debate (cf. Almond 1987; 1991; Pye 1990).

The latest reincarnation of modernisation theory tends to underplay earlier cultural analyses in favour of a focus on the functional aspects of state–society relations and the growing strength of civil society *vis-à-vis* the state (Cheng 1990: 10–16). Pye's recent article is especially interesting in that it claims specific contradictions between authoritarianism and modernisation:

> All governments are put under pressure by the increasingly significant flows of international trade, finance and communications; by the effects of contemporary science and technology; and by all the other elements that make up what we imprecisely call modernisation. But the authoritarian regimes are the most vulnerable and are therefore being seriously undermined (Pye 1990: 6).

He argues that the emergence of a middle class and a technically educated population create new centres of power that cannot easily be accommodated within the centralised structures of authoritarian regimes. This harks back to the theme of developing legal–rational authority, suggesting that democratic forms will emerge as a stage in the development process. It also contrasts with Huntington's recent culturalist position.

Interestingly this recent modernisation position is perhaps closer in its themes to more radical theorists of state and class than to Huntington's and other cultural determinist approaches. There are two such themes: first, the idea that the emergence of complex class systems and technically advanced capitalist industrialisation requires the integration of major social groups within the political system, together with means for mediation, conciliation and accountability; and second, that this will only be possible in situations of high social cohesion and order. However, the problem for modernisation theory is that it maintains an essentially ahistorical dichotomy of tradition–modernity, and is thus unable to explain transitions from one stage of development to another. The more radical theories attempt to do this.

State, capitalism and forms of state power

Modernisation and political order theorists operate within a world of systems, functions, structures and values, examining the conditions for order and chaos through institutionalisation and cultural transformation. However, these factors are not considered as products of any specific set of economic organisation or state structure within any specific historical situation.

Contrasted with this is a set of approaches that are concerned with relationships between various forms of state organisation and arrangements of the social and economic system, in particular historical circumstances. From this perspective, politics is seen as being about policy and concerned with specific decisions which directly and indirectly influence the distribution of wealth, power and the structure of social relationships. Unlike the modernisation approaches, policy formation is not seen to be value-neutral, but is rather seen to take place within the context of specific relations of social and political domination, a system in which the state takes a critical, partisan role.

Theories that conceive of the state in this manner derive from a range of Marxist and Weberian perspectives. These theories variously conceive the state as an instrument of the ruling class, as constrained by the structures of capitalist society and especially the processes of capital accumulation, or as influenced by an identifiable corps of state managers. Examples of these conceptualisations applied to Southeast Asia may be seen in the earlier work of Robison (1978) on Indonesia and in Elliott's (1978a, b) work on Thailand. Another perspective takes a more voluntarist position on the state, developing a state-centred approach which sees the state and/or its higher level officials as autonomous with identifiable interests which may override those of the dominant class (Skocpol 1985; Block 1977; Trimberger 1977). Useful examples of this kind of approach in the Southeast Asian context may be seen in the work of Hans-Dieter Evers (1973) and his colleagues (e.g. Korff 1989).

Both Marx and Weber indicated an Orientalist view that associated authoritarianism with pre-capitalist society and democracy with capitalism and the rise of the bourgeoisie (Turner 1978). For example, Marx's concept of the Asiatic Mode of Production represented the dominance of bureaucrats in situations where the state was the economic and political power, and where private property was relatively unimportant (Miliband 1989: 94). This association of capitalism, the overthrow of Absolutism, and the rise of liberal democracy does little more than reflect the general course of Western European history.

Nevertheless Marx did, in his approach to the Bonapartist state, indicate how an authoritarian regime could come to dominate within a capitalist society. In a time of political and economic crisis, Marx (1969: 373) showed how the bourgeoisie would surrender state power (in the form of a parliament) in the interest of preserving '. . . its social power intact', which meant that '. . . to save its purse it must forfeit its crown'. However, this was seen as a short-term measure, and he assumed that the bourgeoisie would naturally retake the political high ground.

The value of this analysis is that it provides a picture of the dynamics of class-regime relationships. A bourgeoisie is attracted to democratic forms of state power only when these do not threaten the social order in which its dominance is embedded. In situations where socialist or working-class movements threaten to play the determining role in democracies, the bourgeoisie may shift its allegiance to conservative military or single-party regimes. Where the bourgeoisie cannot guarantee its own dominance through its control of society, economy and ideology, it will require the use of the coercive powers of the state. A particular regime, therefore, cannot be understood separately from the structure of social power and conflict and specific class interests. In this view, forms of state power are not functional imperatives of complex forms of society but the political consequence of patterns of social conflict or coalition. However, it is assumed that bourgeois capitalism and liberal democracy will ultimately triumph. This unilinear evolutionism does not satisfactorily explain the variety of forms of state power in capitalist societies. Why has the political role of the bourgeoisie and middle classes been so different in Britain and Japan or even Germany? How do we explain the prevalence of oligarchic or populist forms of state power and fragile democracy in many parts of the Third World? How is it that the Asian NICs exhibit author-itarianism in the presence of strong bourgeois and middle classes? How can the great variations in the organisation of state apparatuses be explained?

A first explanation of these questions identifies the specific loca-tion of individual societies within the international economy as being a major influence upon the nature of political regimes. A second approach rejects social and economic determinism in sug-gesting a 'by chance' explanation. Yet a third perspective emphasises the specific configuration of social power that emerges with the development of capitalism and the social and political context of industrialisation. We will examine each of these in turn.

The world economy and forms of state power

As noted above, dependency theorists considered authoritarianism as virtually an essential element of capitalist underdevelopment. Liberal democracy was only for Western Europe in its particular historical circumstances when capitalism was competitive. Capital went to the peripheries, but not Western European liberal, demo-cratic political institutions (cf. Boron 1981: 52–4).

Dependency theorists considered that the comprador status of the local bourgeoisie meant that it was never able to destroy the old landed oligarchy and dominate the political system. In Thailand, a number of theorists have shown that the major economic elements (Sino-Thai business groups, foreign capital, and the old aristocracy) were unable to organise a satisfactory political alliance, allowing the military to take the leading role (e.g. Elliott 1978b). Like the situation of military alliances in Latin America, this situation was reminiscent of Bonapartism except that dependency theorists tended to see it as a permanent situation of bureaucratic authoritarianism (Schmitter 1973: 187–90). These theorists suggested that bureaucratic authoritarian regimes, as well as maintaining order and the social and economic interests of the dominant classes, enabled structural change in the economy. It is considered that these changes would not have been likely in conditions of competition between the various elements of the dominant classes.

These theoretical approaches were confronted with serious problems as a process from authoritarian to civilian rule and the establishment of democratic processes took place in Southern Europe and Latin America in the 1970s and 1980s. While a number of dependency theorists had given some attention to the emerging economic and political power of the bourgeoisie (e.g. Evans 1979), most were confronted by the sight of the domestic bourgeoisie, which they had understood as a residual, non-determining category, taking a leading role in democratic transformations. Categories such as 'dependent', 'peripheral', 'comprador' were thrown into question, and a shift to a more 'real' analysis took place. This resulted in a less deterministic approach to political change and the position of the state, and a move away from the dependency cul-de-sac.

At the same time, a broad range of Marxist-oriented theories emerged to demolish dependency theory. Led by Laclau (1971), Brenner (1977) and Warren (1973), one strand of this critique produced a complete rejection of the thesis that capitalist industrialisation was not likely in the Third World. Indeed, Warren (1980) argued that rather than impeding capitalist development, imperialism cut a swathe through pre-capitalist social and economic relations to establish capitalism. Following this, a series of influential studies in Africa, beginning with Kenya, clearly demonstrated that a bourgeoisie could develop locally and become vigorous, aided and abetted by the state (Leys 1978; Swainson 1978). While these theorists did not develop a concept of the state appropriate to an understanding of this process, their intervention showed a path out of the dependency straightjacket. Drawing on these studies, Robison (1986) and Hewison (1989b) have demonstrated a similar experience in Indonesia and Thailand. Despite effective demonstrations of the contrary, studies continue to suggest that capitalism is dependent in Southeast Asia (Yoshihara 1988).

As Becker (1984) has noted, the acknowledgment of Third World capitalism allows for the consideration of a 'post-imperialist' phase of 'progressive' capitalism, albeit wasteful, degrading, exploitive and ruthless. Becker suggests three 'post-imperialist' propositions. First, that transnational capital is not always antagonistic to democracy or necessarily supportive of authoritarianism. This has been well demonstrated in Thailand where 'investment strikes' have usually coincided with economic and social disorder rather than having followed the ups and downs of military coups and civilian rule. Second, the presence of transnational capital can be supportive of domestic capital in that it advances investment, technology and skills necessary for industrial deepening (Becker 1984: 426). Here the state plays a crucial role in establishing the conditions for investment and for the expansion of domestic capital. Third, Becker (1984: 428) argues that democratisation is encouraged in this 'post-imperialist' situation because industrial development establishes an industrial proletariat which is technically skilled and industrially disciplined. Hence, the bourgeoisie is less concerned that populist calls to insurrection will be successful. This advanced working class is more likely to see its interests as lying within a representative system. These conditions mean that the bourgeoisie is freer to express its preference for pluralism where, as Therborn (cited in Becker 1984: 428) puts it, each capitalist faction is assured that '. . . its rivals within the class will not capture the ear of the state authorities and, with them, ride roughshod over its particular interests'.

It might also be noted that dependency approaches are unable to cope with situations where imperialist nations are calling for human rights, labour reform and democratic reform in, for example, Indonesia, Thailand, the Philippines and China. One revised explanation is to argue that the United States' interests now lie in removing mercantilist authoritarianisms that have depressed wages and demand and allowing, for example, the Asian NICs to out-compete the US (Cumings 1989).

However, both this revised dependency (even conspiracy) approach and its critics' more materialist approach are rejected by a group of writers who have come to a position that finds all suggestions of strategies or levels of organisation as unacceptable.

There is no plan: Empiricist interventions

In the 1980s a series of publications emerged with the specific objective of explaining the large number of transitions from authoritarianism in Southern Europe and Latin America. The *Transitions* volumes address themselves both to questions of political strategy in ending authoritarian rule and the theoretical aspects of the process.

Following a series of case studies in Europe and Latin America, the *Transitions* group concluded that authoritarian regimes were most successfully transformed through processes of compromise and negotiation whereby constitutional and institutional rights and safeguards are exchanged for the political immunity of former leaders and officials. More significantly, however, revolutionary strategies are rejected in favour of reformist goals (O'Donnell & Schmitter 1986) which means an acceptance of the existing class structure.

The idea that a democratic transformation occurs through negotiation is a clear rejection of any general theory of social or economic determination of political outcomes. This is based on the observation that strong bourgeoisies and middle classes are associated with a range of political regimes. These empirical observations are in marked contrast to earlier post-dependency works by, for example, Stepan (1985) and O'Donnell (1979), where both argued for explanations that specified contradictions between the nature of authoritarian rule and bourgeois class power.

The revised approach argues that social structural factors are not of themselves sufficient to explain or predict the nature of political transitions. Emphasised instead are readily observable factors such as strategies, tactics, ideas, leaders, and even accidents and coincidences. As O'Donnell and Schmitter (1986: 5) explain it:

> This is not to deny that macro-structural factors are not there: world system, class etc. Short-term political calculations are only loosely influenced by such factors and cannot be deduced from or imputed to such structures. Instead, unexpected events, insufficient information, hurried and audacious choices, confusion about motives and interests, indefinition of political identities, talents of specific individuals are all decisive in determining outcomes.

Ironically, this new position reflects some of the very criticisms of O'Donnell's earlier attempts to build an integrated model of state, regime type and economy, particularly his functionalist claims of a relationship between bureaucratic authoritarianism and the stage of industrial deepening. In his critique of the earlier O'Donnell thesis as it applied to the Philippines, Adriano (1984) argued that O'Donnell confused state and regime and demonstrated that the imposition of martial law and the rise of Marcos were not related either functionally to a transition from import substitution industrialisation to industrial deepening, or instrumentally to the political needs of the Philippine bourgeoisie.

This position is taken up most strongly by Przeworski (1986), who argues that an identification of class or group interests has no predictive value in any particular historical circumstances. While Przeworski's thesis appears to support the pluralist and modernisa-

tion theorists' rejection of the concepts of state and class and their
stress on leadership, political organisation and institution-building
in the transition process, he does suggest a property or social power
basis to the transition. He argues that democratic transitions are a
result of negotiation and bargaining between groups intent on maintaining their interests. Democracies protect these interests by leaving
intact the exploitation and social and economic power bases of these
interests. For him, democracy is an on-going process of conflict and
negotiation between competing political forces rather than the attain-
ment of a particular, finite end. The state, far from being neutral,
presides over hierarchies of social and economic power and maintains these (Przeworski 1986: 56–61).

The *Transitions* ensemble appears to suggest at least two useful
points. First, that regimes may collapse internally in a process
seemingly unrelated to social and economic power structures. Hence
the regime's capacity to organise and reorganise itself for the
exercise of power is an important factor in explaining a democratic
transition, or lack of it. This appears a useful explanation of the
Singapore case, where an authoritarian state is maintained despite
industrialisation and a strong middle class. Second, the recognition
that officials are important actors with their own interests, a perspective often lost in earlier approaches, is also an important observation.

Despite these useful points, we believe the *Transitions* approach
to be flawed for two important reasons. First, as Petras (1989: 27)
notes, there is confusion between the concepts of state and regime,
and the implications of differences between them for regime change.
In addition, Petras questions whether subordinate classes gain from
a negotiation and compromise process, especially in situations where
a civilian regime is facilely assumed to be democratic. The Philippines might be considered an example of a 'democratic' regime
where political terror increased after the 'transition' from the authoritarianism of Marcos. Petras (1989: 28–32) calls for attention to be
redirected to state and class. Second, if negotiation, compromise and
chance are to be the factors to explain transitions to democratic
forms, it might be asked why it is that negotiation does not appear
to begin at any time in any country once an opposition adopts a
reformist strategy. Similarly, will an authoritarian regime accept
negotiation at any time, or are there specific preconditions which
might be necessary? And, what factors will determine the direction
of the transition process? The *Transitions* literature would tend to
suggest that the process is very largely voluntarist. This seems
unlikely for a number of reasons.

In the first place, we suggest that the socio-economic environment
is critical. Negotiated democratic transition is clearly facilitated

when an authoritarian regime deals with a reformist bourgeoisie which does not aim to fundamentally alter the social and political order. In other situations, where social or political conflict remains bitter, transition appears considerably more difficult. A good example is Thailand where, when the Communist Party remained active, the development of democratic forms was stalled. However, as the Party collapsed, participatory institutions blossomed. In short, a democratic transition would appear to be contingent on certain social structural preconditions, most notably a conviction that such a transition was not likely to overturn the existing order.

Second, it appears that there are patterns, regionally and over time, in regime type and in transition experience. For example, patterns of authoritarianism exist in Latin America, Northeast Asia and Southeast Asia, even if there appears to be regional variation. Similarly, the patterns of democratic regime in North America, Australia and Britain appear to be resilient and have much in common. In other words, we are suggesting that the coincidence between regimes and social and economic formations appears too consistent to sustain the *Transitions* thesis of chance, strategy, leadership and organisation. It appears that there are a series of structural constraints, imperatives, contradictions and preconditions which influence both forms of state power and the nature of the state itself.

Third, in rejecting arguments that political outcomes result from structural factors, Przeworski (1986: 55) focuses instead on political disintegration and on political factors as decisive. However, he goes on to argue that the social structural level merely sends 'signals' to actors telling them whether to 'shift' or 'remain'. But this appears a rather ambiguous way of introducing social structural factors without actually acknowledging them.

To illustrate this point let us take the example of the fall of Marcos. At one level it may be argued that the collapse of the Marcos regime was due to the internal disintegration of the regime and the desertion of the military leaders Ramos and Enrile to the side of Aquino. After all, weeks of demonstrations by the middle classes had failed to dislodge the Marcos government and bring any real changes in the regime. Limited to expressing their opposition by street demonstrations, they could not move to the next necessary step: the physical overthrow of Marcos. It is also true that Ramos and Enrile were prompted to defect by news of their impending arrest at the hands of their rival, General Ver. However, there was an important 'signal' which came from powerful forces in society. Marcos' policies had led the social coalitions which underpinned the Marcos state, as well as the United States, to conclude that Marcos' rule contradicted and threatened their long-term interests.

For these coalitions, including the most powerful of the land-owning and capital-owning families, the regime had to be changed if the state and the social order it embodied was to survive.

The 'signal', therefore, was that a military revolt in support of a transition to an oligarchic democracy would be supported by the Philippine ruling class and the US; that their financial and ideological resources would be available to a new government and therefore the chances of success would be high. The Philippine case also illustrated what may happen to military moves when no such 'signals' emerge. The lack of success of the Right wing military radicals in the post-Marcos era must surely be considered in the context of the desire of the principal families to reconstitute their rule through the reincarnation of the Congress as the pivotal mechanism of political authority. Their interests clearly lay in oligarchic democracy, not military authoritarianism (cf. Anderson 1988).

The *Transitions* thesis which rejects any notion of structuring, determination or even of conditioning is, as Cumings (1989: 15) notes, a rejection of any explanation that offers a comparative perspective transcending incidents, instances, or coincidences. We are left with no more than a series of empirical events. Building socio-structural factors into explanations of regime formation and democratic transition is a complex task, but some theorists have suggested approaches that do this. One fruitful course has been to examine the ways in which industrial capitalism has interacted with the development of the state and the balance of social forces and their political power.

Forms of state power and historical courses

That an analysis of the historical development of particular social formations and related forms of state power is considered important should be obvious from our previous comments. The need for such an analysis is seen in the different kinds of tensions and challenges facing authoritarian regimes in countries where capitalism emerged under the tutelage of a strong state and well-developed state apparatus as, for example, in East Asia, and those in Latin America where a national bourgeoisie, strong middle class, and landed oligarchies played leading roles. The different historical paths would suggest different approaches to democratic transition.

There has recently been a resurgence of interest in the work of earlier theorists who examined relationships between forms of state power and the historical conjunctures which marked the processes of capitalist development. Barrington Moore's (1966) path-breaking study of the varieties of political outcomes of capitalist development has been influential. He proposed that democracy resulted where there was a strong bourgeoisie, whereas authoritarianism emerged where a bourgeoisie was weak and unable to play a leading role. Later theorists found Latin America difficult to fit into his categories and developed a new paradigm in which the export of Iberian feudalism resulted in a vacuum of power where neither bourgeoisie, traditional oligarchy nor radical forces were able to attain and consolidate social or political hegemony, leaving the way open to military rule. Such an analysis was not necessarily framed in dependency terms (Nun 1968).

Another important approach was that of iconoclast modernisation theorist Gerschenkron (1962) who explored relationships between social structural factors, phases and timing of industrialisation, and the emergence of democratic and authoritarian regimes. He proposed that 'early' industrialisation, following a long incubation period, allowed the bourgeoisie to slowly build industrial capitalism. At the same time this class could eliminate feudalism and its entrenched classes. 'Late' industrialisation, requiring rapid and high investment, left the bourgeoisie behind, together with its free markets and liberal political institutions. In such situations the state and its officials achieved political dominance. Kurth (1979: 330–5) has recently taken up this theme, showing that the consumer goods manufacturers of eighteenth and nineteenth century Britain wanted free markets and had no need for the protection or resources of the state. They found in the institutions of universal suffrage and parliamentary representation a political format that allowed them to undermine both political conservatism and economic protectionism. There was a conjuncture between economic and political liberalism, in contrast to Prussia where the champions of free trade were the conservative landed forces. Thus Kurth argues that in Britain economic liberalism worked to reinforce a political liberalism, whereas in Prussia economic liberalism actually worked to frustrate political liberalism.

Reinforcing these conjunctures of class formation and political power were elective affinities between regime types and phases of industrialisation. Whereas early industrialisation dealt in modest amounts of capital and incremental advances in technology, allowing investment to be mobilised by family firms without resort to major finance banks or the state, late industrialisation was characterised by rapid and large-scale investment in capital goods industries, the establishment of industrial cartels and the active intervention of the state and industrial banks.

The question of authoritarian transformations has been most recently addressed in this context by Cumings. His is a thesis of capitalist maturation, incorporating historical advances within a global context, and attempting to explain political outcomes while

retaining social structural factors at the centre of his analysis. He
argues that the political outcomes of European transitions were the
result of collisions of cultural, economic and political amalgams at
specific points in world history which cannot be repeated in these
forms elsewhere. In North America, for example, migrations from
Europe left the peasantry and aristocracy behind, resulting in the
transplantation of liberalism into a political vacuum, without the
feudal and socialist elements of the European amalgam. By contrast,
the Iberian migrations to Latin America were mainly clerical, rural
and military, bringing together—but never realising—the Southern
European amalgam. Hence, the political history of these places takes
different courses, directed by their divergent amalgams of culture,
economics and politics.

These are important observations. If we apply the notion of
collisions of historical amalgams to the Asian situation, the various
forces involved in the different timing of their collisions help
explain why Asian outcomes, with the notable exception of the
Philippines, differ so markedly from the Latin American experience.
Generally missing in the Asian experience is the hacienda feudalism
and the political power of the church which were important ingre-
dients in the emergence of caudillo politics. Instead, the tradition
of a strong state and powerful officials is entrenched, descending
from the traditional agrarian bureaucracies and the authoritarian
colonial commodity-exporting states. In the post-colonial shake-up,
the authoritarianism of industrial mercantilism or 'command
capitalism' was to predominate. It is the collision of this state-dominated capitalist amalgam with an international, market-based capitalism that constitutes the present set of political tensions. In Asia,
the importance, cohesion and autonomy of an estate of politico-
bureaucrats is generally of a different order to the Latin American
experience and is closer to the sorts of dynamics to be found in
Moore's path to capitalism via 'revolution from above' which
includes the German and Japanese cases. Hence, attempts to represent the Latin American experience as general theory, as has been
the case of dependency theory and later works of O'Donnell and
his associates, must be recognised for what they are.

Cumings (1989: 23) also adds the important point that these
aspects must be considered not only in the context of individual
states, but within a context of sovereign states belonging to a world
system of capitalist commodity production and exchange. It should
be added that class relations also operate within an international
division of labour (Jenkins 1984).

One of the few theorists in this area who raises the question of
culture, explicit in the categories of 'feudal', 'bourgeoisie' and
'liberal' that he uses, Cumings' concept of culture is drawn from

the works of Raymond Williams, E. P. Thompson and Perry Anderson rather than from the school that owes much to Talcott Parsons. For Cumings, culture is integral to the political and material levels of society, so that a bourgeois epoch develops a bourgeois culture. This is in contrast with, for example, Huntington's perspective, where culture has no history, it just is. For Huntington and Cotton, Korean authoritarianism will persist because Korea has an authoritarian culture. For Cumings, however, authoritarianism remains strong because the bourgeois democratic culture is poorly developed in the early, raw, industrial capitalism which exists.

The value of an analysis that examines the historical paths of capitalist development is that it identifies sets of options and constraints for political action that influence the prospects for transition from authoritarianism. In so-called late industrialising societies, capitalist classes are nurtured within the protective framework of authoritarian, neo-mercantilist regimes and thereby constitute its political allies as long as they remain dependent upon the resources and protection of the state. The critical point in the political histories of such societies comes when the development of industrial capitalism and the interests of a bourgeoisie become contradictory to the continued existence of authoritarian forms of state power; when the regime constrains the social order.

Regime vs capitalist development

At what point, if any, do authoritarian regimes collide with the processes of capitalist development and the interests of emerging social forces? Exactly what are the points of contradiction? A first type of contradiction comes when mercantilist and/or patrimonial regimes come into conflict with a capitalist class whose business activities are increasingly focused around regularised processes and market mechanisms. Weber (1964: 357) emphasised this aspect:

> . . . under the dominance of a patrimonial regime only certain types of capitalism are able to develop. It leaves room for a certain amount of capitalistic mercantile trade . . . This is not, however, true of the type of profit-making enterprise with heavy investments in fixed capital and a rational organisation of free labour which is oriented to the market purchases of private consumers. This is altogether too sensitive to all sorts of irrationalities in the administration of justice in other forms of administrative practice and in taxation. For these upset the basis of calculability.

While Weber concentrated on the contradiction between 'rational' capital and patrimonial regime, later theorists, including O'Donnell (1979: 297–8), were to focus upon the nationalism of military regimes and the internationalism of the high bourgeoisie. Harris extends this functionalist analysis to include the whole range of constraints that state capitalism imposes upon an emerging capitalist class. It is an analysis of political transformation which focuses upon the conflicts between regime and capital in the sphere of investment and production, rather than, as Cumings does, in the sphere of international trade. Harris (1988) argues that the development of national capitalism usually needs a phase of state-led development whether this is called economic nationalism or socialism. Import substitution, monopoly accumulators and a system of unequal exchange are all part of this phase. Eventually, however, this state and its system of state-led accumulation come to contradict and constrain critical elements of the emerging capitalist classes:

> However, when the state establishes a system for forced accumulation, this is not simply a set of arrangements that can be changed at will. It constitutes a social order, with a weight of inertia constituted by vested interests, the immediate beneficiaries, that inhibits the creation of any other order. What was set up to speed development becomes an inhibition to growth as capital develops, as output diversifies, as businessmen are increasingly drawn to participate in the world economy, and as the need for the psychological participation of a skilled labour force supersedes the dependence upon masses of unskilled labour: capitalism 'matures'. The old state must be reformed or overthrown, to establish the common conditions for all capital: a rule of law, accountability of public officials and expenditure, a competitive labour market and, above all, measures to ensure the common interests of capital can shape the important policies of the State. Thus, the enemy of capitalism is not feudalism but the State, whether this is the corrupt, particularist State, State capitalism, or, as is more often the case, a combination of these (Harris 1988: 247).

In this view the maturation of capitalism establishes a set of conditions which require changes to state policy and in the nature of the relationship with social forces. Two aspects are of further interest here. First, the state gradually withdraws from direct ownership of capital and from market-place intervention. This occurs as the capacity of private capital to compete locally and internationally and to exploit market opportunities increases. Second, the relationship between state and capital changes as capital becomes a more coherent class. The state is increasingly called upon to manage both society and economy in the interests of capital-in-general rather than for specific client groups.

However, it is clear that this relationship between capitalist maturation and political systems refers to a functional contradiction with implications for the state's managerial role. But there is no necessary link between increased rationalisation and democratisation or the institutionalisation of accountability. Rationalisation of these state managerial activities might just as easily be achieved under a highly organised authoritarian regime—as Harris (1988: 248) explains, 'there is no mechanical or inevitable process at work here'. Indeed, whatever the particular political outcome, it will reflect the balance of social forces and the nature of political struggle.

There is, however, a key factor in the political outcomes—the bourgeoisie. Where it develops its corporate strength and its capital base to the stage where accumulation is facilitated more by competition in a market than by state patronage, there are inevitable pressures for the state to become less interventionist. For the larger corporations a state that provides mercantilist systems of monopolies becomes less useful than one which provides common and predictable rules which guarantee the existence of all capital. Where capitalist growth is vigorous and where the national economy becomes increasingly integrated with the world economy, these pressures become more difficult for regimes to resist. This suggests, then, that there are significant contradictions between authoritarianism and market capitalism. Here we can suggest three. First, the resolution of conflict between competing elements of capital requires mechanisms of mediation which authoritarian regimes find difficult to provide. Second, the new relationship between market capitalism and the state requires mechanisms of accountability inimical to most authoritarian regimes, with Singapore a notable exception. Third, the dismantling of mercantilist state powers seriously weakens the power base of the officials who normally exercise authority within such regimes.

The reorganisation of the regime by capital must, however, be seen in the context of broader sets of social relations. Attempts to resolve contradictions in capitalist development by making regimes more accountable may be restrained if capital fears that accountability will threaten the social order: that it does not have the social and economic dominance *vis à vis* other classes sufficient to enable an opening of state power.

The triumph of capital over state and the question of regimes

How is it, then, that regimes are transformed? We have recounted and criticised the *Transitions* position above as one of negotiation, and the importance of 'developmental elites' for theorists like Huntington and Johnson has similarly been rejected. The problem confronting state theorists here is not only to avoid the pitfalls of these approaches, but to avoid the crude reductionism common to all instrumentalist approaches where the state is seen to be a reflection of its social base.

One approach which partly avoided this is found in the works of 1970s radical dependency theorists. They argued that there was no prospect of a transition to accountable regimes. For example, Schmitter (1973: 188), in explaining the persistence of military regimes in Brazil, argued that the Bonapartist model, where '. . . the only form of government possible at a time when the bourgeoisie had already lost, and the working class had not yet acquired, the faculty of ruling the nation', was the most appropriate model. In this analysis state officials and the state are relatively autonomous of civil society because of the destruction of the local bourgeoisie under conditions of dependency.

Similarly, Alavi viewed state autonomy in post-colonial Bangladesh and Pakistan as arising from a fragmentation of class power and the 'over-developed' nature of the bureaucratic apparatus. Both situations were said to arise as a legacy of colonialism:

> . . . the state in the post-colonial society is not the instrument of a single class. It is relatively autonomous and it mediates between the competing interests of the three propertied classes, namely the metropolitan bourgeoisies, the indigenous bourgeoisie and the landed classes, while at the same time acting on behalf of them all to preserve the social order in which their interests are embedded, namely the institution of private property and the capitalist mode as the dominant mode of production (Alavi 1979: 41–2).

The notion that a 'state class' or 'state bourgeoisie' had emerged as one fragment of a petty bourgeoisie under a deformed capitalism was common. For example, Stauffer (1985) has applied this perspective to the Philippines under Marcos, while Robison (1986) and Feith (1980) writing on Indonesia have reflected on this also. However, none of these approaches presents a theory of state and society that adequately explains transition from authoritarianism.

A group of neo-Weberian state-centred theorists including Skocpol, Block and Trimberger have placed great emphasis on the institutional interests of state officials, and consider that the state may be able to override the interests of capital. While Block suggests that capital retains a veto power over the actions of state officials, state-centred theorists tend to exclude the possibility of structural limitations on state autonomy (cf. Cammack 1989).

Miliband's concept of a 'partnership' between state and class has important advantages for examining state–society–regime relation-ships. In Miliband's (1983: 64) view, the

> . . . relationship between the dominant class in advanced capitalist societies and the state is one of partnership between two different,

separate forces, linked to each other by many threads, yet each having its own separate sphere of concerns. The terms of that partnership are not fixed but constantly shifting. . .

It is a concept which, in Miliband's (1983: 65) words,

seeks to give due importance to the independent and 'self regarding' role of the state and to make full allowance for what might be called the Machiavellian dimension of state action, which Marxism's 'class reductionist' tendencies have obscured.

Miliband argues that the two main impulses generated by executive action within the state are the self-interest of power-holders and officials and a conception of the 'national interest'. The latter, he argues, has largely been defined in capitalist society in terms of the well-being of capitalist enterprise, mainly because this is the system that generates production and wealth in society for which there is no conceivable alternative arrangement. This does not mean that the state cannot work against the short- or medium-term interest of individual capitalists or fractions of capital, or that policy decisions cannot turn out to be wrong-headed and to everyone's disadvantage. Clearly there are tensions between state and capital, particularly over taxation reform and regulation. What it does mean, however, is that the state operates under structural constraints when dealing with the perceived general and long-term interests of capital. It is also difficult for leftist governments to mount an attack on the fundamental interests of a hegemonic capitalist class, not only for fear of capital flight but because '. . . capital also knew that it was only a small part of the state that was now in alien hands; the top reaches of the civil service, the police, the military, the judiciary remained more or less intact and vigilantly concerned to limit the damage which the government might do' (Miliband 1983: 66).

Most important, this analysis avoids the huge waste of time consumed in attempting to develop general theoretical propositions about whether state–society relations are instrumental, structural or state-centred. It enables explanations of state action to be made in terms of all three dynamics—instrumental, structural and state-centred—according to the specific historical factors that prevail.

One critical facet of the Miliband thesis is the link it develops between the existence of a hegemonic class and the prospects for the development of an 'accountable' regime with constitutional checks and balances. Miliband (1983: 61) argues that:

The degree of autonomy which the state enjoys for the most purposes in relation to social forces in capitalist society depends above all on the extent to which class struggle and pressure from below challenge the hegemony of the class which is dominant in

such a society. Where a dominant class is truly hegemonic in
economic, social, political and cultural terms, and therefore free
from any major and effective challenge from below, the chances are
that the state itself will also be subject to its hegemony, and that it
will be greatly constrained by the various forms of class power
which the dominant class has at its disposal. Where, on the other
hand, the hegemony of a dominant class is persistently and strongly
challenged, the autonomy of the state is likely to be substantial, to
the point where, in conditions of intense class struggle and political
instability, it may assume 'Bonapartist' and authoritarian forms, and
emancipate itself from constraining constitutional checks and
controls.

Clearly, like most theorists who have concentrated on the history
of capitalism in Europe, Miliband associates authoritarianism with
the sort of autonomy that derives from an absence of an hegemonic
class. Interesting for its further exploration of this theme is Fatton's
(1988) analysis of class and state in Africa, which supports the main
thrust of Miliband's argument. However he cautions against any
assumption that the autonomous, Bonapartist state is the only explanation of authoritarianism in emerging capitalist societies. The
authoritarian state, he argues, may be the product, not of autonomy
from but of subordination to a dominant class dependent upon state
power to ensure its social, economic or cultural means to sustain
its dominance within the sphere of society; it does not dominate the
institutions or ideologies of society (Fatton 1988).

In Fatton's African examples, the officials of the state are not
autonomous and the nature of the struggle is not one between state
and the bourgeoisie, or between state and civil society. The struggle
is between classes, one of which imposes its dominance via a narrow
instrumental control over the state and uses the state's coercive
powers in its own interests. It follows that the shift to a more
accountable state may come only when the increasing hegemony of
the dominant class makes coercion less essential, that is, when the
class's interests and ideologies are embedded in the legal, religious,
educational, industrial and media institutions of society. Fatton's
thesis is that any understanding of the state requires an initial
deciphering of class power and the processes of class formation.
While Miliband might disagree with Fatton's instrumentalism, he
would support this idea of analysing class power in order to determine how it comes to be transformed into political power.

The authoritarian states of Africa, so apparently autonomous in
their violent and coercive relations with much of society, are, Fatton
argues, a very narrow form of class rule in a situation where the
ruling class has not yet attained social and ideological hegemony,
and where class power is totally dependent upon control of the state

and the use of state power for narrow corporate interests. This proposition leads Fatton (1988: 254) to a general thesis about the relationship between the maturation of class hegemony and the transformation of narrow, class-based dictatorships to more democratic and autonomous institutions:

> The non-hegemonic status of the African ruling classes deprives the state of the relative autonomy that makes reform possible, despotism unnecessary, and liberal democracy viable. The state is almost exclusively an authoritarian structure of dominance; expressing the narrow corporate interests of the ruling class, it has failed to become integral. The integral state is the state of a hegemonic ruling class and as such is capable of 'expansion'. It is capable of integrating and coopting into its own institutions potential allies and even antagonistic elements. The integral state is thus relatively autonomous since it can extract certain sacrifices from the ruling class and make certain concessions to the popular classes. The integral state, however, is not above society; it is integral precisely because the ruling class has achieved hegemony. In other words, the integral state can only emerge when the ruling class has consolidated its rule to the point where its material, intellectual and moral leadership is unquestioned or at least consensually accepted by the subordinate classes.

Miliband and Fatton do, however, make a common point: that the accountable or integral state is possible only in societies where the ruling class is not only dominant but hegemonic, and that authoritarian forms are more likely where no class enjoys hegemony.

This is a critical point. It was important, for example, that significant sections of the British ruling class supported political reforms in the nineteenth century because they were assured that the extension of the franchise would not threaten the existing social order. Liberals like Bentham and Mill justified their arguments in favour of reform in precisely these terms, assuring the conservatives that the newly enfranchised masses would be 'responsible' (Macpherson 1977: 37, 42). The importance of hegemony has also been recognised in one way or another by most of the theorists dealt with in this chapter. Although expressing the concept of hegemony in terms of the notion of political order, Huntington recognised that political reform was unlikely where deep and bitter social divisions existed and were manifest in political conflict. It is central to Stepan's explanation of why the bourgeoisie in Uruguay, for example, was more ready to abandon the military junta in that country than their class counterparts in Chile who remained in fear of the strong working-class and revolutionary movements.

Within the advanced industrial economies, ruling-class hegemony in the social sphere is considered by many theorists to have become so all-encompassing that politics has receded in importance. With the incorporation of the proletariat into the capitalist project, we might add, political parties, both conservative and reformist, find themselves competing largely on the basis of their capacity to effectively manage the capitalist process of economic growth—reduced in ideological terms to Tweedledee and Tweedledum. Cumings (1989: 21) notes that, in the United States today, the capitalist order is so thoroughly secured at the social and economic level that '. . . hardly anyone believes that we can solve our problems through the architecture of politics. That is why we derive the President-as-curiosity. . .'.

Concluding comments

Any resolution of this debate or progress towards definitive sets of propositions must come from comparative analysis of dynamics underlying the resilience or reorganisation of regimes in industrialising capitalist societies. Clearly, different situations present different problems for theory. How do we explain Indian democracy in a context of what appears to be a relatively chaotic configuration of social power? Why does an authoritarian form of state power persist in the advanced capitalism of Singapore? Does the Singaporean case reinforce the emphasis upon organisation, strategy, leadership and political voluntarism of the *Transitions* thesis? Do the democratic transitions in Korea or Taiwan indicate the decreasing relevance of the state to the process of capitalist accumulation or to the political dominance of the bourgeoisie? Are there specific problems of transformation or resistance in 'late-industrialising' economies? Is democratisation in this economy a process of re-organisation of regime to save the state carried out by the dominant coalitions of social power? To what extent do popular forces play any decisive role?

Through this collection of Southeast Asian case studies we hope to advance the basis for comparative analysis in addressing the above, and other, questions. Although the different authors do not adopt identical frameworks in the respective chapters, they are nevertheless guided by certain common questions which logically derive from the above critical survey. In particular, the question of political change is viewed as inseparable from socio-economic and historical considerations. At its broadest level, this involves recognition that the general context of political power here is capitalism—and an emerging capitalism that is rapidly taking an industrial form.

This is not to suggest that the form and nature of power is totally shaped by such a context, but the options and constraints facing exponents of power in such societies cannot be understood without specification of the dynamics of capitalism. These dynamics are central to the ability or otherwise of existing regimes to reproduce themselves. However, as will be demonstrated in the subsequent chapters, these dynamics do not manifest themselves in the same fashion from one society to another. Rather, different class structures, variations in the relationships between classes and states, as well as related contrasts in economic structures, all serve to complicate, though not necessarily diminish, the significance of capitalist development for the exercise of power. The impact of capitalist development on political regimes is thus a thematic consideration in this collection, even if that impact may be far from uniform. Indeed, the purpose of the collection is to explore the potential and limits of capitalism in its current phase for political and social change in Southeast Asia.

References

Adriano, Fermin 1984, 'A Critique of the Bureaucratic Authoritarian State Thesis: The Case of the Philippines', *Journal of Contemporary Asia*, vol. 14, no. 4, pp. 459–84

Alavi, Hamza (1979), 'The State in Post-Colonial Societies: Pakistan and Bangladesh', *Politics and the State in the Third World*, ed. Harry Goulbourne, Macmillan, London

Almond, Gabriel A. 1991, 'Capitalism and Democracy', *PS: Political Science & Politics*, vol. 24, no. 3, pp. 467–74

—— 1987, 'The Development of Political Development', in Weiner and Huntington eds (1987), pp. 437–90

—— & Coleman, James S. 1960, *The Politics of Developing Areas*, Princeton University Press, Princeton

Amin, Samir 1974, *Accumulation on a World Scale*, 2 vols. Monthly Review Press, New York

Anderson, Benedict 1988, 'Cacique Democracy in the Philippines: Origins and Dreams', *New Left Review*, no. 169, pp. 3–31

—— 1990, 'Murder and Progress in Modern Siam', *New Left Review*, no. 181, pp. 33–48

Becker, David G. 1984, 'Development, Democracy and Dependency in Latin America: A Post-Imperialist View', *Third World Quarterly*, vol. 6, no. 2, pp. 411–31

Block, Fred 1977, 'The Ruling Class Does Not Rule: Notes on the Marxist Theory of the State', *Socialist Revolution*, no. 7, pp. 6–28

Boron, Atilio 1981, 'Latin America: Between Hobbes and Friedman', *New Left Review*, no. 130, pp. 45–66

Brautigam, Deborah 1991, *Governance and Economy: A Review*, World Bank Policy Research Working Papers WPS 815, Washington DC

Brenner, Robert 1977, 'The Origins of Capitalist Development: A Critique of Neo-Smithian Marxism', *New Left Review*, no. 104, pp. 25–93

Burris, Val 1986, 'The Discovery of the New Middle Class', *Theory and Society*, vol. 15, no. 3, pp. 317–49

Cammack, Paul 1989, 'Review Article: Bringing the State Back In?', *British Journal of Political Science*, vol. 19, no. 2, pp. 261–90

Cheng Tun-jen 1990, 'Is the Dog Barking? The Middle Class and Democratic Movements in the East Asian NICs', *International Studies Notes*, vol. 15, no. 1, pp. 10–16

Cotton, James 1989, 'From Authoritarianism to Democracy in South Korea', *Political Studies*, vol. 37, no. 2, pp. 244–59

Cumings, Bruce 1989, 'The Abortive Abertura: South Korea in the Light of the Latin American Experience', *New Left Review*, no. 173, pp. 5–32

Elliott, David 1978a, *Thailand: The Origins of Military Rule*, Zed Books, London

—— 1978b, 'The Socio Economic Formation of Modern Thailand', *Journal of Contemporary Asia*, vol. 8, no. 1, pp. 21–50

Evans, Peter 1979, *Dependent Development. The Alliance of Multinational, State, and Local Capital in Brazil*, Princeton University Press, Princeton

Evers, Hans-Dieter 1973, 'Group Conflict and Class Formation in South-East Asia', *Modernization in South-East Asia*, ed. Hans-Dieter Evers, Oxford University Press, Singapore

Fatton, Robert 1988, 'Bringing the Ruling Class Back In', *Comparative Politics*, vol. 20, no. 3, pp. 253–64

Feith, Herbert 1980, 'Repressive Developmentalist Regimes in Asia: Old Strengths, New Vulnerabilities', *Prisma*, no. 19, pp. 39–55

Frank, Andre Gunder 1969, *Latin America: Underdevelopment or Revolution?*, Monthly Review Press, New York

Geertz, Clifford ed. 1963, *Old Societies and New States: The quest for modernity in Asia and Africa*, The Free Press, New York

Gerschenkron, Alexander 1962, *Economic Backwardness in Historical Perspective*, Harvard University Press, Cambridge

Goldthorpe, J.H. et al. 1969, *The Affluent Worker in the Class Structure*, Cambridge University Press, Cambridge

Haralambos, Michael 1980, *Sociology: Themes and Perspectives*, University Tutorial Press, Slough

Harris, Nigel 1988, 'New Bourgeoisies', *The Journal of Development Studies*, vol. 24, no. 2, pp. 237–49

Hewison, Kevin 1989a, *Politics and Power in Thailand*, Journal of Contemporary Asia Publishers, Manila

—— 1989b, *Bankers and Bureaucrats: Capital and State in Thailand*, Yale University Southeast Asia Monographs No. 34, New Haven

Higgott, Richard 1983, *Political Development Theory*, Croom Helm, London

Huntington, Samuel 1968, *Political Order in Changing Societies*, Yale University Press, New Haven

—— 1984, 'Will More Countries Become Democratic?', *Political Science Quarterly*, vol. 99, no. 2, pp. 193–218

—— 1987, 'The Goals of Development', in Weiner & Huntington eds (1987)

Jenkins, Rhys 1984, 'Divisions over the International Division of Labour', *Capital & Class*, no. 22, pp.28–57

Johnson, Chalmers 1987, 'Political Institutions and Economic Performance: The Government–Business Relation in Japan, South Korea and Taiwan', *The Political Economy of the New Asian Industrialism*, ed. Frederic C. Deyo, Cornell University Press, Ithaca

Keesing, Roger 1991, 'Asian Cultures?', *Asian Studies Review*, vol. 15, no. 2, pp. 43–50

Korff, Rudiger 1989, *Bangkok and Modernity*, Chulalongkorn University Social Research Institute, Bangkok

Kurth, James R. 1979, 'Industrial Change and Political Change: A European Perspective', *The New Authoritarianism in Latin America*, ed. David Collier, Princeton University Press, Princeton

Laclau, Ernesto 1971, 'Feudalism and Capitalism in Latin America', *New Left Review*, no. 67, pp. 19–38

Leys, Colin 1978, 'Capital Accumulation, Class Formation and Dependency— the Significance of the Kenyan Case', *The Socialist Register 1978*, eds Ralph Miliband & John Saville, Merlin Press, London

Macpherson, C.B. 1977, *The Life and Times of Liberal Democracy*, Oxford University Press, Oxford

Marx, Karl 1969, 'The Eighteenth Brumaire of Louis Bonaparte', from excerpts in *Marx and Engels: Basic Writings on Politics and Philosophy*, ed. Lewis S. Feuer, Fontana, London

Miliband, Ralph 1983, 'State Power and Class Interests', *New Left Review*, no. 138, pp. 57–68

—— 1989, 'Marx and the State', *Democracy and the Capitalist State*, ed. Graeme Duncan, Cambridge University Press, Cambridge

Moore, Barrington 1966, *The Social Origins of Dictatorship and Democracy*, Penguin, Harmondsworth

Nun, Jose 1968, 'A Latin American Phenomenon: The Middle Class Military Coup', *Latin America: Reform or Revolution?*, eds James Petras & Maurice Zeitlin, Fawcett, New York

O'Donnell, Guillermo 1979, 'Tensions in the Bureaucratic Authoritarian State and the Question of Democracy', *The New Authoritarianism in Latin America*, ed. David Collier, Princeton University Press, Princeton

—— & Schmitter, Philippe C. 1986, 'Tentative Conclusions about Uncertain Democracies', in Guillermo O'Donnell, Philippe C. Schmitter & Laurence Whitehead eds (1986)

——, Schmitter, Philippe C. & Whitehead, Laurence (eds) 1986, *Transitions from Authoritarian Rule: Tentative Conclusions about Uncertain Democracies*, The Johns Hopkins University Press, Baltimore

Olson, Mancur 1982, *The Rise and Decline of Nations*, Yale University Press, New Haven

Petras, James 1989, 'State, Regime and the Democratization Muddle', *Journal of Contemporary Asia*, vol. 19, no. 1, pp. 26–32

Przeworski, Adam 1986, 'Some Problems in the Study of Transition to Democracy', in O'Donnell, Schmitter & Whitehead eds (1986)

Pye, Lucien 1990, 'Political Science and the Crisis of Authoritarianism', *American Political Science Review*, vol. 84, no. 1, pp. 3–19

Riggs, Fred W. 1966, *Thailand: The Modernization of a Bureaucratic Polity*, East-West Centre Press, Honolulu

Robison, Richard 1978, 'Towards a Class Analysis of the Indonesian Military-Bureaucratic State', *Indonesia*, no. 25, pp. 17–40

—— 1986, *Indonesia: The Rise of Capital*, Allen & Unwin, Sydney

Schmitter, Philippe C. 1973, 'The "Portugalization" of Brazil', *Authoritarian Brazil*, ed. Alfred Stepan, Yale University Press, New Haven

Skocpol, Theda 1985, 'Bringing the State Back In: Strategies of Analysis in Current Research', *Bringing the State Back In*, eds Peter B. Evans, Dietrich Rueschemeyer & Theda Skocpol, Cambridge University Press, Cambridge

Stauffer, Robert 1985, 'The Philippine Political Economy: (Dependent) State Capitalism in the Corporatist Mode', *Southeast Asia: Essays in the Political Economy of Structural Change*, eds Richard Higgott & Richard Robison, Routledge & Kegan Paul, London

Stepan, Alfred 1985, 'State Power and the Strength of Civil Society in the Southern Cone of Latin America', *Bringing the State Back In*, eds Evans, Rueschemeyer & Skocpol, Cambridge University Press, Cambridge

Swainson, Nicola 1978, 'State and Economy in Post-Colonial Kenya, 1963–1978', *Canadian Journal of African Studies*, vol. 13, no. 3, pp. 357–81

Taylor, John G. 1979, *From Modernization to Modes of Production*, Macmillan, London

Trimberger, Ellen Kay 1977, 'State Power and Modes of Production: Implications of Japanese Transition to Capitalism', *The Insurgent Sociologist*, vol. 7, Spring, pp. 85–98

Turner, Bryan 1978, *Marx and the End of Orientalism*, George Allen & Unwin, London

Warren, Bill 1973, 'Imperialism and Capitalist Industrialisation', *New Left Review*, no. 81, pp. 3–44

—— 1980, *Imperialism: Pioneer of Capitalism*, Verso, London

Weber, Max 1964, *The Theory of Social and Economic Organisation*, The Free Press, New York

Weiner, Myron & Huntington, Samuel (eds) 1987, *Understanding Political Development*, Little Brown, Boston

Yoshihara, Kunio 1988, *The Rise of Ersatz Capitalism in Southeast Asia*, Oxford University Press, Singapore

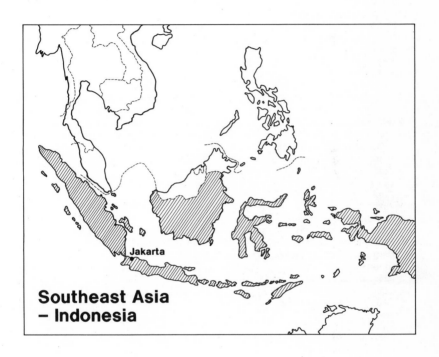

**Southeast Asia
– Indonesia**

Jakarta

Indonesia: Basic social and economic data

Population (1989)	179.1m
Population density (1990)	95 persons per sq. km
Average annual population growth (1982–89)	1.8%
Urban population (1990)	26%
Total labour force (1990)	76.1m
Major ethnic groups	Javanese, Sumatran
Capital city	Jakarta
Population (1985)	7.9m
Land area	1 948 000 sq. km
Official language	Bahasa Indonesia
Other main languages	Javanese, Sundanese, Sumatran, other local languages
Administrative division	Provincial divisions based on large islands or groups of islands
Education, enrolments	
Primary (1990)	30.02m
Secondary (1990)	4.48m
University (1990)	1.83m
Adult literacy rate (1990)	74%
Health	
Life expectancy (1990)	59 yrs
Infant mortality/1000 (1989)	66
Persons/hospital bed (1989)	1814
Persons/physician (1989)	9464
Economy	
GNP at market prices (1989)	US$87.9 bn
Real GNP per capita (1989)	US$490
GNP growth rate (1989)	7.4%
Trade	
Exports, value (1990)	US$25.7 bn
Imports, value (1990)	US$21.8 bn
Main imports (1990)	Machinery & transport equipment 42.7%, manufactures 16.3%, chemicals 15.5%
Main exports (1990)	Mineral fuels 43.8%, manufactures 33.2%, food & animals 9.0%
Foreign debt (1989)	US$53.1 bn
Foreign reserves (1990)	US$8.6 bn
Energy consumption/capita (kg coal equiv. in 1989)	274
Communications	
Rail (1990)	4784.8 km
Roads, paved (1990)	50 749 km
Religion	Predominantly Muslim

Sources: Far Eastern Economic Review Asia Yearbook 1991; The Far East and Australasia 1992 (Europa Publications); United Nations Economic and Social Commission for Asia and the Pacific *Newsletter, Key Indicators of Developing Asian and Pacific Countries* 1991, Asian Development Bank.

3 Indonesia: Tensions in state and regime
Richard Robison[1]

In Marx's celebrated analysis of the Bonapartist state, the French bourgeoisie found it necessary for their survival as a class that parliamentary democracy be replaced with an authoritarian regime. Unable to rule in their own right as revolutionary challenges mounted, they were prepared, in Marx's words, to forfeit the crown in order to save the purse, to hand power to an individual at the head of a huge and parasitic state bureaucracy (Marx 1962: 288).

To an extent, the Bonapartist dynamic also underlay the collapse of the democratic experiment in Indonesia in the 1950s and the subsequent rise of authoritarianism. While admittedly not a bourgeoisie, a fractured and rambling coalition of petty propertied classes, middle-class professionals and state officials generally drawn from the remnants of the old agrarian bureaucracies had dominated the parliamentary regime. Unable to organise themselves into a cohesive class coalition, to reconstitute the crumbling colonial economy or to hold back the rising tides of revolution and reaction, they were overtaken first by a populist form of authoritarianism under Sukarno and then a narrower and more centralised authoritarianism under General Soeharto.

At this point, however, there are important divergences between Marx's model and the Indonesian reality. The Bonapartist regime proved ultimately unable to manage the affairs of the bourgeoisie which eventually stepped in again to reconstitute the regime into its 'appropriate' bourgeois form: a parliamentary democracy. In the Indonesian case, however, the authoritarian regime of President Soeharto became much more than a military dictatorship. It developed a highly complex and politically effective set of ideological and institutional structures. More important, the New Order state became integral to the development of capitalism and an Indonesian capitalist class.

41

The ideological base: The organic state

The ideological basis of Indonesian authoritarianism is the notion of the organic, or integralist state, a pre-Weberian political concept which emerged within the declining absolutist regimes of industrialising continental Europe. It was developed in Indonesia in the late colonial and early republican periods by two nationalist and aristocratic Javanese political thinkers, Supomo and Ki Hadjar Dewantoro. The central features of the organic state thesis are its functional concept of social structure and organisation and its view of the state as transcending particular vested interests within society but embodying its common interests. Such an ideology, the antithesis of bourgeoisie liberalism, provides the ideal legitimation of authoritarian rule and the denial of legitimate political activity outside structures defined by the state. It has obvious and universal utility for ruling elites whose power base resides within the state apparatus itself rather than in mass-based political movements and who depend upon the pre-eminence of values of hierarchy and authority within political culture.

The organic state ideology in its Indonesian manifestation was drawn from several sources. One source was a type of nationalist cultural relativism in which 'Eastern' society was viewed as one characterised by ideals of harmony and consensus, while 'Western' society was considered to be based on individualism, confrontation and materialism. A second source was the political culture of the Javanese aristocrat officials (of which Supomo and Ki Hadjar Dewantoro were representative)—order, authority and hierarchy balanced by the mythology of aristocratic obligation as contrasted to 'western' or 'liberal' government which was seen to be the institutionalised conflict of vested interests (Reeve 1978). These views proved extremely compatible with the conservative, organic political theories of the declining aristocracy of Bismarckian Germany and other European authoritarian monarchies and this may explain their impact on the thinking of Supomo.

The Indonesian liberal democratic experiment of the 1950s saw a series of governments based on complex and fragile party coalitions rise and fall with startling rapidity. In the context of serious and sustained economic decline, endemic corruption and mismanagement, as well as the threat of an increasingly coherent and popular Indonesian Communist Party (PKI), the commitment to democracy by the propertied classes evaporated. Thus there emerged a political opportunity for Sukarno and the military to make a strike against the parliamentary regime. After assuming power, Sukarno progressively institutionalised key aspects of the organic state concept within a new political regime which he termed 'Guided Democracy'. In 1959 the original republican constitution of 1945 was restored and in 1960 the parliamentary model was formally replaced with a presidential system, while the concept of representation shifted from popular elections and cabinet government to representation through 'functional' groups. Hence the new, and appointed, parliament included nominated representatives both of the old parties and of 'functional' organisations established to represent farmers, workers, civil servants, intellectuals, veterans, the military, etc., defined and sanctioned by the state. The possibility for legitimate and independent political organisation outside these state-sanctioned and controlled groups was progressively constrained (Feith 1963; Reeve 1979). Most important, the problem of representation was solved, as Reeve (1978: 94) points out, by divorcing functional representation from access to decision-making. Political power was to reside firmly in the hands of the President and the officials of the state.

The fatal flaw of Guided Democracy was that Sukarno took the ideology of the organic state seriously. He attempted to contain within the state a variety of contradictory and irreconcilable political and social forces: capitalist, petty mercantile capitalist, and communist. The seizure of power by the military in 1965 and the elimination of the PKI resolved the major contradiction. While the fall of Sukarno gave middle class liberals and the Muslim petty bourgeoisie hopes for a broader democratic regime, these were short lived. On the contrary, Soeharto's great political achievement has been to develop a regime that represents a much more sophisticated institutionalisation of state authority over civil society.

The institutional base: Authoritarian corporatism

In the early years of the New Order, the expectation that elections, parties and parliament would be reinstated presented obvious problems for the new government. These were ingeniously resolved in the early 1970s by a series of initiatives carried out under the direction of General Ali Moertopo, through the Special Operations Office (OPSUS). A selected number of the old political parties were permitted to reform and compete electorally under strict government control, but their activities were confined to the actual election period, ensuring that the masses were not diverted from the more urgent tasks of economic development (the so-called floating mass doctrine). This eliminated the political party as a permanent organisation of cadres continually active at all levels on behalf of a coherent set of social interests. Perhaps the most important step was the creation by the state of a party—Golkar—to contest elections and take parliamentary seats on behalf of the state. With the resources, both political and financial, of the military, the presidency and the state bureaucracy—through its functional group KORPRI— Korps Pegawai Republik Indonesia (Corps of State Employees) Golkar was to consistently win large majorities in all of Indonesia's elections (Reeve 1990; Ward 1974; Boileau 1983: 59–121). It was this guarantee that elections would not produce a hostile parliament or constitute an arena for opposition that made elections possible.

The second major advance was to remove any possibility for legitimate political organisation outside the state apparatus and in contradiction with state ideology. The state ideology of Pancasila played a critical role in this process. It is not the policy content of Pancasila that is important, this being fairly bland generalisations about national unity, social justice and belief in one God which may be found in most statements of national principles. What is important about Pancasila as interpreted and propagated by the New Order is that it legitimises authoritarianism as a mechanism that achieves the common will of society through consensus under the tutelage of a state in the possession of its own officials.

Of greater immediate political utility, Pancasila defines what are not legitimate political objectives and values: liberalism, laissez-faire capitalism, communism or, indeed, any exclusive religious, racial or ethnic/regional position. In 1983 legislation was introduced requiring all political parties to adopt Pancasila as their sole ideological basis (Azas Tunggal). This particularly damaged the Muslim political party which was prohibited from claiming any special representation of Islam or carriage of Islamic values. Similarly no potential social reformist party would be permitted to claim to specially represent the interests of the working class or to have a special concern for social justice. In effect, all political parties were now required to accept Pancasila ideology and platform, permitted to differ only in their claims to be its most effective implementers. In 1985 the Azas Tunggal principle was extended to all non-government organisations under the terms of the ORMAS—Organisasi Masyarakat (Social Organisations) legislation (Lubis 1990: 166–72, 212–45).

The dominance of the state and its strata of officials, and the ideology of the state as guardian of the general interests of society, also existed in the economic sphere. What were considered to be the destructive tendencies of economic self-interest embedded in laissez-faire liberalism were to be subordinated to the broader social interest through the stewardship of the state. In practice, Indonesian *dirigisme* meant a wide variety of mercantilist state interventions from direct ownership to nationalist strategies of industrial planning, and state authority over a range of economic activities from trade to investment. This gave state bureaucrats a strategic grip on the commanding heights of the economy and opportunities to cultivate not only the authority of state over market but to build important alliances between themselves and corporate capitalist clients.

The New Order does not fit easily into recognised categories of political regime or state. For example, there is no dominant party similar to that found in the classic fascist, corporatist dictatorships of Spain, Portugal or Italy or even of Syria or Iraq today. In these countries the party exercised authority over the state apparatus whereas in Indonesia it is the officials of the state apparatus who create the state party as its instrument. Nor is the state the arena of dominant landowning or capitalist families as it has tended to be in Latin America or the Philippines. Neither can the Indonesian state be compared with the powerful industrialising states of Japan, Korea, Taiwan or Singapore where the position of the bureaucracy is cast much more within a legal-rational framework. The fundamentally unique feature of Indonesia's New Order is that the source of political power and political leadership lies within the state apparatus itself, and that political power and bureaucratic authority are appropriated and integrated by the officials of the state.

Both the language and institutions of the New Order are corporatist in their insistence on the existence of a common national good and the purported organisation of political activity into functional units rather than competing interests. Schmitter's (1974: 96) definition of corporatism captures the appearance of political organisation under the New Order:

> Corporatism can be defined as a system of interest representation in which the constituent units are organised into a limited number of singular, compulsory, noncompetitive hierarchically ordered and functionally differentiated categories recognised or licensed (if not created) by the state and granted a deliberate representational monopoly within their respective categories in exchange for observing certain controls on their selection of leaders and articulation of demands and supports.

In reality, Indonesian corporatism is less concerned with interest representation than with state control and social discipline. The non-competitive political organisations within which political activity is confined do not constitute a classical tripartite bargaining arrangement between labour, capital and the state but, rather, a mechanism for domination by an authoritarian regime. This distinction between corporatism as an instrument of authoritarian political control and as a form of social bargaining is similar to that made by Schmitter in his contrast of what he calls state corporatism and the societal corporatism of some advanced industrial economies, and by Lehmbruch who contrasts authoritarian corporatism with liberal corporatism (Cawson 1986: 68–9).

State and society

Political authority within the New Order resides in the hands of a dominant stratum of bureaucrats who not only have a political identity but a coherent set of values and interests. The regime, which might be termed authoritarian corporatism, provides it with a set of institutional structures and constitutional relationships within which it exercises political authority. But the regime cannot be understood as solely the vehicle of a bureaucratic elite; it is integral to the broader system of state power and the social relations embedded within it. The tensions in the New Order cannot be represented as simply a contest between the state and civil society, notably the bourgeoisie. On the contrary, important segments of the bourgeoisie and the middle classes strongly support the state.

Although the regime is not accountable to these supporting coalitions through formal constitutional and institutional processes, it operates in a framework of constraints and obligations which require it, among other things, to maintain economic growth—which means providing a conducive environment for capitalist investment and production—and to cultivate at least some degree of legitimacy with the propertied and middle classes and with the Muslim leadership closely associated with the landed and entrepreneurial petty bourgeoisie.

But there has also emerged a more instrumental link between state and the bourgeoisie. Over the past quarter century state officials have built for themselves a new dimension of social power and identity as families of the middle class and bourgeoisie. Linkages with the major conglomerates, primarily Chinese but also *pribumi* (indigenous) are institutionalised in common shareholding and joint ventures. Large numbers of bureaucrat families have directly entered the world of business, led by the Soeharto family itself but repeated on a descending scale down to local and regional officials. Hence, the most powerful of the politico-bureaucrats tend to have quite direct interests in ensuring capital accumulation, not only as a general proposition but for specific corporate entities; an interest which sometimes conflicts with that of maintaining the autonomy and authority of the state.

On the part of the bourgeoisie and the middle classes, there has been a general accord with both state and regime. However, there are internal tensions over the issues of arbitrary exercise of state power, official corruption, constraints on freedom of speech and relations between the state and the conglomerates because these are not to the advantage of liberal elements of the middle class, foreign investors and sections of the Muslim petty bourgeoisie. However, the emerging and established corporate conglomerates, the dominant elements of the Indonesian bourgeoisie, continue to rely heavily upon these very factors. Above these internal tensions, this broad social coalition is bound to the New Order because it provides political stability—meaning protection from popular and populist political challenges—and economic growth.

The political structures, economic strategies and social alliances which constitute the New Order are now confronting several challenges which are the product of internal contradictions. First, as the Soeharto presidency prepares to enter its final term of office, the regime must contemplate the capacity of its political institutions and constitutional arrangements to manage change from one government to the next and thereby guarantee the long-term existence of the state. As it stands there are no formal mechanisms of negotiation, accountability or participation, however limited, able to mediate and resolve conflicts between contending factions and provide an institutional base for alliances. Second, the capacity of Indonesian *dirigisme* to provide a framework for economic growth in the post-oil era is under serious question. Pressures for economic reform strike at one of the central terminals of bureaucrat power: its mercantilist and neo-patrimonial control of the economy. Third, the emergence of a new and powerful class in the form of an alliance of bureaucrat families and corporate conglomerates has given rise to social tension within the social coalitions that support the New Order. Pressure to regularise relationships between state and capital threaten this social dimension of bureaucrat power.

Challenges to the regime

The President's dilemma

Within the state apparatus the critical and focal point of power lies with the President. Part of this ascendancy is embedded in the constitutional authority of the office itself: its autonomy and ascendancy in relation to the parliament and in the power to select a cabinet. However, the real basis of Soeharto's power is the institutional arrangements and political alliances he has constructed in the past twenty-six years. These are elements of power that would not automatically be transferred to any successor. In the early years of the New Order, Soeharto developed extra-constitutional instruments of rule under his direct authority or that of his close associates. These included the security apparatus, Kopkamtib, his inner circle of advisers, ASPRI—Asisten Pribadi (Personal Assistant), and the strategic and political body, OPSUS, under the leadership of General Moertopo (Crouch 1978: 221–72). Soeharto also secured effective authority within Golkar as head of its Control Board (Dewan Pembina—DP), a position that enables him to determine selection of Golkar office-holders and candidates (Jenkins 1984: 127). This meant that Soeharto wielded substantial control over the membership of both the parliament (DPR) and the People's Consultative Assembly (MPR), the body that meets every five years to elect the President and set the guidelines of state policy for the coming five-year presidential period.

The President also has very substantial resources of patronage which he has used to attract considerable support from local officials and leaders of local communities as well as more powerful figures in the bureaucracy and the military. He has at his disposal several important sources of funding. Banpres (Presidential Assistance) is a fund within the state budget, operated by the State Secretariat, which allocates funds to local and regional communities for schools, hospitals and public works. However, it is perhaps the tax-free charitable foundations (Yayasans), controlled by Soeharto, that provide the most important source of funding and reveal the full complexity of the President's power base. It is estimated that eighteen Yayasans have been established by Soeharto for purposes ranging from building mosques and funding Golkar to assisting destitute children. Office-holders in the Soeharto Yayasans include state officials, family members and business associates, and the Yayasans are both investors in businesses and recipients of fees and contributions paid by companies, many of them in monopoly positions (*Far Eastern Economic Review [FEER]* 4 October 1990; Yoon 1989: 247–8). The Yayasans are a unique amalgam of public and private power which are tied to Soeharto and not the office of President. This is nowhere better illustrated than in the case of Yayasan Dakab where public officials and private citizens, including members of the Soeharto family and business figures, are shareholders and office-holders in a foundation established to provide funds to the state political party, Golkar (Indonesia 1985: 1–7).

Soeharto has also been able to greatly increase the institutional power of the presidency through the development of the State Secretariat (Sekneg) as the instrument of direct presidential control over important sectors of the state apparatus, including the military. Banpres, the National Economic Planning Board (Bappenas), the Investment Co-ordinating Board (BKPM), the State Logistics Board (Bulog), and the Technology Research and Development Board (BPPT) which now encompasses state-owned strategic industries, are all responsible to the President and administered through Sekneg (Pangaribuan 1988: 9–10). In addition, the passing of Presidential Decisions (Keppres) 14A and 10 in 1980 gave Sekneg control of allocation of contracts for supply and construction related to gov-

ernment projects. Between 1980 and 1986, Rp.39.5 trillion (approximately US$20 billion) worth of contracts were processed
(Pangaribuan 1988: 205). The point of contact between both international and domestic business and the state was firmly established
in Sekneg in this period. A most important consequence of this was
the exclusion of the military from key sources of patronage and
economic influence.

At the age of seventy, Soeharto now finds himself faced with the
problem of organising a succession of power to the next President.
There are several difficulties in this exercise. Because Soeharto's
power is comprised largely of networks of political and economic
alliances, systems of patronage and sources of finance which are
not bestowed by the formal constitutional powers of the President,
whoever replaces him will inherit only a fraction of his real political
power. It is therefore unlikely that the configuration of power will
remain the same. New alliances in which the position of the President is less dominant and more accountable are probable. It must
be emphasised that this is not to suggest a new state but, on the
contrary, a reorganisation of the regime to preserve the existing state
and hold intact its social and political hierarchies.

A major difficulty is that the formal institutions and mechanisms
through which the process of selecting a new President takes place
are weak. With no party structure within which political alliances
may be forged and guarantees for stable support for the incoming
President negotiated, the process must take place informally. As the
late General Simatupang pointed out, the lack of formal mechanisms
for organising the succession opened the way for an era of new and
shifting political alliances unconstrained by structures and regulations, '. . . a kind of anarchy with everyone manoeuvring for
position' (*FEER* 18 January 1990).

Struggle within the regime: Soeharto and ABRI

The political struggle between elements of ABRI (Armed Forces of
the Republic of Indonesia) and the factions surrounding the President which have taken place in the past decade has been focused
around the constitutional power of the presidency and the political
power of Soeharto rather than any fundamental differences over the
nature of the autonomy and authority of the Indonesian state. The
major question that comes out of the conflict is whether it will lead
to political consequences unforeseen by its agents and open the
regime to new alliances and new constitutional forms.

ABRI is a complex institution. Most of the leading figures in
Indonesian politics, including Soeharto himself, Internal Affairs
Minister Rudini and, indeed, Sudharmono, are former military

officers. A distinction must be drawn between those whose power lies outside the institutional structures of ABRI, however much they rely on its coercive power for their political dominance, and those whose interests lie within ABRI as an institution. This latter group is primarily to be found within ABRI's command structure and the Ministry of Defence. Its leading figures include General Moerdani and General Sudradjat and a broad range of retired and serving officers, many of them in parliament, committed to the institutional interests of ABRI. It was these elements who were to become increasingly critical of the President in the post-1988 era and to call for political and social reforms. Even this division of interest within ABRI is problematic. Important officers in the command structure, including the present ABRI commander, General Try Sutrisno and several officers recently appointed to very strategic commands, are regarded as Soeharto appointments and dependent upon patronage from this source.

ABRI has long considered that it has a legitimate right to participate in political life as guardian of the revolution it felt it had made possible. To some extent, this claim has been recognised in the institutional arrangements of the New Order. Representation is reserved in the DPR for ABRI which also plays a leading role in Golkar. Key senior positions in the state apparatus and the Ministries, particularly in the areas of political, legal and security affairs, have tended to be filled by military officers. ABRI's influence in the early period of the New Order was diluted as other centres of power and influence emerged. These included General Ali Moertopo's 'Special Operations' organisation, Opsus in the 1970s, the State Secretariat in the 1980s, as well as the economic technocrats in the Economic Planning Board, Bappenas. ABRI's position received a major setback in 1974 when the head of the military-dominated security apparatus, Kopkamtib, General Soemitro, was defeated in a power struggle with General Moertopo, resulting in a major shift of power and influence to the Presidential Palace. By the 1980s the privileged position of ABRI as an institution within the state apparatus had become increasingly ambiguous.

Its long political decline was, in part, the consequence of protracted conflict between ABRI and Sekneg, which, under Sudharmono, had done much to undermine ABRI's political and economic power in the 1980s. Keppres 10 and 14A, discussed earlier, had effectively cut the military out of that strategic intersection where contracts for supply and construction were decided. At the same time the military's lucrative forestry and transport monopolies had largely evaporated as better capitalised conglomerates and new family enterprises moved in. Since his appointment as Head of Golkar in 1983, Sudharmono had set about reducing military influence and introducing civilians into key positions within the state party. This was clearly a move to develop Golkar as an alternative channel to the military for producing the cadres and leadership of the New Order.

The year 1988 was a particularly bad one for ABRI. Powerful ABRI Commander, Moerdani, was made Minister for Defence, an effective downgrading of his power. The military-dominated security command, Kopkamtib, was replaced by a new organisation, Bakorstanas, which reported directly to Cabinet and to the President. Many of its previous security functions were transferred to the police. The military were no longer actively to intervene in what were now defined as civil matters, including student demonstrations and Muslim protests. The new body, although still headed by the armed forces commander, was more accountable and subject to formal legal constraints, a change in status which represented a major downgrading of the autonomy and civil power of the military (*Tempo* 17 September 1988; 19 November 1988; *FEER* 22 September 1988). Significantly, the new arrangements, under Keppres 25 of 1988, were announced by State Secretary Moerdiono.

The most dramatic confrontation came when ABRI failed in a very public attempt to block the appointment of State Secretary Sudharmono as Vice President after Soeharto's 1988 election. That the President simply overrode their objections brought home to them the realisation that their power and influence was less than they had assumed and that while the President clearly relied upon the military as the coercive base of the New Order their access to the levers of power and influence had never really been guaranteed. This began a long struggle on the part of ABRI leaders to regain influence within the New Order.

The events of 1988 were not all negative for ABRI. Sudharmono's elevation to the Vice Presidency was a two-edged sword. It effectively separated him from his power base—Sekneg—and gave him a largely ceremonial role in politics. By 1992 ABRI had seized back much of the ground gained by Sekneg whose strategic control of the allocation of government contracts had been ended and influence within Golkar curtailed. Nevertheless, it had become clear that ABRI was no longer a centre of power that set the policy agenda but, increasingly, the bodyguard of the regime. Political reform involving the imposition of some form of accountability and transparency upon the state apparatus, especially the Presidency, could therefore be seen from ABRI's point of view as a means of redressing this imbalance of intra-regime power in its favour.

A second dimension of the ABRI/Presidential conflict has been the question of social justice, particularly the economic dominance of the Chinese business conglomerates and the position of the

President's family in the world of business. Given that President Soeharto is extremely vulnerable on this issue, the focus on social justice is an obvious strategy to undermine his political position. However, the attack by ABRI on the new bureaucrat–capitalist alliance is not simply a cynical device in the struggle between competing bureaucratic institutions. While ABRI clearly sees the emerging bourgeoisie, embodying the integration of conglomerate wealth and bureaucrat authority, as an amalgam of power likely to further marginalise its own institutional position, this political hostility also derives from a genuine tradition of petty bourgeois populism within ABRI.

One channel of protest for the reformist ABRI critics has been the military party in the DPR (F-ABRI—Armed Forces Fraction). In a forum usually noted for its supine nature, F-ABRI members, notably Police Colonel Roekmini Soedjono and General Samsudin, were to take the lead in using the DPR as the vehicle for public discussion of a range of issues including government controls on press freedom, the accountability and transparency of the bureaucracy and its operations, and the subordination of parliament to the bureaucracy (*Kompas, Pelita, Merdeka* 28 June 1989; *Tempo* 8 July 1989). As Chairman of the DPR's Second Commission, under the Chairmanship of Samsudin was used as a forum for public airing of these issues (*Tempo* 8 July 1989; 15 July 1989).

Social issues were also targeted by the F-ABRI which was more active than the other parliamentary fractions in receiving disputants to the DPR, particularly those protesting compulsory land acquisitions. General Samsudin was to shake the DPR with the claim that ' . . . the land in Irian Jaya has already been divided up by elements from Jakarta' (*Tempo* 15 July 1989). Although this was public knowledge, such matters were particularly sensitive given the identity of those 'Jakarta elements' who were expropriating Indonesia's land. These allegations therefore constituted a direct assault upon those leading political and business figures who could be seen increasingly to constitute a putative ruling class.

Outside the DPR the reformist position in both its political and social dimensions was propagated within military staff college seminars and in public statements by Moerdani, Sudradjat and other senior officers. These were widely reported in the media and tended to focus upon three major themes: the need to move from authoritarianism to a more open political system that would nurture initiative and new ideas in society; the need to abandon feudal attitudes in favour of a more modern, rational approach in the bureaucracy; and the need to eliminate gross distortions in wealth and to protect the weaker sections of society against the wealthy and powerful (*FEER* 18 January 1990; 3 August 1989; *Kompas* 28 June 1989; 13

November 1990; 12 January 1991; *Suara Pembaruan* 25 May 1991; *Jakarta Post* 4 March 1992). ABRI has pointedly refrained from endorsing Soeharto as a candidate for the Presidency in 1993 (*Editor* 23 June 1990).

The most detailed exposition of the approach taken by reformist ABRI elements has come from the retired General Soemitro. In his view, now that communism has been destroyed and Pancasila has been established as the sole basis for politics, there is no need for the strict control and management of the DPR and the parties currently exercised by the government. Further, he has argued, political parties should now be mass-based with the initiatives coming from the bottom rather than being imposed from above. This not only applies to the non-government parties but to Golkar, whose subordination to the state apparatus through such institutions as Korpri should be ended. Political leadership, he proposes, should be cultivated within the parties. Experience in the DPR and MPR he sees as a pre-requisite for candidacy to higher office (Soemitro 1989; 1990).

However, ABRI's vision of political reform is framed by an insistence that it will not involve any disturbance of the existing social and political hierarchies. Soemitro argued for the reduction of some presidential powers, including the power to nominate the membership of the DPR and Golkar, because, in his view, the successful implementation of Pancasila now means that these authoritarian controls are no longer necessary to guarantee continuation of the existing policy regime or to protect the social order. His democracy is predicated upon the Pancasila vision that all parties are dedicated to the 'national interest' and not to sectional interests.

Senior ABRI officers, including ABRI Commander Sutrisno and Army Commander Sudradjat, have endorsed openness but with the proviso that it did not interfere with economic development, bring about a fundamental change of values (liberal, 'western'), or disturb national discipline and order. That Sudradjat did not have liberal reform in mind is illustrated by his claim that the concepts of majority and minority did not concern Indonesia which adheres to the family principle (*Kompas* 19 December 1990). Sutrisno was anxious that in any political reform everyone continued to '. . . know his place, function and responsibility' (*Kompas* 10 December 1990). A range of military spokesmen expressed concern that vigilance be exercised to ensure that 'openness' was not exploited by 'small groups' (*Kompas* 7 August 1987; 9 November 1990; 17 November 1990; 21 November 1990; 9 December 1990; *Kedaulatan Rakyat* 3 August 1987).

The ABRI dilemma, therefore, is to reconcile greater political

openness and the reduction of presidential power with the maintenance of the existing social order and the prevailing political ideologies and state policies; to change the regime and preserve the
state. In the system of Pancasila democracy, some centre of power
must fulfil the role of arbiter and enforcer of the 'national interest'.
Just as the populist social reformism of ABRI poses no real blueprint
for greater social justice other than moral exhortation or arbitrary
expropriations, ABRI presents no real solution to the political
dilemma.

Apart from these inconsistencies, however critical, the capacity
of the ABRI reformers to influence the course of events is unclear.
On the one hand, there is little doubt that ABRI is the one political
institution able to guarantee the succession by ensuring a solid base
of power and support for a new presidential incumbent. On the other
hand, ABRI's unity is not assured. Although there appears to be an
accord between Moerdani and Soemitro, previously in hostile
camps, control of the military does not rest unambiguously in the
hands of the reformers. President Soeharto remains the central
source of patronage and influence. The present ABRI commander,
General Try Sutrisno, is considered a Soeharto appointment and
several recent controversial appointments to two key positions
reflect the hand of Soeharto rather than the decisions of the Army
Command. The new commander of the Jakarta regional command,
Kentot Harseno, is a former adjutant of Soeharto, and the new
commander of the strategic reserve, Kostrad, Wismoyo
Arismunandar, a relative of Mrs Soeharto and former commander
of Soeharto's personal bodyguard (*Editor* 11 August 1990; 18
August 1990; *Tempo* 18 August 1990).

In the final analysis ABRI's reformism is severely constrained.
On the one hand, in order to reduce the power of an authoritarian
Presidency, which it sees as being increasingly a component of a
hegemonic alliance of corporate conglomerates and powerful
bureaucrat families, it must open the political system and enter into
alliances with social forces outside the state. On the other hand,
these strategies must, by their very nature, undermine the political
dominance of the state and its strata of bureaucrats. As Levebvre
(cited in Hobsbawm 1990: 133) observed in the case of the French
revolution, '. . . the revolution was launched by those whom it was
going to sweep away, not by those who were to be its beneficiaries'.
Yet the military has little choice but to move in the current direction.
The long-term significance of its intervention may well be to
provide the catalyst for a political transformation within which its
own power is fundamentally reconstituted.

Political reform and the bourgeoisie

Barrington Moore's (1969: 418) dictum, 'No bourgeoisie, no democracy', may well be true but it does not follow that the presence of a bourgeoisie necessarily implies liberal democracy or that this class will support democratic reform in all situations. In the classic English case, the emerging industrial bourgeoisie was truly the political force behind liberalism, not only because the absolutist state represented mercantilist and *rentier* interests which restrained the growth of industrial capital but because the English bourgeoisie largely provided its own capital and funded its own infrastructure. In terms of international trade, the English bourgeoisie required laissez faire, not protection. In short, the new bourgeoisie did not need mercantilist absolutism. In later cases of industrialisation in Germany, Japan and more recently, Korea, the development of capitalism was achieved under the state umbrella and with state finance. The bourgeoisie in these situations found its interests embedded in states and regimes that were *dirigiste* and authoritarian (Kurth 1979). Broadly speaking the Indonesian bourgeoisie finds itself in this latter pattern.

The *dirigisme* of the New Order has two facets: mercantilist and patrimonial/rent-seeking. On the one hand the state intervenes in mercantilist fashion to protect national enterprise and national economic agendas, including the development of such upstream manufacturing industries as steel and petrochemicals, through tariffs, monopolies and state-funded industrial projects. In another dimension, its officials appropriate state resources and authority on behalf of specific political and corporate interests. Under this *dirigiste* regime the growth of a capitalist class has proceeded with great rapidity. Between 1977 and 1990 approved domestic investment increased from Rp.574 billion to 59 878 billion (World Bank 1991: 206) with the private sector share now clearly outstripping that of the state sector both in terms of capital formation and share of value added (Soesastro 1991: 70; Pangestu 1991: 45).

Dirigisme has been critical to the power and autonomy of the state and its bureaucracy. We have seen how Sekneg controlled the allocation of contracts for supply and construction for much of the 1980s. Levers of economic power have also resided with a range of government departments and corporations including the departments of Industry and Trade, the state oil company, Pertamina, and the state agency controlling pricing and distribution of essential commodities, Bulog. These presided over strategic monopolies and allocated contracts providing the state and its bureaucrats with sources of revenue and economic power.

Within this framework of state protection and bureaucrat favour, domestic corporate capital grew strongly. The largest of the domestic corporate groups are now international conglomerates with interests in a range of sectors including manufacturing, property, banking, construction, forestry and trade. The vast bulk of these are Chinese-owned. Below the major conglomerates are a broad group of mainly Chinese manufacturers in textiles, engineering, footwear and food-stuffs who are providing the cutting edge of non-oil exports (Robison 1986: 271-322; Yoon 1989: 321–86).

Indigenous (*pribumi*) capitalists are a much smaller component of the domestic bourgeoisie and have tended to emerge from various state policy offensives to stimulate *pribumi* capital. There are still to be found a few whose rise was launched by the Benteng policy of the 1950s which attempted to channel trade monopolies to *pribumi* entrepreneurs. Pertamina in the early 1970s and Sekneg in the 1980s were two more recent sources of contracts, concessions and licences which were to underpin the rise of *pribumi* capitalists. It was through these channels that an extensive, and potentially cohesive category of *pribumi* capitalists has emerged. Several came from established indigenous capitalist families, including Bakrie, Kowara and Kalla, while others have risen from outside although managing to gain access to important facilities: Iman Taufik, Fahmi Idris, Fadel Muhammad and others in the so-called Kodel group (*Prospek* 18 May 1991). Many have important links with Soeharto family business groups.

Other *pribumi* capitalists more immediately connected to the centres of power were able to obtain facilities that transcended any formal policy initiatives. The bulk of this category of *pribumi* capitalists are from bureaucrat families, notably the Soeharto children—Sigit, Bambang, Tommy, Siti Rukmana—and various other relatives including Probosutejo, Sudwikatmono, Sukamdani and numerous players on the shadowy margins such as Ibnu Hardoyo. The children of other bureaucrat families, including the Sutowos and Sudharmonos are also prominent in business.

The interests of this bourgeoisie and the set of state–capital relations that sustain it appeared threatened by the substantial struc-tural changes and economic deregulation which followed the col-lapse of oil prices in the mid-1980s. Not only was the state less able to finance the major industrial projects which had been at the heart of domestic corporate activity in the 1980s, it was forced to abandon much of its mercantilist policy thrust in order to stimulate an internationally competitive non-oil sector (Robison 1987). The economic reforms introduced in the past five years have dismantled trade monopolies, deregulated banking and relaxed foreign invest-ment regulations (Pangestu 1989: 218–33).

Liberal intellectuals, including such prominent public commentators as Sjahrir, Kwik Kian Gie and Christianto Wibisono, and several of the editorial writers of the major newspapers and weekly political and economic journals, have seen deregulation as a powerful force for broader liberal transformation. Transparency and accountability imposed in the sphere of economic management, they assumed, would spill over into the political sphere as a consequence of the remorseless march of rational behaviour and the structural weakening of the power of bureaucrats as their control of economic resources and patronage networks declines (*Tempo* 6 January 1990).

Their expectations have been in part fulfilled as the economic power of various government departments and instrumentalities, including Industry, Trade, Customs and Sekneg, was substantially eroded. Some moves have been made towards privatisation and the ending of state monopolies in certain areas, notably television broadcasting. However, other elements within the state apparatus have remained unscathed. Most important in this category is Habibie's Department of Research and Technology and the 'strategic' industries that have been brought under its umbrella.

The attitude of the various elements of the bourgeoisie towards deregulation is a critical factor in deciding the extent of the transition from *dirigisme* to market and whether reform in the economic sphere will lead to political liberalism and to democracy. Has the Indonesian bourgeoisie reached a stage where growth and expansion can be more profitably sought through competition in the marketplace, utilising capital and organisational resources rather than access to political favours in a patrimonial/rent-seeking state structure? Does the bourgeoisie now require a state that is accountable to the requirements of the market and does this involve mechanisms for ensuring political accountability and transparency which may involve representative processes?

There are undoubtedly segments of the bourgeoisie that seek a more liberal economic regime. Downstream manufacturers have welcomed deregulation and the erosion of the trade monopolies which sustained high input costs throughout the 1980s (Robison 1992: 73–82). International capital and international institutions such as the World Bank have long called for deregulation and the ending of *dirigisme*. Even the major conglomerates have found that deregulation has benefited them in some sectors. Deregulation of the financial sector has enabled an unprecedented expansion of investment in the past few years although this is bringing problems in increased levels of debt (*FEER* 12 October 1989; 20 December 1990; Taubert 1991). Some capitalists have benefited from the ending of state monopolies in certain sectors, notably airlines and television, while, on the other hand, deregulation threatens to bring hard times to domestic investors in the automobile industry.

For the largest conglomerates, however, *dirigisme* continues to provide a necessary and critical basis for business success although often in a changed form. The ending of import monopolies in sectors critical to broader industrial production, notably plastics, cold-rolled steel and petrochemicals, has seen a shift of former monopoly-holders into upstream manufacturing in those sectors. The massive investments in industrial projects over the past five years, estimated at US$70 billion in 1991, have been dominated by the largest of the Chinese conglomerates, especially Prajogo's Barito group and Liem Sioe Liong's Salim group as well as Bambang Soeharto's *pribumi* group, Bimantara. The key to this investment has not been ability to secure a formal monopoly but access to finance from the state banks, which have been the major funding source for investment in this sector. Government banks and departments have reportedly channelled Rp.90 trillion into non-*pribumi* companies in the context of current development projects (*Tempo* 20 July 1991).

With the exception of the Bimantara and Humpuss groups, which have received generous state bank finance for petrochemical and other ventures, including Tommy Soeharto's cloves monopoly, *pribumi* capitalists have not been at the centre of the explosion of conglomerate wealth in the deregulation period. However, this has not led them to demand an ending of *dirigisme* and the subordination of state to market but, on the contrary, has led to demands for the *dirigiste* regime to take greater account of their interests. Most important was the visit to the President by a group of seventeen prominent *pribumi* capitalists in July 1991 protesting the flow of offshore and state bank loans to Chinese conglomerates and demanding greater access for *pribumis* (*Tempo* 20 July 1991).

There is, therefore, little evidence to suggest that either the largest corporate groups or the most politically important elements among the Indonesian bourgeoisie have reached a stage where their continued expansion requires a fundamental change from *dirigisme* to the triumph of market over state. Even less so is there any evidence that this bourgeoisie is pressing for liberal reform at the political level. For the Chinese conglomerates, their position is so vulnerable to social resentment that political stability takes clear precedence over any preferences for state accountability or the establishment of liberal or democratic reform. Hence, the greatest concern of Chinese businessmen in Jakarta today is that the succession should be achieved without prejudicing either the social order or the economic and political environment provided by the current amalgam of authoritarianism and *dirigisme*.

As now recognised by earlier, enthusiastic, liberal commentators the assumed link between economic deregulation and the emergence of a liberal economy is problematic (*Tempo* 6 January 1990; Soesastro 1989). The major political and business associations representing the *pribumi* bourgeoisie rely upon state intervention on their behalf to enable their very survival in a corporate world dominated by the Chinese conglomerates. These organisations include Kadin (the Indonesian Chamber of Commerce and Industry), the elite organisation, HIPMI (the Young Indonesian Businessmen's Association), and the conservative, chauvinistic HIPPI (the Businessmen's Association of the Sons of Indonesia). None of these advocate economic liberalism and deregulation for the simple reason that *pribumi* business continues to be largely sustained by state protection and favour. Since the ending of Keppres 10 in 1988 and the decline of Sekneg as a source of patronage, many larger *pribumi* businesses have become increasingly involved in co-operation and joint ventures with Chinese conglomerates. There has been a recent discernible softening of anti-Chinese rhetoric among these groups, reflecting this new reality (*Prospek* 18 May 1991).

If the assumption that deregulation equals economic liberalism is flawed, then the assumption that deregulation will somehow lead to political liberalism is an even more tenuous proposition. The *pribumi* bourgeoisie has not been active in pursuing liberal and democratic reform in the political sphere. In the 1980s prominent *pribumi* capitalists threw their support behind Golkar while it was under the tutelage of Sudharmono. Their membership and financial support for the party came at the time of Sekneg's sponsorship of Keppres 10 and 14A, the most interventionist of policies which had provided the basis upon which the latest wave of *pribumi* capitalists were to consolidate their position (*Prospek* 18 May 1991).

Within the Youth front organisations associated with Golkar a new and interesting political grouping emerged, comprised of the children of retired ABRI officers, many of them involved in business (FDPPI—Discussion Forum of the Sons and Daughters of the Retired Military Officers of Indonesia). By all accounts this is not a well organised group. Nevertheless, it is a significant organisation because it involves members of the leading political and bourgeois families organising on the basis of their common membership of a social elite rather than their common membership of an institution such as ABRI, KORPRI or Kadin. It represents, however poorly organised and understood by its own members, a bourgeois political organisation. Yet its position remains intensely reactionary (*Jawa Pos* 2 November 1987; *Tempo, Kompas* 7 November 1987). This is an important reminder that the bourgeoisie in history has more often played the role of right-wing conservative than liberal reformist.

Why is this the case in Indonesia? Put simply, none of the

fractions of the Indonesian bourgeoisie are yet able to dispense with the *dirigiste* and authoritarian regimes which constitute the New Order. Their hegemony is not established in either social or economic life nor has the bourgeois ideology of equality before the law replaced the hierarchical organic outlook that sustains corporatist authoritarianism. The institutions of bourgeois society—rule of law, accountability and transparency in economic activity, the legal basis of contracts and property and the authority of civil courts—remain poorly developed. Bourgeois institutions which normally reside outside the state, such as the stock exchange, schools and universities, the press and the media, remain weak and subordinate to state control. Capital continues to rely on the military to control organised labour and impose its dominance in industrial relations. Without the coercive power of the state their capacity to prevail over reactionary petty bourgeois populism, which, in Indonesia, has a close political and ideological association with Islam, is uncertain.

Political and democratic reform and the middle classes

Public criticism of authoritarian rule and demands for liberal and democratic reform in post-colonial, and indeed, in late-colonial Indonesia, have come primarily from within intellectual and professional elements of the middle classes rather than the bourgeoisie. Reformist academics, lawyers, political and cultural figures, popular entertainers, Muslim preachers and economic commentators enjoy high profiles in the media and have achieved celebrity status. Non-governmental institutions (NGOs), with a leadership drawn predominantly from the urban middle classes, increasingly constitute the institutional channels for reform in a variety of areas from conservation and environmental policy to legal and human rights.

However, the middle class has not constituted an effective and coherent force for political change in Indonesian political history. Reformist elements have been a minority within its ranks while the majority have supported the political option that appeared to them to guarantee the social order and the process of economic growth. In the 1950s, the party that most concentrated reformist middle-class elements, the PSI (Indonesian Socialist Party), proved unable to forge effective political alliances and was quickly swept from influence by the political machines associated with the state bureaucracy, the Muslim petty bourgeoisie and the PKI. Soeharto's surge to power in 1965 and 1966 was swept along by popular middle-class support despite its military and anti-liberal character. Since then the New Order has increased its control and containment of middle-class reformists by forcing political organisation into state-sponsored structures and by legislating to limit expression in the press and on university campuses.

Nevertheless, there is a body of belief current among liberal reformers that political liberalisation is an unstoppable global trend swept along by the internationalisation of the market and the exponential growth of a middle class. It is variously argued that European historical experience shows that the growth of a middle class (and here the term 'middle class' is usually used to conflate the middle class and the bourgeoisie) brings demands for increased surveillance of government and legal guarantees for private and business rights. This process, it is alleged, is hastened as governments are increasingly required to develop a broad revenue base—the expectation being that people who pay taxes expect to have a say in policy (*Tempo* 8 July 1989). In the Indonesian case, income tax, non-oil company taxes and consumption taxes have accelerated as a proportion of total tax revenue since the mid-1980s but the impact on structural political change is not yet evident. Democratic politics is also claimed to be a necessary factor of international economic competitiveness by some commentators, a puzzling conclusion in the light of the experience of the Asian NICs (*Suara Pembaruan* 23 October 1989).

Some commentators are hopeful that the Indonesian middle class will play this increasingly effective political role in forcing liberal reform. Taufik Abdullah, for example, has been strongly critical of the way in which authoritarianism has been associated with Indonesian cultural traditions and argues that democracy is also an Indonesian tradition. Further, he proposes that intellectuals have a greater potential to make the reformist breakthrough than businessmen (*Kompas* 15 August 1987). To this point in the history of the New Order, however, reformist elements of the middle class have only been able to operate effectively where the ruling bureaucratic elite is split and where factions of the military offer protection and encouragement for their activities.

The picture of the middle class as an inherently liberal and reformist class is difficult to sustain. Although little substantive research has been done in the area, the available work suggests that the vast bulk of the Indonesian middle classes is depoliticised and materialist and remains driven by the political ideals of authoritarianism and nationalism rather than any democratic vision (*Kompas* 2–3 October 1989; *Editor* 18 August 1990). Student organisations, formerly the preserve of critics of the regime, now include many unashamedly dedicated to careers and 'pragmatic' politics, a development familiar to Western observers. Prominent economist and former student activist, Dorodjatun Kuntjorojakti, dismissed many of the current student leaders as '. . . bourgeois brats' (*FEER* 24

October 1991). With a primary concern for accumulating wealth, improving living standards and carving out lucrative careers in the era of rapid economic growth that has accompanied the New Order, the fear of chaos and disintegration and the value placed upon political order and social stability outweighs liberal concerns for many members of the rising generation of the Indonesian middle class—at least so long as economic growth is maintained.

We are therefore confronted with the fact that the middle class cannot be regarded *sui generis* as a class with natural predilections for any particular form of political regime. While middle-class individuals constitute the leadership of such reformist political movements as the Petisi Limapuluh group, the Legal Aid Institute and the Forum Demokrasi, middle-class people staff a variety of organisations and think-tanks integral to both the state and the regime. The state has its own conservative and nationalist middle class to carry out the intellectual, technical and managerial functions of the state. State technocrats, both *dirigiste* and free-market, may be regarded as middle class. Golkar civilian leadership is largely middle class and devoted to the Pancasila ideal. What, we might ask, is the social identity of the military and bureaucrat families? Are they not middle class?

This is not to say that middle classes, whether they be managerial, technical, professional or 'intellectuals', have no core of abiding interests deriving from the very nature of their social position. Although they are found as the *apparatchiks*, the experts and the technicians within a range of regimes—authoritarian, liberal, capitalist, petty bourgeoisie and communist—middle classes ideally require at least some degree of legal protection from arbitrary rule, some basic civil rights, and some organised framework within which skills, qualifications, credentials and expertise might be expected to prevail over political whim. This is why China's cultural revolution with its 'red' versus 'expert' conflict remains today the most bitter memory of the Maoist period for the Chinese middle class. Beyond this core of necessary interests, which may be guaranteed by a range of political regimes, it is difficult to argue that liberal reform, including freedom of speech and the press, political representation and democracy are inherent to the 'middle class' interest.

Why do some elements of the Indonesian middle class pursue a liberal reformist line while others remain determinedly conservative, repelled by liberal notions of freedom of the press and popular, representative democracy, or have various populist perspectives? The key is the nature of the political and economic forces and structures to which they have become historically attached.

That much of the middle class is conservative in outlook is no surprise given the critical importance of the state bureaucracy in

Indonesian political life and the degree to which employment, education and development funding derives from the state. That stratum of state bureaucrats, almost a class in itself, constitutes the social and ideological environment within which much of the current middle class was nurtured and given their ideological and cultural outlook.

Reformist elements are to be found primarily in those sections of the middle class located outside the state—in the professions and among the intelligentsia. These have tended to be urban and elitist with no mass base, in the secular tradition of the PSI, which provided the political vehicle for this social and ideological force in the 1950s. Muslim middle-class reformers are also to be found in urban-based elite movements such as the Petisi Limapuluh group and the ICMI (Indonesian Muslim Intellectuals' Association) group. Increasingly, however, middle-class reformists have begun to make alliances with broader social organisations. Whereas student movements in the 1970s sought to remove corruption and other 'aberrations' from the regime, Max Lane (1989a,b) notes that the new student activists of the 1980s were more convinced that the so-called 'aberrations' were part of the system and were concerned to become involved in broader social conflicts such as those relating to land alienation and forced relocation of peasant farmers. Similarly we find that Abdurahman Wahid, leader of the Muslim Nadhatul Ulama, has integrated urban middle-class reformism with the moderate populist aspirations of the Muslim rural middle classes and petty bourgeoisie. In the Muslim *pesantren*—rural Muslim schools and colleges—he has a highly developed institutional base.

Although in both cases, middle-class reformism risks being overwhelmed by populist or radical tendencies as were the Narodniks of nineteenth century Russia, these new alliances make them much more formidable political forces and much less susceptible to the tactics of co-option or exclusion which have been used so successfully on ICMI and Petisi 50.

Two other recent developments in middle-class politics are of significance. First, the formation of the Forum Demokrasi. This movement is described by its own members as merely a vehicle for raising the public consciousness of political issues and not a political party. It has no prospects of even securing representation in parliament under the present political arrangements. Nevertheless it is a movement that unites Muslim and secular middle-class reformers and operates outside the prescribed institutional framework of the New Order's corporatist institutions and outside the ideological constraints of Pancasila—hence, the hostile reception it received from leading military and political figures (*Kompas* 9 April 1991). From this vantage point it has been able to raise and pursue issues not possible within the approved parties and front organisations, including the issue of the constitutional position of the presidency.

One of the short-term strengths and long-term vulnerabilities of the New Order is that it has denied the possibility of working for reform within the system. While its domestication of the political parties, the parliament, the campuses and the press and its control of professional associations, notably the journalists and lawyers, have been regarded as important victories for the New Order, they have merely served to demonstrate that little worthwhile reform can be undertaken inside the system. This is why the major Muslim political party, Nadhatul Ulama, withdrew from the formal system of parties and elections and why reformers established the Forum Demokrasi outside the system, forgoing the right to compete in elections. Middle-class activists focusing upon the environment, legal reform and most student organisations no longer bother with the legitimate arena. In opting out they are freer to form alliances with those forces traditionally outside the social and political alliances that have sustained the New Order: workers and peasants. This extra-corporatist sector of middle-class activity is increasing rapidly as the middle class grows. Ten years ago environmentalism was almost non-existent in Indonesia. Today there is a flourishing movement produced, admittedly, by the sheer scale of depredation occurring, but also by the burgeoning of a class of educated people able to become concerned with general social questions.

From rule by bureaucrats to bourgeois rule?

Whether they are yet conscious of it the critical problem that will progressively confront the generation of military and civil bureaucrats who have established themselves as capitalists is the forging of a new relationship with the state. The interests of generals and bureaucrats in maintaining the institutions of state power and the political and ideological regime that guarantees autonomy for the state apparatus will not necessarily guarantee the class position of the newly emerged capitalist families. In other words, the leading elements of the bureaucrat capitalist families and the major client *pribumi* bourgeoisie are faced with the problem of making the state accountable to their class interests as their patrons retire from office. At this juncture, the logical action is for Soeharto to construct a bourgeois political party. It is in this context that the development of Golkar over the past decade has been so interesting.

The origins of Golkar lay in ABRI's need to combat the capacity of political parties, including the PKI, to mobilise and control social organisations, and the New Order's need to guarantee its dominance of the elections it had promised when it came to power. Golkar triumphed in the 1971 elections as the instrument of ABRI and KORPRI, and an assortment of state-sponsored social organisations incorporating labour (FSBI), veterans (KOSGORO), and youth (KNPI). Control over Golkar remained in the hands of Soeharto and the military through the Supervisory Board, Dewan Pembina (DP), which exercised authority over the selection of candidates and officials and the policy set by the Board of Management (DPP) (Reeve 1990: 151–73).

An important change of direction was to take place in 1983 with the appointment of Sudharmono as Chairman. Sudharmono's objective soon became clear; it was not to transform Golkar into a bourgeois party but to establish it as an alternative mechanism for regenerating the leadership of the New Order. He brought into the party several prominent civilian politicians and businessmen. The most politically influential of these were Sarwono Kusumaatmadja and Rachmat Witoelar, members of the so-called Bandung group, former student activists in 1966. Although careful to acknowledge the prevailing political and ideological realities it was clear they held a somewhat different vision of what Golkar should be. For them the two major issues were to be Golkar's independence from outside control and its internal democracy. In essence they were proposing nothing less than that Golkar should become a new and independent source of power in the New Order based on the direct mobilisation of popular support—even though it may have been in the corporatist rather than the liberal model—rather than functioning to exclude and subordinate civil society (*Tempo* 2 July 1988; 16 July 1988; 23 July 1988; *Kompas* 2 August 1988; 16 October 1988).

A first step in this process, carried through against the bitter opposition of conservatives in ABRI, KOSGORO and FSBI, was to reorganise Golkar's membership basis from organisations to individuals. The implications of this were significant. Power theoretically shifted from the member organisations, notably ABRI and KORPRI, to the leadership of Golkar. While intellectual circles in Jakarta spoke enthusiastically of Golkar becoming an instrument for democratisation (*FEER* 20 October 1983; 1 December 1983) it was more realistically a case of whether Golkar was to become the party of the emerging ruling class, separate from those institutions within the state apparatus from which it had emerged.

Under Sudharmono's management Golkar flourished. Its financial base was substantially strengthened with contributions from the Yayasan Dakab and from increasing business donations (*Prospek* 7 September 1991). With the political demise of the Islamic party, Nadhatul Ulama, several nationally prominent NU figures came into

Golkar, including Abdurahman Wahid and Atakib Ali (*Jawa Pos* 28 September 1987).

As 1988 and the five-yearly Golkar conference (Munas IV) approached, ABRI and other conservative forces became increasingly restive at the prospect of an independent party with access to mass politics. From ABRI's point of view, Golkar was also another arena for its struggle with Sudharmono and Sekneg for hegemony within the state apparatus. Conservatives organised to reimpose upon Golkar tighter military control and greater conformity to the organic political vision. Figures such as General Hasibuan, Chairman of the intellectuals' functional group in Golkar, Jusuf Wanandi of the Centre for Strategic and International Studies, the architect, with Ali Moertopo, of the 'floating mass' concept and the 1971 Golkar triumph, and Internal Affairs Minister Soepardjo argued that Golkar's function was primarily that of unifying and drawing in the various social groups rather than representing interests. It was an anti-liberal vision of a party whose function was to integrate, institutionalise and secure political stability.

The primary theme of conservative views expressed before and during Munas IV was opposition to any moves for autonomy from ABRI and any moves towards liberal reform of the party's function. In particular there was a move to stop 'newcomers' and 'fence-jumpers' from gaining executive positions over long-term Golkar *apparatchiks* (*Kompas* 2 August 1988; 16, 19 October 1988; *Tempo* 29 October 1988). Soeharto's speech gave no comfort to the reformers, when he spoke of Golkar's role in the most orthodox language of organic political ideals as embodied in the concept of Pancasila Democracy (*Kompas* 15–16 October 1988).

The outcome of Munas IV was a comprehensive victory for the conservatives and a re-establishment of ABRI authority over the party. Sudharmono was replaced by General Wahono as Chairman, a low-profile military officer generally regarded as cautious, conservative and unlikely to take dangerous initiatives. A ten-year membership requirement was introduced for appointment to executive positions, effectively locking out the newer civilian members, especially prominent figures like Abdurahman Wahid. Although Rachmat Witoelar was nominated as Secretary, Sarwono and Akbar Tanjung were elevated out of Golkar to the Ministry and none of the prominent younger reformers, notably Marzuki Darusman or Theo Sambuaga, was moved on to the DPP. Significantly, ABRI nominees were to secure around 70 per cent of regional Golkar seats, a major setback for civilian members (*Tempo* 29 October 1988; 17 December 1988; *FEER* 10 November 1988; *Kompas* 16 October 1988).

The position of the ABRI conservatives was always clear: Golkar was an instrument for ensuring social control and consolidating rule by the state bureaucrats. Sudharmono may have sought to develop Golkar as an alternative mechanism for renewal of the political leadership but neither he nor Soeharto had ever contemplated the prospect of Golkar as a new source of power independent of the state. Golkar remained firmly in the grip of the state. Its controlling board was not elected by the party but comprised the President as Chairman and, essentially, the Ministry as Deputy Chairs and members. As the prominent political commentator, Rachman Tolleng, pointed out, Golkar is not the ruling party but the party of the rulers; it does not determine the membership of the government but on the contrary its membership is determined by the government (*Kompas* 16 & 20 October 1988).

Financially, Golkar remained dependent upon sources whose interests lay firmly in retaining the organic model of authoritarianism: Yayasan Dakab, under the directorship of Soeharto which was to provide Rp.50 billion in the period 1988-93; and private business, primarily the major Chinese conglomerates, which were expected to provide Rp.30 billion for the same period. Another Rp.20 billion was to be raised from other business sources (*Prospek* 7 September 1991). The political interests of these business groups was not to transform Golkar into an independent bourgeois party but to ensure it remained an effective institution for stability and order.

Despite the retreat from discussions of autonomy and internal democracy in Golkar's position in regime and state, several Golkar members remained outspoken critics of land expropriations, press censorship and the subordination of the DPR to the bureaucracy. However, even this role as a forum for critics has been ended. With the elections of 1992 looming and the Presidential nomination following in March 1993, Soeharto has obviously decided that the democracy debate needs to end. The most outspoken of the Golkar members and potential candidates, including Marzuki Daroesman, Christianto Wibisono, General Saiful Sulun, Ny. Roekmini and Anang Adanansi, were either dropped from the Golkar lists or placed so far down that their chances of election were minimal (*FEER* 26 September 1991). Golkar is clearly not intended to be part of the national political debate in the critical period ahead.

The Golkar experience is instructive. Political power, for the time being, is to remain in the hands of the state bureaucrats and Golkar is to remain a party designed to extend the state apparatus into the social sphere and to prevent the operation of popular politics. Within Indonesia, the only route to power and influence is through the organs of the state apparatus. Golkar is once again confirmed as one of the channels of the state apparatus albeit one giving access to those outside the bureaucracy. Because Golkar is not an autonomous political institution it offers no career for the political agent, the party boss, the mobiliser of votes or the dealer in patronage because it has no power independent of the bureaucracy.

Putting the lid on debate

Soeharto's response to the tensions causing, and exacerbated by, the debates over democratisation and succession has been, after some confusion, to reconfirm the Pancasila model and to increase anti-liberal rhetoric. In broad terms, Soeharto and leading Ministers, including Rudini and Moerdiono, were to argue: that liberalism is destructive and conflictual (Soeharto 1990: 12; *Kompas* 6 June 1989); that Pancasila Democracy is the form of political democracy best able to harmonise with Indonesian cultural values of consensus and the family system (*Suara Pembaruan* 13 May 1989); and is the form of democracy which enables political stability, social order and economic development to be appropriately balanced with freedom (Soeharto 1990: 16; *Kompas* 21 October 1990; *Suara Pembaruan* 13 May 1989; *Suara Karya* 28 June 1989).

For Soeharto, the successful implementation of Pancasila, with its embodiment of the propositions of the organic state, has enabled Indonesia to reach a stage where there is no longer any need to fear the emergence of ideas in society. In other words, ideas can be tolerated now that they harmonise with Pancasila and do not challenge the existing state or regime (*Kompas* 29 June 1990). If there are problems in the day-to-day operation of the regime these are, according to Moerdiono and Rudini, not inherent but remnants of feudal culture and behaviour which can be eliminated (*Suara Pembaruan* 13 May 1989; *Kompas* 5 July 1989; *Suara Karya* 28 June 1989).

Apart from indicating his uncompromising stance in relation to liberal reform, Soeharto was well aware of the more immediate dangers posed by the political fluidity and the manoeuvring generated by the succession issue: the atmosphere of speculation, the changing alliances and the attractiveness of destabilising tactics to the players in the game. The general air of uncertainty was made worse by the confusion surrounding the Presidential election process. Soeharto claimed the present system is clear and adequate. The factions in the next MPR, he argued, should agree on one candidate through a process of consensus. In the meantime there was no point in discussing the issue. His increasing irritation with public discussion became more apparent as the DPR became more outspoken and the press probed the confusion. This was increased as sensitive issues, including the Soeharto family businesses, were brought into the public arena. On 3 May 1989 Soeharto made a major statement to Cabinet calling for an end to public discussion and, at an airport press conference, threatened potential challengers. He stressed the need for continuity and stability in the elections for the next President (*Kompas* 6 June 1989; *FEER* 28 September 1989, 18 January 1990; *Kompas* 9 January 1991).

However, the constitutional questions about the succession kept resurfacing, an indication of how crucial they were. The whole system had been built upon the assumption that the MPR would be presented with a single candidate, agreed on by all the major groups. If no such agreement could be reached and a vote had to be taken, the nature of the MPR would be transformed from a rubber stamp into an arena for political competition. Neither Soeharto nor Sudomo seemed clear on what would happen if the factions in the MPR could not come to a consensus on one candidate. How many candidates could there be? Would there be a vote? Would voting contravene the whole basis of the organic, Pancasila state? (*Kompas* 13 April 1989; 6 June 1989; 17 January 1991; *Suara Pembaruan* 19 January 1991; *Pelita* 3 July 1991).

In the volatile political context it was clear that no agreement between the major political forces had been put in place to guarantee support for a successor to Soeharto. Nor was it the ideal time to reach such an agreement. In this situation there is little alternative for Soeharto but to declare his candidacy for another term. To a large degree his candidacy is made virtually unassailable by the very difficulty of replacing him. In the absence of a clear alternative candidate with widespread support, the threat of a power vacuum and a split in the regime is a central concern for the current rulers and for the social coalitions supporting the New Order.

Nevertheless, Soeharto has been unable to take his position for granted, perceiving a need to broaden and consolidate his political and social support. This calculation was reinforced in the wake of the *demokrasi ekonomi* debate of the late 1980s in which attention was drawn to the inconsistencies between the government's egalitarian rhetoric and the reality of a rapacious capitalism dominated by Chinese corporate conglomerates in league with the leading bureaucrat families. It is in this context that Soeharto's dramatic decision to transfer a percentage of the shares of the large, and overwhelmingly Chinese-owned, corporate conglomerates to cooperatives must be seen (*Kompas* 2 July 1990; *Editor* 31 March 1990). This move, however irrelevant to the realities of the distribution of corporate ownership, undermined the effectiveness of attempts by some critics, including sections of the military, to mobilise anti-Chinese and anti-conglomerate sentiment in the political debate.

Cultivation of the Muslim community had for some time been conducted by Soeharto through a mosque-building programme financed by his Yayasan Amalbakti Pancasila and the increasingly pious demeanour of some of the family members, especially the eldest daughter and businesswoman, Siti Hardijanti Rukmana. This appeal for Muslim support was given greater public profile with the long-awaited decision to undertake the *haj*. Sponsorship of the Organisation of Muslim Intellectuals (ICMI) followed (*FEER 19 March 1991*). These, however, were moves concerned with the question of legitimation rather than structural change in the regime that would give Muslim political groups any different institutional position.

Long-term challenges

It is not so much the next presidential election that is the problem but the following one. In the intervening period Soeharto will have to find and negotiate broad support for a candidate if the existing system is to be retained, or to build a new set of structures if it is not. This task will be carried out in a set of circumstances different from those that have prevailed to this time. Economically, the pressures for sovereignty of capital over state will increase and in the political sphere the change will be undertaken as the power of the President progressively fades. In the very apt analogy of Liddle (1992) it will be the era of a dying king.

The unique concentration of power and patronage focused in the hands of Soeharto was forged in the context of a particular historical conjuncture of factors which no longer exist. Soeharto came to power in 1965 in a situation of revolutionary threat, economic chaos and disarray among the propertied and middle classes. Today, in the absence of a serious revolutionary challenge to the capitalist social order, the compulsion for authoritarian rule is lessened. Even ABRI does not see the regime as it is now constituted as essential to maintaining the social order. At the same time, business and the middle classes are larger and more highly developed and there is a strong framework of political institutions and forces entrenched. Consequently, the next President will move into a relatively more powerful political and social environment where negotiation for support and alliances can be expected to extract a higher price in terms of accountability.

Even though the economic reforms of the late 1980s have left intact much of the *dirigiste* character of the state and the dominant position of the politico-bureaucratic stratum, there are continuing pressures to establish a regime of accountability and transparency of process which guarantees the common interests of capital and subordinates the state and its bureaucrats to regulation and law. These pressures are fuelled by the need to generate competitive non-oil export industries, to maintain external inflows of investment and to secure sources of state revenue through efficient tax systems. The need for investment, revenue and productivity are in contradiction with continued bureaucrat appropriation of the state apparatus and nationalist, mercantilist policies. The battles are now being fought for control of customs regulation, monitoring of forestry exports, collection of taxes, regulation of the capital market and the authority of the finance ministers over vested corporate interests in the areas of credit policy and production monopolies.

Although this paper has focused upon tensions and contradictions within the state and its supporting social coalitions, social forces have grown outside these structures quite rapidly in the past two decades and are becoming more cohesive and better organised. The activities of organised labour have recently entered a new phase. There have also been signs of real cohesiveness within the Muslim middle class/petty bourgeoisie under the leadership of Abdurahman Wahid, which signals a shift from the rather disorganised iconoclasm of earlier Muslim political organisations. The old formulas for regulating relations between state and civil society will become increasingly inadequate.

Finally, as Indonesia is increasingly integrated into the structures of the global capitalist economy and becomes more reliant on international negotiation and agreement and less able to isolate itself from the flow of information and ideology, both the *dirigiste* and organic aspects of the regime come under increasing pressure. This is especially so given the importance of foreign aid and investment, the former constituting just under 25 per cent of central government receipts in 1990–91 and the latter providing approximately US$9 billion or 25 per cent of total approved investment in 1990. Despite the government's recent nationalist gesture (for internal consumption) to refuse Dutch foreign aid and reject Dutch leadership of the consortium of foreign creditors because of human rights conditionality, the government is less able to ignore international pressure. It still accepts loans from the World Bank and the Asia Development Bank which increasingly embody conditionality, particularly in regard to structural change. Indonesian awareness of external pressure is evident in its reactions to recent international condemnation of the Dili massacre.

The Indonesian outcome will not be determined by the rational choices of modernising bureaucratic elites or by voluntarist political negotiation for a withdrawal from authoritarianism or by chance, accidents and coincidences. Nor will there be a spontaneous democratisation flowing from the emergence of a more rational and modern society. It will be a long and complex struggle with the President and the ruling stratum of bureaucrats the focal point. In the 1970s the capacity of the bureaucratic stratum to maintain its power through mercantilist and corporatist policies was underpinned by the boom in oil revenues which gave it financial power and independence. The system may be perpetuated in the future by a populist alliance of bureaucrat and petty bourgeoisie or even an increasing resort to nationalist policies. On the other hand, the accountability of the state and its stratum of officials may be enforced if reformist forces are able to forge effective political alliances and develop a mass base of support in the context of a split within the ruling alliance. This is the level where the autonomy of politics asserts itself. While the nature of the tensions within, and constraints upon, political action may relate to social and political environments, these factors may be accommodated in a variety of political outcomes.

It is also important to remember that political reform involving a greater accountability of the state to social forces cannot be conceived solely in terms of the liberal democratic model. Indonesia's prevailing structure of social and political power and the historically strong position of the state and its corps of bureaucrats would indicate that different sorts of democratic arrangements, for example, that which occurred in post-Bismarckian Germany, may be a more helpful model. The state and its military and civil bureaucracies will remain a political force in themselves for the foreseeable future and one that will require continued accommodation.

Note

1   The critical comments provided by Vedi Hadiz, Ian Chalmers, Garry Rodan and Kevin Hewison on earlier drafts of this chapter were greatly appreciated.

References

Boileau, J. 1983, *Golkar: functional group politics in Indonesia*, Centre for Strategic and International Studies, Jakarta

Cawson, Alan 1986, *Corporatism and Political Theory*, Basil Blackwell, Oxford

Crouch, Harold 1978, *The Army and Politics in Indonesia*, Cornell University Press, Ithaca

Feith, Herbert 1963, 'Dynamics of Guided Democracy', *Indonesia*, ed. Ruth McVey, Human Relations Area Files, New Haven

Hobsbawm, Eric 1990, *Echoes of the Marseillaise*, Verso, London

Indonesia 1985, *Anggaran Dasar Yayasan Yayasan, Yayasan 'Dana Abadi Karya Bakti' (Yayasan 'Dakab')*, Tambahan Berita-Negara, 57

Jenkins, David 1984, *Suharto and His Generals: Indonesian Military Politics, 1975–1983*, Cornell Modern Indonesia Project Monograph No. 64, Ithaca

Kurth, J. 1979, 'Industrial Change and Political Change: A European Perspective', *The New Authoritarianism in Latin America*, ed. David Collier, Princeton University Press, Princeton

Lane, Max 1989a, 'Students on the Move', *Inside Indonesia*, no. 19, pp. 10–15

—— 1989b, 'State, Society and Democratisation in Contemporary Indonesia: A Class Approach', unpublished mimeo, Canberra

Liddle, R. 1992, 'Regime in Crisis? Presidential Succession, the East Timor Massacre and Prospects for Democratisation in Indonesia', Paper presented at the 44th Annual Meeting of the Association for Asian Studies, Washington DC, April 2–5

Lubis, T. M. 1990, 'In Search of Human Rights: Legal-Political Dilemmas of Indonesia's New Order, 1966–1990', University of California, Berkeley, PhD thesis

Marx, Karl 1962, *Karl Marx and Frederick Engels: Selected Works*, Foreign Languages Publishing House, Moscow

Moore, Barrington 1969, *Social Origins of Dictatorship and Democracy: Lord and Peasant in the Making of the Modern World*, Peregrine Books, Harmondsworth

Pangaribuan, R. 1988, *Perkembangan Kekuasaan Sekretariat Negara Dalam Jajaran Politik Nasional Periode 1945–1987*, Universitas Indonesia, Fakultas Ilmu Sosial dan Ilmu Politik, Skripsi Sarjana, Jakarta

Pangestu, Mari 1989, 'Economic Policy Reforms in Indonesia', *Indonesian Quarterly*, vol. 17, no. 3, pp. 218–33

—— 1991, 'The Role of the Private Sector in Indonesia: Deregulation and Privatisation', *Indonesian Quarterly*, vol. 19, no. 1, pp. 27–51

Reeve, David 1978, 'Sukarnoism and Indonesia's "Functional Group" State: Developing "Indonesian Democracy" ', *Review of Indonesian and Malay Affairs*, vol. 12, no. 2, pp. 43–94

—— 1979, 'Sukarnoism and Indonesia's "Functional Group" State: Implementing "Indonesian Democracy" ', *Review of Indonesian and Malay Affairs*, vol. 13, no. 1, pp. 53–115

—— 1990, 'The Corporatist State: The Case of Golkar', in Arief Budiman ed., *State and Civil Society in Indonesia*, Monash University Centre of Southeast Asian Studies, Monograph No. 22, Clayton

Robison, Richard 1986, *Indonesia: the Rise of Capital*, Allen & Unwin, Sydney

—— 1987, 'After the Gold Rush: the politics of economic restructuring in Indonesia in the 1980s', in Robison, Hewison & Higgott (1987)

—— 1992, 'Industrialisation and the Economic and Political Development of Capital', *Southeast Asian Capitalists*, ed. Ruth McVey, Cornell University, Southeast Asia Program, Ithaca

——, Hewison, Kevin & Higgott, Richard eds 1987, *Southeast Asia in the 1980s: The Politics of Economic Crisis*, Allen & Unwin, Sydney

Schmitter, Philippe 1974, 'Still the Century of Corporatism?', *Review of Politics*, no. 36, pp. 85–101

Soeharto 1990, *Pidato Kenegaraan Presiden Republik Indonesia Soeharto 16 Augustus 1990*, Departemen Penegaraaan, Republik Indonesia

Soemitro 1989, 'Aspiring to Normal Politics' *Far Eastern Economic Review*, 6 April, pp. 22–4

—— 1990, 'Pembangunan Politik Sesudah Tahun 1993', *Analisis CSIS*, vol. 19, no. 1, pp. 47–53

Soesastro, H. 1989, 'The Political Economy of Deregulation in Indonesia', *Asian Survey*, vol. 39, no. 9, pp. 853–69

—— 1991, 'Capital Formation and Equal Distribution', *Indonesian Quarterly*, vol. 19 no. 1, pp. 62–73

Taubert, A. 1991, 'Liberalism under pressure in Indonesia', *Southeast Asian Affairs 1990*, Institute of Southeast Asian Studies, Singapore

Ward, Ken 1974, *The 1971 Election in Indonesia: An Indonesian Case Study*, Centre of Southeast Asian Studies, Monash University, Monash Papers on Southeast Asia No. 2, Clayton

World Bank 1991, *Indonesia: Developing Private Enterprise*, The World Bank, Washington DC

Yoon, H. S. 1989, 'Demystifying the Capitalist State: Political Patronage, Bureaucratic Interests, and Capitalists-in-Formation in Soeharto's Indonesia', Yale University, PhD thesis

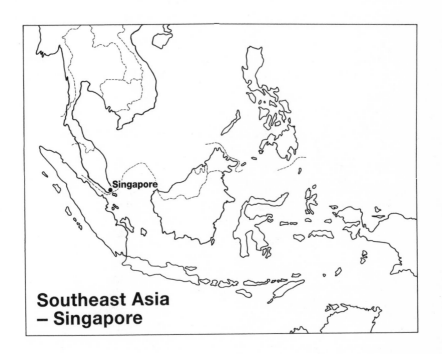

**Southeast Asia
– Singapore**

Singapore: Basic social and economic data

Population (1990)	2.7m
Population density (1990)	4358 persons per sq. km
Average annual population growth (1982–89)	1.5%
Urban population	100%
Total labour force (1990)	1.35m
Major ethnic groups	Chinese, Malays, Indians
Capital city	Singapore
Land area	622 sq. km
Main languages	Bahasa Malaysia, English, Chinese dialects, Tamil
Administrative division	Island city state

Education, enrolments
Primary (1990)	257 833
Secondary (1990)	166 274
University (1990)	50 756
Adult literacy rate (1990)	87.6%

Health
Life expectancy (1989)	74 yrs
Infant mortality/1000 (1989)	7.0
Persons/hospital bed (1989)	247
Persons/physician (1989)	837

Economy
GNP at market prices (1989)	US$28.06 bn
Real GNP per capita (1989)	US$10 450
GDP growth rate (1990)	8.3%

Trade
Exports, value (1990)	US$52.8 bn
Imports, value (1990)	US$60.9 bn
Main imports (1990)	Machinery & transport equipment 44.7%, manufactures 22.4%, mineral fuels 15.8%
Main exports (1990)	Machinery & transport equipment 50.1%, crude materials 18.2%, manufactures 15.9%
Foreign debt	Nil
Foreign reserves (1990)	US$27.7 bn
Energy consumption/capita (kg coal equiv. in 1989)	4979

Communications
Rail	50 km
Roads, paved (1990)	2836 km
Religions	Buddhism, Islam, Hinduism, Christian

Sources: Far Eastern Economic Review Asia Yearbook 1991; The Far East and Australasia 1992 (Europa Publications); United Nations Economic and Social Commission for Asia and the Pacific *Newsletter, Key Indicators of Developing Asian and Pacific Countries 1991,* Asian Development Bank.

4 Preserving the one-party state in contemporary Singapore
Garry Rodan[1]

In the recent growth of literature examining political change in Latin America and Asia, the transition to civilian, and particularly parliamentary, rule has been considered a crucial measure of the decline of authoritarianism. In the case of Singapore, however, a Westminster-style parliamentary system has been in operation for the duration of self-government, with some recent modification to incorporate an elected President with significant powers (Cotton 1992). Hence, government has been determined in Singapore by popular elections since 1959, with parliament and political parties, rather than military juntas, prevailing. Yet despite such democratic appearances, an authoritarian regime has managed to successfully coexist with these political forms in Singapore. Here the definitive feature of authoritarianism is the extra-parliamentary constraint on challenges to the ruling People's Action Party (PAP). This has at times involved crude measures like the detaining or imprisoning of opponents, but more commonly it has involved techniques of greater sophistication that systematically obstruct counter views and institutionalise the PAP's ideology.

Successive PAP administrations have exercised state power in accordance with a system of restrictive rules and regulations. That system or mode of administering state power which governs the daily lives of all Singaporeans can be referred to as an 'authoritarian regime'. It is at the same time the 'PAP regime' because it is the extensive influence of the Party in all exercises of state power that makes the systematic and comprehensive imposition of a particular set of restrictive rules and regulations possible. In other words, the particular form that authoritarianism takes in Singapore is largely shaped by the PAP.

With the existence of such a regime, parliamentary elections constitute a stunted political expression—they are not the end product of broader contests over social and political power but rather the only contest. Contestation outside a narrowly defined formal politics is severely limited. But even in this sphere, the PAP sees little margin for opposition, continually arguing the importance of the 'dominant-party system'. This system is a critical element in what is effectively a one-party state.

Nevertheless, as elsewhere, the conditions under which the PAP attempts to reproduce the authoritarian regime have undergone considerable change in the last decade or more. No longer is Singapore at a rudimentary stage of economic development, as it was in the 1960s when the regime was established. Rather, it is now a reasonably affluent society with a sizeable middle class and much greater exposure to the lifestyles and political cultures outside the city-state. Much of this exposure has to do with the emergence of qualitatively new forms of integration with the international economy. Though the precise influence of any of these factors is unclear, there is reason to speculate that the authoritarian rule, which has proved so effective in political and economic terms in the past, may have a problematic future in Singapore. After all, since the early 1980s, the PAP has experienced a sustained electoral decline, leading to a range of political reforms at the initiative of a second and third generation of party leaders.

It is the purpose of this chapter to evaluate these reforms and their significance for the exercise of power in Singapore. The argument to be developed is that, although they do represent a conscious break from the more extreme state paternalism of the past, these changes are intended above all else to preserve the essence of the authoritarian regime—the one-party state. The idea is to broaden the scope of the state in an attempt to co-opt disgruntled elements of the newly emerging middle class and pre-empt democratic reforms which might genuinely threaten the one-party state.

More precisely, the strategy attempts to channel dissent and disaffection through the PAP or institutions through which it can exert an influence, and away from opposition political parties or non-government civil organisations. Moreover, while this strategy may not be proving as successful as the leadership would like, since the PAP has been unable to halt its electoral decline, the regime is not facing the sort of challenge likely to force more dramatic changes in the near future. Emerging social forces are not on a collision course with the regime. On the contrary, the substantial middle class, which some theorists regard as a critical prerequisite for political liberalisation, may be irritated by aspects of authoritarian rule, but its material interests and social position are also shored up by the essentially elitist policies enacted through this regime. Indeed, the PAP state is very much a 'middle-class state', in which decision-making is dominated by technocrats and professionals and rationalised in terms of 'meritocracy', a concept supportive of the social position of this class. However, this is not to suggest that the middle class's privileged position is reliant upon authoritarian rule; the social position currently enjoyed by the middle class, while bolstered by the PAP's rule, also owes something to the relatively advanced nature of the Singapore economy and the related social and technical divisions of labour. Rather, the persistence of the particular form of rule in Singapore under the PAP is primarily a function of the latter's party–political ambitions.

Furthermore, as a city-state with an export-oriented industrialisation strategy in place since the mid-1960s, Singapore has long been reliant upon integration with the international economy. The domestic bourgeoisie did not have sufficient interest or capacity to contest this. Consequently, the PAP has championed internationalisation ahead of economic nationalism. Moreover, the regime has derived much of its political legitimacy and its effectiveness in attracting capital from the fact that Singaporean authoritarianism has embodied efficient, regularised and relatively corruption-free bureaucracy. Hence, the political pressures emerging in Indonesia (Robison 1988) and South Korea (Cumings 1989) for either an opening up of the economy or a more regularised bureaucracy are not in evidence in Singapore.

This is not to suggest, however, that the path ahead for the PAP and its mode of administration is without trepidation, nor that significant political change—if not liberalisation—is inconceivable. Tremendous social and economic change provides a quite different backdrop against which official policy and related ideological pronouncements are now interpreted within Singapore. Certainly there seems little demonstrable need for the extent of control and discipline exerted by the regime in contemporary Singapore. In the past, developmentalism and anti-communism have been politically effective rationales for such a regime, but they would appear to have little currency left in them. In this climate, are we to see some xenophobic variant surface which emphasises the threat to Singapore's 'Asian' heritage, or an even greater emphasis than already exists on the state as a manager of ethnic sensitivities? The widening income gap associated with Singapore's economic development might also add fuel to a critical re-evaluation of the regime's self-justification and possibly provide a stimulus for more concerted attempts to form independent civil and interest-group organisations (Rodan 1992a). Such a development is a necessary pre-condition for a more fertile environment for organised political alternatives to the PAP. It is precisely the PAP's appreciation of this point that informs much of its current political strategy—a strategy that involves the introduction of new political structures intended to undercut such alternatives.

Establishing the authoritarian regime

When the PAP stormed to victory in the 1959 elections that brought self-government, it carried with it serious internal divisions. In the postwar nationalist struggle against the British, the PAP was formed out of a marriage of convenience between a left-wing Chinese-educated working-class movement and a more conservative group of English-educated middle-class nationalists led by Lee Kuan Yew. The former had the organisational structure and mass support and the latter the appearance of respectability in the colonialists' eyes. The early 1960s was thus an intense period of strategic jockeying for ascendancy within the Party. The authoritarian regime in Singapore was born out of this contest and was essentially the mechanism by which it was resolved in favour of Lee's faction.

Despite the paucity of organisational structures or any serious social base behind it, Lee's faction was in charge of the Party executive in 1959. Though this had been accepted by the left as a temporary expedient to win office, Lee demonstrated clearly that possession was nine-tenths of the law. Having already reformed the party structure to centralise power in the hands of the executive (Turnbull 1982: 266), Lee and his colleagues also fashioned the post-colonial state to the same end. For instance, upon taking office the PAP abolished local government and in 1960 also disbanded all management committees of community centres. The latter had been established in the 1950s to encourage grassroots participation in community developments but were brought under the central control of a new statutory body, the People's Association, whose staff reported directly to the Prime Minister's office.

After pursuing a series of policy directions at odds with the left, Lee's faction prompted a showdown within the Party by its enthusiastic support for political union with Malaya in the Malaysian federation. The left saw this as a means through which it would be comprehensively purged by the right-wing central government. The result was the formation in 1961 of a separate party, the Barisan Sosialis (BS), which drew the vast bulk of the Chinese working class, students and intellectuals from the PAP, leaving Lee and his colleagues without significant organisational support at the grassroots level.

The PAP dealt with this vulnerability on a number of fronts. First, it used the various repressive mechanisms of the state, either directly or indirectly, to whittle away the leadership and organisational structures of the BS. The most conspicuous such exercise was Operation Cold Store in 1963 which resulted in the arrest of 111 people by the Special Branch, including 24 executives of the BS,

50 executives of thirteen trade unions within the Singapore Association of Trade Unions (SATU) sympathetic to the BS, five left-wing journalists and eleven students from the Nanyang University (*Far Eastern Economic Review [FEER]* 21 February 1963).

Second, the PAP turned very deliberately to the civil service as a political ally, improving allowances and conducting propaganda sessions through the Political Study Centre. The hitherto lukewarm relationship with the conservative bureaucracy naturally benefited from the sharp break with the left. But it also benefited from the expansive role it was to enjoy due to the social and economic policies subsequently pursued by the PAP.

A third and not unrelated point was the further centralisation of Party responsibilities. With grassroots organisational structures decimated, the PAP executive harnessed the machinery of the state to traditional Party functions. No longer was there any notion of the Party organisation assisting in the formation of policy. Rather, this was the exclusive domain of the executive. What Party organisation existed was intended only to convey and promote executive decisions (Bellows 1973: 28–9). But this task was increasingly to be undertaken by the institutions of the state, notably the public bureaucracy, which came to be almost indistinguishable from the PAP. This was most conspicuous in the harnessing of the Community Centres and Citizens' Consultative Committees (CCCs) to the task of mobilising support for the PAP,[2] but it extended to all other aspects of the public sector. To deal with the bureaucracy was to deal with the party and the regime at the same time. Public appointments were invariably viewed by the PAP as a strategic opportunity to consolidate both a particular set of policies and a mode of implementation. Without PAP membership or sanction it was not possible to exert any real influence through the state. The state-owned media were also creatively employed to the PAP's advantage. Possibly one of the greatest political achievements in the 1960s, however, was the PAP's supplanting of effective independent trade-union organisations with a state-sponsored National Trades Union Congress (NTUC) (Deyo 1981).

This meshing of the PAP with the state was rationalised through a corporatist ideology which soon became institutionalised. Various arguments were advanced in support of this, including: the precariousness of the city-state as a political entity following the failed merger with Malaysia; the sensitive ethnic and geopolitical context of Singapore; and the potential for political pluralism to frustrate the urgent task of economic development. This systematically restricted policy debate and marginalised organisations, individuals and viewpoints at odds with Lee and his cohorts (Rodan 1989). Civil society was naturally a casualty in this process. The very idea of social organisations and associations voluntarily formed for self-protection and self-interest, and enjoying more or less autonomy from the state, was incompatible with the evolving regime structure.

However, the political strategy of the PAP did not rest exclusively on a combination of intimidation on the one hand and ideological production on the other. Rather, there was the simultaneous development of social and economic policies intended to give substance to the notion that political curbs were part of a trade-off for material benefits. Substantial expenditure on public housing and education, for example, did demonstrate a commitment to transforming conditions for the masses and helped build working-class electoral support for the PAP. These social reforms, nevertheless, took a particular political and ideological form—enhancing the control of the PAP over the population through the latter's dependence on the former (Chua 1991a). The general pervasiveness of the state in the social sphere has indeed been one of the central features of the regime (Chan 1978). Similarly, successful policies to attract capital investment, especially towards the end of the 1960s when the export-oriented industrialisation (EOI) strategy gathered momentum, earned the PAP wide support. The authoritarian regime was fundamentally in place before the EOI programme took root, but the political pre-conditions for success as an exporter of low-cost, labour-intensive manufactures destined for world markets—notably docile or compliant labour—reinforced such a regime. This meant the PAP's own political objectives could be presented as economic imperatives.

Clearly the PAP leadership comprised capable administrators who also happened to be adept at various techniques of social and political control. However, these points must be placed in context, otherwise the character of the party and the political basis of it can be distorted. First, the essentially middle-class leadership owed its political pre-eminence in part to peculiar socio-historical circumstances and not entirely to its own qualities. In the lead-up to self-government, the domestic bourgeoisie, whose interests were structurally linked to those of colonial capital, could neither appreciate nor accommodate the overriding nationalist sentiment of the population. Thus, with self-government in 1959, it found itself without an effective political voice. However, if the middle-class leadership of Lee Kuan Yew and others had attained power without reliance upon capital's support, with the breakaway of the left to form the BS, before long it could also, indeed had to, distance itself from labour as an independent political force. The consequent high degree of relative political autonomy enjoyed by the PAP facilitated decisive public policy, something that was portrayed by the government as demonstrative of the rational, rather than sectional, decision-making process. The technocratic administration thus had a broader foundation than the abilities and inclinations of the leadership itself.

Second, we must keep in mind that the seemingly rational decision-making process was nevertheless fundamentally oriented towards maximising private capital accumulation. Indeed, private investment levels and economic growth rates were the determining criteria by which good government was consistently measured. In pursuing these goals, policymakers chose to promote those fractions of capital, and the attendant middle class, that could most effectively integrate Singapore with the global economy through export-oriented industrialisation. In this sense, despite the PAP's political separation from capital, it very consciously and actively presided over a capitalist state. To lose sight of this in favour of emphasising the PAP as an almost autonomous modernising elite is to ignore the structural constraints and opportunities taken into account by the PAP in its exercise of power. Certainly the PAP leadership had its own vision of society, one that reflected broader concerns than capital accumulation *per se*, but the pursuit of this entrenched the social and economic power of others outside the state and party. The PAP thus constituted a wider set of interests than is captured by the notion of a modernising elite, even though it enjoyed an unusual degree of relative political autonomy from capital and labour.

Against the above background, the PAP has enjoyed remarkable electoral success. After the internal split in 1961, the PAP secured re-election in 1963 with 46 per cent of the vote. From then until 1984, it averaged 75 per cent of the total vote in general elections. The PAP also held every parliamentary seat from the general election of 1968 until a by-election in 1981. Whatever observations we might make about the regime, throughout this period the PAP's political legitimacy in government was almost unquestioned within Singapore. However, since the early 1980s reproduction of the PAP's absolute political monopoly has become a more difficult task, giving rise to new strategies to preserve the one-party state, and its associated authoritarian structures, over the longer term.

End of the parliamentary monopoly

The PAP's by-election loss in Anson in 1981 to Joshua Jeyaretnam of the Workers' Party (WP) came as a shock to a party that had become accustomed to a total dominance of parliamentary seats. Moreover, it provided the occasion for a series of explicit public statements by the PAP leadership about political opposition in general and within Singapore in particular. According to the then Prime Minister, Lee Kuan Yew (*Straits Times [ST]* 15 December 1981), '. . .an opposition, if we are lucky, makes no difference to good government'. His Old Guard colleague, Second-Deputy Prime Minister Sinnathamby Rajaratnam, held the concept in even less regard, claiming 'the role of the opposition is to ensure bad government' (quoted in *FEER* 7 May 1982). The intensity of the PAP's reaction to the breaking of their parliamentary monopoly, expressed in its hostile and dismissive attitude to Jeyaretnam both inside and outside Parliament, reflected more than resentment and bitterness. The concerted attack on individuals by the PAP represents a not uncommon strategy to destroy any potential focus of opposition *per se*.

The PAP's insistence on its exclusive right to power was further underlined at the 1982 Biennial Conference of the PAP where the Party redefined itself as a 'national movement'. According to the official PAP organ, *Petir*, 'No fly-by-night political parties, committed only to the politics of dissent, which are devoid of capable leaders and credible alternative policies, can run the country'. However, it was also at this conference that Lee Kuan Yew floated the seemingly contradictory idea of ensuring that several 'better and more intelligent opposition members are in Parliament' (quoted in *Asia Research Bulletin* January 1983). Lee claimed that the existence in Parliament of a few opponents might help to sharpen up the skills of the PAP's emergent new generation of leaders, the so-called New Guard. Subsequently, in 1984, Singapore's Constitution was amended to provide for up to three of the highest opposition losers in general elections to be non-constituent members of Parliament (NCMPs). This was increased to four in 1991. However, the voting rights of NCMPs were restricted, since they could not vote on money or constitutional bills, although they could speak on these issues.

This apparent contradiction was actually an attempt by the PAP to stem the tide of serious opposition on the one hand, yet to project an image of political tolerance on the other. It did not take long for the attacks on Jeyaretnam to evoke widespread public sympathy and admiration for the PAP critic. What most worried the PAP was the apparent support for the liberal notion of opposition as a positive element in a political system. In this climate, the PAP turned its attention to shaping the form of political opposition. The 'better and more intelligent members' to whom Lee referred would of course be so because they would not, like Jeyaretnam, openly confront and challenge the PAP. The idea was to have more accommodative individuals if there was to be opposition at all.

While the PAP did not take the Anson loss lightly, to some extent

it could attribute i   :ctorate, including
the effect of evic   Port of Singapore
Authority residen   13 per cent swing
against the PAP in the subsequent 1984 general elections represented
a decisive shift in Singapore politics that indicated a more
generalised alienation with the party than the PAP previously perceived. The NCMP provision had not blunted voter enthusiasm for
legitimately elected representation. This election not only saw the
return of Jeyaretnam but the entry of Chiam See Tong of the
Singapore Democratic Party (SDP) to Parliament. However, the
first-past-the-post voting system meant that the PAP's 62.94 per cent
of the vote gave it the remaining 77 seats.

One factor in the PAP's declining electoral fortunes was the
apparent alienation of the now substantial middle class.[4] Singapore's
rapid economic growth and successful industrialisation had brought
with it a significant expansion in the number of technicians and
professionals and a general increase in educational levels. According
to census data, administrators, executives and managers, professionals and technicians collectively accounted for 18 per cent of the
workforce in 1980 and reached 24 per cent by 1990. Many of these
people undertook tertiary education and/or employment overseas,
and were thereby exposed to different social and political systems.

Though the middle class was the principal beneficiary of the
PAP's policies, elements of it were increasingly finding the ideological pronouncements and authoritarian excesses of the PAP objec-
tionable. Lee Kuan Yew's stance on eugenics in August 1984, for
example, led to a flurry of dissenting opinion in the English-lan-
guage daily *Straits Times* newspaper, bearing witness not just to
dismay at Lee's views but to the greater preparedness to publicly
criticise the government and its leaders (Rodan 1989: 183–6). One
of the contradictions operating here was that, on the one hand, the
social and economic status of this class was reinforced by state-
sponsored ideologies about 'meritocracy', yet, on the other hand,
public policy treated these people in the same patronising way it
did the rest of the population. If they were encouraged to see
themselves as the talented and gifted upon whom the rest of the
population depended, then it was only natural that they would come
to resent the state's all-pervasive influence. They also tend to enjoy
a comparatively high degree of autonomy in the workplace (Wright
1978), something that stands in sharp contrast with their social and
political experiences in Singapore.

However, disaffection with the PAP was not confined to the
middle class in the 1984 election. The policies of the so-called
'Second Industrial Revolution' strategy, adopted in 1979 to acceler-
ate Singapore's transition to a more sophisticated technological base,

adversely affect   ic bourgeoisie who
felt this represe   treatment for for-
eign-based trans   were also concerns
among middle- and low-income earners in particular about proposals
mooted by the government to raise the age from 60 to 65 years at
which withdrawals could be made from the compulsory superannu-
ation scheme, the Central Provident Fund (CPF) (*Asiaweek* 4 January 1985).

In general, though, the middle class, being more inclined to
articulate viewpoints through conspicuous channels like letters to
the daily English press, possibly had greater visibility in its dissent.
Certainly the trade union movement, through the NTUC's dominance, did not engage in open contest over government policy on
behalf of the working class.

The 1984 election result set in train a significant modification in
the PAP's political strategy. By this time, a stage-managed handover
of senior positions to the New Guard was well advanced. Led by
Lee Kuan Yew's anticipated successor, Goh Chok Tong, there was
an explicit attempt to demonstrate that the leadership transition
marked the opening up of politics in Singapore. The 'new' PAP
would be a more consultative and tolerant one. Goh also raised
expectations of a society in which the state's circumscription of the
individual would be relaxed (*FEER* 24 January 1985; Goh 1986).
The assumption underlying this programme of political reform was
that the bulk of the PAP's electoral decline stemmed from a perceived authoritarianism, with Goh quite openly conceding in the
wake of the 1984 election result that the government needed to more
widely consult and involve people in the decision-making process
(*FEER* 21 February 1985). This perception was thought to be
concentrated among Singapore's younger—just over 50 per cent of
the 1.5 million eligible voters in the 1984 election were under 35
years of age—and better educated voters, of which the fast-growing
middle class was a major and strategic component. Accordingly, the
latter was targeted in the range of measures introduced from the
mid-1980s.

It is of course to be expected that any political party will endeav-
our to arrest its electoral decline. The distinctiveness of the PAP
response to the 1984 election lies more in the effect the reforms
were intended to have on the way politics was conducted. The idea
was to provide more elaborate mechanisms for political expression
outside the party system rather than to elevate competition between
parties. The latter was incompatible with the *de facto* one-party state
to which the PAP was still totally committed. It is the constancy of
this objective that explains why Lee Kuan Yew has been prepared
to take a back seat during the New Guard experiment. Where there

were modifications to the regime governing social and political life in Singapore, they did not contradict this basic aim.

Consultative government under the New Guard

The major initiatives by the PAP since the mid-1980s to provide alternative avenues for public involvement in policy debate include: the establishment of the Feedback Unit in 1985; the phased introduction of Town Councils which began in 1986; the introduction of Government Parliamentary Committees (GPCs) in 1987; the creation of the Institute of Policy Studies (IPS) in 1988; and the establishment of a new category of parliamentarians—nominated MPs (NMPs)—in 1990. A complementary 'national ideology' has also been promoted to encourage a political culture that excludes 'confrontationalist' politics.

The Feedback Unit is an extra-parliamentary body headed by a government MP. Its four stated objectives are: to receive suggestions from the public on national problems; to gather information on existing policies; to facilitate prompt responses by government departments to public complaints; and to instigate public information programmes. Between 1985 and 1990, a total of 109 'dialogue sessions' were conducted with a range of professionals, grassroots leaders, trade associations, small business groups and others. Professional groups have, however, been disproportionately represented at these forums, leading to charges that the unit is fundamentally targeting the English-educated middle class (*Straits Times Weekly Overseas Edition [STWOE]* 21 April 1990). The intention, it would seem, is to provide both an opportunity for these people to air their views and feel that they are being taken into account, and at the same time for the government's case on policy to be sympathetically put.

The introduction of Town Councils between 1986 and 1991 resulted in a decentralisation of various administrative activities previously centralised under the Housing Development Board (HDB). Town Councils were attached to the different electorates and became the responsibility of the local MP. This change was presented as an opportunity for greater community participation in the allocation of public resources. At the same time, though, it tested the commitment of the electorate to its preferred candidate. As Lee Kuan Yew argued, constituencies that reject the PAP cannot expect to be insulated from 'bad choices' (*ST* 2 July 1989). In practice, however, the Town Councils have been more significant as a demonstration that the PAP has no monopoly on administrative competence, rather than as a breakthrough in participatory democracy,[5] with no evidence to date of either inferior services or efficiency in their delivery in the opposition SDP Town Council of Potong Pasir. Indeed, according to a survey published in the *Straits Times* (*STWOE* 28 December 1991), 48 per cent of respondents believed that Town Councils would be run the same regardless of whether the local MP was from the PAP or another party.

GPCs, like the Feedback Unit, were also heavily geared towards tapping the expertise of professionals. By 1988, ten such committees were established, each comprising five or six MPs who can appoint a resource panel of up to twelve members from outside parliament. Goh Chok Tong (*ST* 14 February 1987) explained that the 'most compelling' reason for GPCs was 'the need for a new political formula that would take Singapore into the next century'. These committees were supposedly the means by which both backbenchers inside and experts outside parliament could increase their participation in the policy process. However, as is generally the case with GPCs in other political systems, they can also enable the government to set the agenda for public debate and steer attention to problems of policy implementation ahead of basic questions of political philosophy and direction.

Launched with a S$4 million government grant and the declared intention of becoming an independent 'think-tank', the IPS has two functions, according to Goh Chok Tong (*ST* 16 January 1988). The first is to educate younger Singaporeans in public administration and private sector management about Singapore's political history. The other is to foster open public debate. By its very nature this institution is again one that primarily targets the educated elite. To date it has published some interesting work on matters of public importance (see Low & Toh 1989; Tan 1990; Ooi 1990; Phua 1991), but it remains to be seen whether it can genuinely initiate issues for public debate not already on the government's agenda.

The one reform that caused a significant degree of controversy within the PAP itself was the introduction of NMPs. The bill, introduced to parliament in late 1989, provided for the appointment of up to six NMPs, each for a renewable two-year term and with the same voting rights as NCMPs. The appointments were to be made by the President on the advice of a special select committee which was in turn appointed by the PAP-dominated parliament. Goh Chok Tong explained that there was a need to correct popular misconception that the PAP was closed to alternative viewpoints when deciding policy. Through NMPs, people who had excelled outside parliament or had special expertise could directly enter political debate. Most importantly, these NMPs were to be non-partisan. According to Goh (*Parliamentary Debates, Singapore* 29 November 1989, column 705) they would thus 'concentrate on the substance of the debate rather than form and rhetoric', as opposition MPs supposedly did. Brigadier-General (BG) Lee Hsien Loong, Trade and Industry Minister and son of Lee Kuan Yew, quite explicitly expressed the hope for NMPs to halt the growing support for opposition candidates (*STWOE* 9 December 1989).

A significant number of backbenchers within the PAP expressed concern about the NMP provision, many viewing it as an easy route to parliament that belittled their onerous constituency work. Some even criticised the departure from the principles of representation and accountability embodied in appointed MPs (Rodan 1992b). However, the bill was finally passed with a proviso that future parliaments could vote on whether or not to exercise the legislation. Thus, in 1990, two NMPs entered parliament.[6]

The common theme to all of these reforms was a determination by Goh and his colleagues to direct dissent and dissatisfaction with the PAP or particular government policies through institutions controlled by the party or institutions with a potential to depoliticise debate. The clear aim was to foster an alternative to the increasing recourse by Singaporeans to opposition political parties.

It should be pointed out that the more consultative style of the New Guard extended to the government's dealings with the private sector. Indeed, the first evidence of the PAP's preparedness to consult more widely was provided through the operations of the Economic Committee, appointed in March 1985 to review the Singapore economy and the strategy underlying it. The Committee was headed by Lee Hsien Loong, but comprised representation from the Singapore Manufacturers' Association, the Singapore Federation of Chambers of Commerce and Industry and various leading local entrepreneurs. In turn, this committee was serviced by eight subcommittees including heavy representation from the domestic business community.

Subsequently, under the auspices of the Economic Development Board and with the involvement of six government agencies, the Small and Medium-Sized Enterprises (SME) Committee put together a master plan intended to make the Economic Committee's 1986 recommendations for a stronger local private sector a reality. This was followed by a national forum involving hundreds of local business representatives. More recently, the local private sector has been involved in the government's economic blueprint for the next two decades, the Strategic Economic Plan (SEP), which was announced in late 1991. Work on the SEP began in 1989 under the Economic Planning Committee (EPC) within the Ministry of Trade and Industry. Through its different sub-committees the EPC comprises over 110 members, a substantial proportion of which is private sector representation (Phua 1991: 1).

Certainly this degree of consultation with the local private sector is unprecedented in the post-1959 Singapore public policy process. In part it is a function of the government's desire to diversify Singapore's economic base in the wake of the mid-1980s recession. That experience clearly highlighted the existing vulnerabilities of heavy dependence upon a small range of manufactured exports. With the new emphasis on regional economic integration, and special emphasis on the services sector, the domestic bourgeoisie now assumes greater strategic relevance to official plans. It is in this sector that it has tended to be most numerous and competitive. At the same time, the policies of the Second Industrial Revolution since 1979 had served to compound the difficulties of the domestic bourgeoisie (Rodan 1989: 142–88). In a context of electoral decline, the concerns of this class found a slightly more receptive ear from government than in the past. However, it should also be kept in mind that the New Guard is generally less suspicious of local business than Lee Kuan Yew's generation of leaders who observed ties between some of its elements and the BS in the early 1960s. Over time, however, more business people have made their way into the PAP so that now a significant, but by no means overwhelming, number of MPs hold directorships on various companies. In fact, in 1991, the question of MPs simultaneously serving as directors on company boards became a public issue. Goh Chok Tong was himself in favour of more MPs being on company boards (see *Business Times* 14 February 1991; *STWOE* 23 February 1991). Thus, a number of factors have combined to facilitate greater consultation with the local private sector.

Alongside these political reforms and modifications to the government's style, the New Guard was also responsible for the ambitious project of establishing an official national ideology, or what came to be officially referred to as a set of 'shared core values'. Drawing on the work of George Lodge and Ezra Vogel in a book entitled *Ideology and National Competitiveness,* Goh (1988) lamented that over the last decade there had been a clear shift in the dominant values in Singapore, away from group interests or 'communitarianism' in favour of self interests or 'individualism'. The supposed shift was depicted as a drift from 'Asian' to 'Western' values, a theme that Lee Kuan Yew (*STWOE* 20 August 1988) had himself taken up in the same year. The *Shared Values* White Paper (1991), eventually completed in early 1991, identified five essential values: placing society above self; upholding the family as the basic building block of society; resolving major issues through consensus instead of contention; stressing racial and religious harmony and tolerance; regard and community support for the individual.

The 'national ideology' was a sensitive one for Singapore's Malay community, who feared the government's exercise might result in the institutionalisation of Confucianism and thereby elevate the cultural position of the Chinese. However, the PAP's concern was primarily with the possibility that a new set of cultural values and an associated political culture was evolving, contributing to the increasing support for opposition political parties. The 'shared core values' statement was intended to assert Singapore's distinctiveness and thereby discourage any emulation of other 'Western'—notably pluralist—political systems. The political significance of the document was that it opened the possibility for the PAP to portray challenges to itself as challenges to the national consensus or the collectively shared values of Singaporeans. If there was to be opposition in Singapore, the PAP was determined to ensure that it took a 'non-confrontational' form (Clammer 1992).

Keeping the lid on civil society

Clearly, then, the period since the mid-1980s has witnessed a range of initiatives from the PAP to increase consultation. But these should not be interpreted as a fundamental recasting of the regime. Strict limits continue to be placed on civil and political life. Indeed, during the same period, a number of measures were also adopted by the New Guard to curtail and structure critical debate in the public domain. One of these involved amendments to the *Newspaper and Printing Presses Act* in early 1986 which empowered the Minister of Communication and Information to restrict the circulation of publications considered 'engaging in the domestic politics of Singapore' (*Asiaweek* 15 June 1986). *Time, Asiaweek,* the *Asian Wall Street Journal* and the *Far Eastern Economic Review* were all victims of the new legislation within 18 months.

The new Singapore has so far retained the rigid distinction between political and civil society that Lee Kuan Yew's generation had enforced. When the President of the Law Society and former solicitor-general, Francis Seow, issued a press release on behalf of the Society, criticising the amended legislation for containing 'ambiguities' and affording the minister 'too wide' an authority to limit publication sales without any appeal process, he was sternly reminded of that distinction. His criticisms were not seriously debated. Instead, the Minister for Communications and Information, Wong Kan Seng, emphasised that 'public policy is the domain of the government. It isn't the playground of those who have no responsibility to the people, and who aren't answerable for the livelihood or survival of Singaporeans' (quoted in *FEER* 12 October 1989). Professional societies, he added, should not 'get involved in issues of public policy which do not affect their professional interests' (cited in *FEER* 12 October 1989). The concern was that the Law Society was attempting to assume the role of a pressure group, something that still could not be accommodated within the Singapore political system. Following this incident, legislative amendments resulted in the establishment of a new Academy of Law whose governing body is almost entirely comprised of government appointees. The intention appeared to be to erode the power and status of the Law Society. Legislation covering other professional organisations has also subsequently been reviewed to safeguard against similar incidents of public criticism.

Probably the clearest indication that the PAP has not, since the mid-1980s, completely overhauled its previous political strategy is the exercise of the *Internal Security Act* (ISA). This was used in 1987 to imprison without trial 22 people allegedly involved in a Marxist conspiracy to overthrow the state. The essence of the problem, according to a 19-page statement from the Ministry of Home Affairs, was that Catholic organisations such as the Young Christian Workers' Movement, the Catholic Welfare Centre and the Catholic Centre for Foreign Workers, were being used as 'a cover for political agitation' (*FEER* 4 June 1987). The arrests became an international embarrassment for the government, with allegations by Amnesty International (1987), and later Asia Watch (1989), of coercion to elicit 'confessions'. By the end of 1987, the confrontation with the church had worsened, with five Christian missionaries expelled and the dissolution of the Christian Conference of Asia on charges of involvement in Singapore's domestic politics (*FEER* 14 January 1988). Not coincidentally, the government subsequently passed the *Maintenance of Religious Harmony Act* in late 1990. This legislation empowers the Minister for Home Affairs to prohibit religious workers deemed subversive or threatening from addressing congregations and holding office in religious publication organisations. Like other aspects of civil society, religion is expected to be clearly demarcated from politics. But the concern about religion is more than this. Through the various organisations of the Catholic Church, Singapore possibly had the embryo of genuine non-government organisations (NGOs) with grassroots links. Elsewhere in Asia, notably Indonesia, the Philippines and Thailand, NGOs have become politically significant precisely because of grassroots connections with groups that cannot find effective representation or expression through mainstream channels.

Despite the various legislative amendments since the mid-1980s to enforce the demarcation of political and civil society, together with the abandonment of the armed struggle by the last vestiges of the Malayan Communist Party (MCP), the ISA itself is not seen to be any less important to contemporary Singapore. Rather, the new leaders have not only argued a case for its continued existence but have taken steps to consolidate the executive's powers under the Act. Through legislation introduced in 1989, the executive's judgment over the use of the ISA is now clearly above any legal scrutiny (Rodan 1992b).

What all of this indicates is that the PAP's strategy since the mid-1980s has been a dual one. On the one hand, it has opened up avenues for greater, albeit conditional, public consultation in the policy process, while on the other hand, it has tried to reinforce the strict separation of political and civil society. The importance of the latter for the former is that, if successful, it safeguards the PAP's ability to continue to define the boundaries of public debate. In such a climate, the risk of the various consultative mechanisms backfiring on the PAP is greatly reduced. With this in mind, it is interesting to reflect on the extent and nature of NGOs since the mid-1980s. Despite the experience of religious workers and the Law Society, some noteworthy organisations have surfaced, raising the question of whether, difficulties notwithstanding, there is an opening in the new style of government under Prime Minister Goh for a more flourishing civil society than has hitherto been possible. NGOs that stand out over the recent years include the Malayan Nature Society (MNS) or the Nature Society of Singapore (NSS) as it has been known since 1992, the Association of Women for Action and Research (AWARE) and the Association of Muslim Professionals (AMP).

Significantly, both MNS/NSS and AWARE have deliberately shied away from public disagreement with the government. The former's lobbying is done primarily through private correspondence and the presentation of documented material. The latter, whose declared strategy is 'to take a low profile' (AWARE 1988a: 46), has been slightly more adventurous. Its executives have written letters to the *Straits Times*, conducted public forums and even produced a critical paper in response to the government's procreation policy (AWARE 1988b). Importantly, though, to date neither organisation appears in any way to facilitate the growth of oppositional politics—either in the sense of adopting a confrontational posture or in the sense of providing avenues for members of opposition political parties to advance their causes. On the contrary, to some extent these organisations provide feedback for the government which its own party structure is unable to deliver. But, above all else, neither organisation has been involved in the development of grassroots linkages in a way that would threaten the PAP's control over the political process. Such factors temper the PAP's otherwise sceptical attitude to these NGOs (Rodan 1992a).

The AMP is the exceptional case. It was formed in 1990 in a climate of Malay discontent with Mendaki, the officially sanctioned council for the development of the Muslim community. In particular, the dominance of that association by PAP MPs, who had endorsed rather than challenged government policies seen as detrimental to the Malay community, came in for criticism (Chua 1991b: 261–2). The initiative to break away from Mendaki and form a separate association was surprisingly supported by the government. Here the government was faced with a choice of risking an open and sustained attack on PAP MPs through an attempted transformation of Mendaki, or tolerating a separate organisation with greater independence. The government chose to actively support the latter, with the provision of matching funds on a dollar-for-dollar basis for the AMP. Primarily this represented an attempt to depoliticise the matter. Already concerned about the level of Malay support for opposition political parties, the government was keen to pre-empt any further drift in that direction. Moreover, the form of official support for the AMP was also functional for the government's current policy objective of stronger community-based, rather than direct state, welfare. Brown's (1992) argument that the government has entered a new corporatist phase in its handling of ethnicity seems applicable here.

The point about these NGOs, then, is that although they can find a degree of space within which to operate, they have a somewhat conditional existence: the right to public comment is limited and contingent upon acceptance of the government's ground rule of 'consensus' ahead of 'confrontation', a rule that appears to disqualify grassroots linkages that modify the existing political process. This raises the question of just what the then acting, and now appointed, Minister for Information and the Arts and increasingly one of the government's leading ideologues, George Yeo, had in mind in mid-1991 when he called for the development of civic society. According to Yeo (1991a: 4):

> Yes, the state is strong. The family is also strong. But civic society, which is the stratum of social life between the state and the family is still weak. Without a strong civic society, the Singaporean soul will be incomplete. If the creation of the strong state was a major task of the last lap, the creation of a strong civic society must be a major task of the next lap.

Here Yeo seems to be drawing on Huntington's (1965; 1968) notion of authoritarianism in a developing society playing an historically necessary role in laying the basis for a more liberal future. But what does he mean by the 'weakness' of civic (read civil) society? Does he really mean by this that the avenues for political engagement are underdeveloped?

It is interesting that Yeo portrays the family as a distinct realm, separate from civil society. In this conception, it would appear that civil society is expected to be harmonious with family, and state for that matter. Yet in concrete terms 'family' here refers to a particular social construction—patriarchy—and Yeo is effectively endorsing its entrenchment. What space would there be then for a feminist civil organisation, for example, to question patriarchal relationships? Nevertheless, Yeo had a number of different functions in mind for civil organisations. One was to 'give individuals and families their sense of place and involvement in the larger community' (Yeo 1991a: 5). Another was the role they could play in increasing people's self-reliance and independence, which had become a casualty of the all-pervasive state; a state that must now 'withdraw a little and provide more space for local initiative' (Yeo 1991a: 8).

Yeo's speech was certainly an attempt to address the real problem of alienation within Singapore that is manifest not only in the PAP's electoral slide, but also in the high levels of emigration—in 1988 alone 4707 families emigrated—that have occurred side-by-side with Singapore's economic success (cf. *Asian Wall Street Journal*, 9 October 1989). It recognises the need to ensure a sense of belonging that cannot necessarily be assured by material satisfaction. In the process, though, it recommends a political solution: the arresting of the state's intrusion in the everyday lives of Singaporeans. But what are the areas in which the PAP is prepared to curb state paternalism and hand responsibility to individuals and civic organisations? And what sort of 'local initiatives' are compatible with the insistence on a strict separation of civil and political society?

The speech, interestingly enough, comes on the heels of and amid some significant policy developments that involve the state's social and economic functions. These include the full or partial privatisation of various government companies, statutory boards, public hospitals and the education system (Ng 1989; Thynne & Ariff 1988). But more particularly, in the government's eagerness to pre-empt any pressure for a significantly expanded welfare system it has begun actively encouraging civic organisations, especially those that are ethnic-based, to explore this area (*ST* 8 July 1991; 20 July 1991). To differing extents, these policies have been at least partly explained by the government in terms of the need to reduce state paternalism and increase the space for individual entrepreneurs, consumers or groups to take initiatives. Yet even if we accept this as evidence of reduced paternalism, it does not automatically follow that such changes represent political liberalisation. They may in some instances widen the choices of certain consumers, but these sorts of reforms do not necessarily diminish the political power of

the state, nor significantly empower individuals or groups outside
the state. What they do, however, is selectively transfer various
costly economic and social functions and responsibilities from the
state to individuals and communities.

While Yeo's concept of strengthening civil society does not
appear, then, to be an invitation for interest or pressure group
formation or a re-evaluation of the separation of political and civil
life, it contains ideas that are nevertheless functional for the PAP's
own policy objectives. It appears that a 'strong' civil society is one
that can be relied upon to produce spontaneous agreement with, or
acceptance of, the PAP agenda. Interestingly, Lee Kuan Yew
(*STWOE* 6 July 1991) has recently suggested that civic society may
never develop in Singapore because of deep-rooted cultural resistance to self-determination in favour of strong government.

Given Yeo's observations elsewhere about democracy, his current
push for particular forms of civil society is also linked to
Singapore's economic development. In reference to the apparent
trend in various parts of the world towards greater democratisation,
Yeo attributed this to 'the way technology is transforming the world
economy' (Yeo 1991b: 167). According to Yeo (1991b: 22):

> Without a widening circle of popular representation and
> participation, no national economy can advance very far. Some
> countries may initially go through a Pinochet-phase which helps to
> get the market economy going, but once a middle-class emerges and
> property ownership is dispersed, democracy becomes essential.

Again, the resonance with Huntington's (1984: 201) notion that
economic development 'compels the modification or abandonment
of traditional political institutions', and the strategic role of the
middle class as a potential democratising force is strong. As Yeo
sees it, though, Singapore is already democratic, and distinctively
so, but there will need to be constant adaptation of the political
system to ensure its functional relationship with the dynamic economy. The question is whether the sort of adaptations that have either
been implemented or projected are consistent with the aspirations
of the electorate.

1991 election: Evaluating the new strategy

The results of the 1988 election were mixed for the PAP. On the
one hand, it returned all but one seat and managed to arrest the
swing against it to 1.7 per cent. On the other, in eight seats,
including six in two of the newly created group representation
constituencies (GRCs),[7] the PAP vote dropped below 55 per cent

and thus made them potentially vulnerable in the next election. The government seemed to take encouragement that it was on the right track in its strategy of political co-option and continued to search for new mechanisms in this vein. However, the snap election of mid-1991 in which the government's share of the total valid vote dropped from 63.2 per cent to 61.0 per cent, thus continuing the steady erosion of PAP support post-1984, came as a genuine shock to a PAP leadership that expected to reverse the trend. This necessarily raised serious questions about the effectiveness of the prevailing strategy. Arising out of this election, the opposition political parties now have four MPs and the PAP's anxiety about the reproduction of the one-party state has been further heightened.

The 1991 election was announced by Goh Chok Tong as a test of the electorate's response to his consultative style of leadership. Goh had been Prime Minister since November 1990 and claimed he needed a mandate to continue down this path. He warned that in the absence of a strong personal mandate there was a risk that the PAP would return to the more authoritarian ways of the past. This led to speculation that Goh was alluding to internal divisions and related pressure from Lee Hsien Loong for the top spot (*FEER* 12 September 1991). Goh was to be more explicit following the election when he commented that 'BG Lee is more conservative in values', then drawing a badminton analogy: 'He is more ready to smash' (*STWOE* 7 September 1991) than retrieve. In any case, Goh was particularly appealing to the educated middle class whom the various consultative mechanisms were principally targeting. However, as the results were to suggest, not only did these mechanisms fail to dissuade voters from supporting the PAP's opponents, they exposed as invalid the assumption that electoral alienation stemmed mainly from the middle class.

The opposition parties' success can in part be attributed to their clever tactic of allowing 41 of the 81 seats to go uncontested. This was not just for lack of resources and because the government gave only nine days' notice of the election. Rather, they argued that voter interest in genuine, as opposed to manufactured, political opposition could therefore be expressed without any fear of the 'freak election' scenario PAP leaders regularly caution against. With the opposition picking up three additional seats and consolidating the existing one of Potong Pasir, this approach was vindicated and cast doubt on the effectiveness of the government's process of co-option. Moreover, while there was some evidence of middle-class disaffection with the PAP in the opposition vote, this factor was uneven across electorates and not a dominant theme. The bulk of the electorates in which there were significant swings against the PAP contained high percentages of constituents with average and below-average incomes who were either blue-collar workers or non-supervisory white-collar workers (Rodan 1992a). In other words, there was a discernible anti-PAP vote from the working class. It had long been presumed that this was the faithful core of the PAP vote. The failure of the PAP to anticipate this change reflects on its relationship with the trade union movement. Arguably a genuinely independent trade union movement would have given greater expression to the concerns and criticisms of this class in advance of the elections.

Naturally there were various factors at work in this election result, including electorate-specific ones like the linguistic capacities and related campaign effectiveness of individual candidates.[8] However, to generalise about the electorates that fell to the opposition, they were those in which many people, by virtue of their socio-economic positions, would have been hard hit by recent increases in the cost of basic services such as health, transport, housing and education, some of which stemmed from privatisations in part intended to facilitate wider choices for the wealthy middle class.[9] In this climate, elitist policies such as independent schools, the gifted education programme and incentives to encourage graduate marriages, which were principally geared to the middle class, caused some irritation. Indeed, during and after the election, Goh and his government have publicly conceded a need to address perceptions of inequality and elitism (*STWOE* 17 August 1991). The PAP leadership is at pains to emphasise, however, that this must not involve an expansive public welfare programme nor any holding back or discouragement of Singapore's talented (*STWOE* 30 November 1991; 18 January 1992; 25 January 1992). In other words, neither redistribution at the expense of the middle class, nor the compromising of 'meritocracy' is acceptable.

Goh's immediate reaction to the 1991 election results was to interpret them as a rejection of his style of government, raising doubts about his intentions as leader and the direction of the Party: 'In my view, life cannot go on as it did before. Certain things have to change now. How they would change I do not know tonight' (quoted in *Sunday Times,* 1 September 1991). After some reflection, however, Goh came to the view that issues other than his style of leadership were determinant in the result.[10] But at the same time, he clearly saw the need for a change of focus. In a reference to the Chinese-educated working class, Goh remarked: 'The group which we are not reaching wants firm government; all they are interested in is steady progress and prosperity. They do not care how we are running the place' (cited in *Australian Financial Review* 6 September 1991). Subsequently, a review of many government charges was announced along with the above-mentioned exploration of commu-

nity-based welfare and some selective non-means-tested increases
to state welfare.

Goh's prediction that internal PAP dissent over the political reform
agenda of the last eight years would be given a fillip by support
for the opposition parties seems to have some basis. In the post-
election period Lee Kuan Yew, for instance, has pushed the view
that the English-educated have had too much attention paid to them,
by way of liberal reforms, at the expense of the Chinese-educated
working class. Such comments run the risk, of course, of alienating
this strategic social force. He has also commented 'those ministers
who are able to read and able to keep close contacts with the
Chinese (grassroots)—their views must be given more weight
because they represent a larger segment of the population' (quoted
in *FEER* 10 October 1991). In this category we would have to
include the two Deputy Prime Ministers Lee Hsien Loong and Ong
Teng Cheong as well as Foreign Minister Wong Kan Seng. Ong in
particular has come out strongly after the election with a similar
message to Lee's (*STWOE* 21 September 1991). He used the case
of the relaxation of censorship laws on Restricted (R) films as an
example of the government's excessive accommodation of a vocal
English-educated minority view.[11] Ong has also urged greater determination to arrest the erosion of Chinese culture. Not coincidentally,
a strong advocate of the preservation of traditional Chinese culture
and values, Ow Chin Hock, has been appointed the new Chairman
of the Feedback Unit's supervisory panel. Whether or not this
juxtaposition of a liberal-minded English-educated minority against
a more conservative Chinese-educated majority accurately accounts
for the election results, it is clearly an influential position within
the party that expresses reservation about the 'softening' of the PAP.

While the depiction of divisions between the Chinese-educated
and the English-educated in terms of cultural values may be super-
ficial, the election results do pose the question of whether the
traditional capacity of the PAP to simultaneously win the support
of the differing classes is being eroded. In the earlier developmental
phase, the Chinese-educated within the working class and small
businesses, predominantly in the retail and wholesale trading sectors, benefited appreciably from the general expansion in employment, consumer spending and public housing. However, in
Singapore's more technologically advanced period of economic
development since the early 1980s, the differential benefits of
economic growth have become more conspicuous in class terms
(Rodan 1992a). Emphasis on a clash of cultural values of course
plays down such class antagonisms.

Nevertheless, seemingly in an attempt to demonstrate that the PAP
has not 'gone soft', subsequent to the 1991 election Goh's govern-

ment modified its film censorship laws (*STWOE* 7 September 1991; 15 February 1992), temporarily suspended the publication of *Women's Affair* (a monthly lifestyle magazine) for a seemingly innocuous article that contained interviewee comments critical of the government's women MPs (*FEER* 5 December 1991), and banned the sale of chewing gum (*STWOE* 4 January 1992).

The depth of any gulf between informal factions in the PAP is difficult to ascertain. It would, for reasons already argued in this chapter, be exaggerated to portray Goh as a liberal flanked by a dissenting group of more authoritarian malcontents. What is clear is Goh's concern, and that of his cabinet colleagues, with the emergence of a more substantial opposition in parliament. Shortly after the election he condemned the use of the ballot to apply pressure on government and stated quite explicitly that he was against the principle of political opposition: 'It will divide the country. I'm not in favour of confrontational politics, so I'm not in favour of opposition' (*STWOE* 7 September 1991). He also argued that 'It would take another 15 to 20 years before Singapore society was cohesive enough to be able to afford a multi-party system' (quoted in *STWOE* 25 October 1991).

Consistent with these statements, Goh has threatened to cut community services to opposition wards and give opposition wards lower priority in the HDB's recently announced refurbishing programmes (*STWOE* 7 September 1991; 18 April 1992). As Goh sees it, people who reject the PAP cannot expect to benefit from PAP-run services. The problem here, of course, is the close intermeshing of the PAP with the state; an intermeshing that is so complete as to seriously hamper initiatives within opposition constituencies to respond to such threats. For instance, it was decided, in late 1991, that capital grants by the state for private kindergartens would be withheld for two years. This, together with new rules preventing political parties from using the open space on the ground floors (void decks) of HDB flats, would, as Heng has argued (*Sunday Times* 29 December 1991), appear to hamstring the opposition Town Councils in providing one of Singapore's most important community services.

Clearly the PAP, even under Goh's leadership, remains reluctant to accept the electorate's verdict in favour of elected opposition MPs. But if the current strategy of co-option has failed to stem the electoral drift against the PAP, the 1991 constitutional change empowering an elected President to veto government spending and senior public service appointments has the potential to limit the impact of any 'freak' election at some future point that might happen to result in a PAP loss of government. To be eligible to stand for the Elected Presidency, candidates must be citizens with no less than three years' experience as senior government officials, chairs or chief executives of large Singaporean companies or government agencies, and meet the approval of a Council of Presidential Advisers.[12] This effectively disqualifies anyone outside the PAP establishment. The Elected Presidency was first mooted by Lee Kuan Yew in 1984 (*FEER* 6 September 1984), leading to widespread speculation that his impending retirement as Prime Minister would simply lead to occupancy of a new and possibly more powerful post. Though Lee has since said that he would not be the first elected President, it remains possible that he could subsequently fill the job. Throughout, however, the argument has remained that Singapore's considerable foreign reserves could be squandered by a reckless and, by implication, welfare-oriented, alternative government.

Institutional modifications are becoming an increasing feature of the Singapore political landscape as support for opposition candidates grows and Lee Kuan Yew's anxieties about the capacities and directions of the new leadership intensify. As Cotton (1992) expresses it: 'wherever possible institutions must be found to ensure that Lee's legacy lives beyond the present generation'. From such a perspective, this institutionalisation is intended to preserve rather than transform the political system. But according to Cotton (1992), the desire to depersonalise the system is greatly complicated by the fact that Lee nevertheless 'remains at the centre of the network of patronage and personal relations which animates Singapore's party and state'.

Chua (1991c) has also observed an increased institutionalisation and move away from exclusive reliance on the personal integrity of the leadership as a basis of government that has coincided with the leadership transition. However, he links this with Goh Chok Tong's declared intention 'to enlarge the middle ground through a more accommodative and participatory style of government that seeks to include rather than exclude the greatest number of Singaporeans in the political process' (cited in Chua 1991c: 22). The different MP schemes, the GRC scheme and the Elected Presidency are, for Chua, all consistent with Goh's particular vision of political transformation of Singapore.

But the point to underline is that Goh's conception of 'middle ground' prescribes a politics that is limited in content to the PAP's philosophy. For instance, the Elected Presidency provisions appear to a large extent motivated by a desire to restrict the scope for a more expansive state welfare system. In the PAP view, welfarism is extreme politics. By contrast, the institutionalisation of social justice conceptions and the attendant welfare systems in the advanced industrial societies play a critical role in ensuring a middle ground or consensus on which stable democracies are built. Do Goh and the PAP leadership conflate the stability of the PAP's political monopoly with the stability of the social and economic order, as if anything that challenges the former must threaten the latter? Could it be that Goh and his colleagues are anxious to develop a particular set of mechanisms for greater consultation and participation in the public policy process precisely to preserve the PAP's ability to define what is extreme politics and what is not?

Clearly the above analysis emphasises the PAP's attempts to resist political liberalisation. Yet in this pursuit the PAP is nevertheless having to initiate certain forms of political change. In itself, the widening process of co-option is a significant political shift, even if it does not amount to a fundamental transformation of the political system. It represents a new set of political relationships and a potentially new basis for the PAP's political legitimacy.

We should also keep in mind that the adoption of more comprehensive techniques of co-option stems from electoral pressure. The PAP's electoral margin has not been reduced to the point that it is in danger of losing office in the foreseeable future. There are, in any case, as we have seen above, continued obstacles to a flourishing civil society on which opposition political parties can draw that limit the potential for coherent and comprehensive alternative political programmes to those of the PAP. However, the PAP is increasingly responsive to electoral pressure in its own way. Though its leadership still insists that it is a party committed to taking the long view and the hard but necessary decisions in the national interest, there is a greater preparedness to modify policies and make concessions to disaffected groups than in the past. In the 1980s this included modification to the graduate mothers policy. More recently, in the wake of the 1991 election, there has not only been a concerted attempt to address the perceived loss of support among the Chinese-educated, including an easing of the intense campaign to promote the widespread adoption of Mandarin at the expense of dialects,[13] but symbolic gestures to those left behind in Singapore's rigid meritocracy. This includes a provision in the 1992–93 budget for the government to pay the December HDB services and maintenance fees for low-income residents (*STWOE* 29 February 1992). Despite all the rhetoric about the perils of welfarism, this is clearly a means-tested subsidy that departs in principle from the general pattern of across-the-board, non-discriminatory public subsidies in areas like transport, education and health.

The PAP leadership's enthusiasm for the ballot has clearly waned in the last decade, but for the time being it is a fixture in the political system that must condition the PAP's strategy to retain its political supremacy.

Conclusion

To return more directly to the theoretical debates over the dynamics of regimes in industrialising capitalist countries, the recent political developments in Singapore suggest a number of points. First, to understand the persistence of the authoritarian regime in Singapore it must be appreciated that this is principally a function of the PAP's insistence on the continuance of a virtual one-party state. It does not spring from any fundamental need on the part of any fraction of the bourgeoisie or the middle class. Especially now that Singapore's industrial competitiveness derives more and more from productivity-enhancing and technology-intensive inputs, rather than simply lower labour costs, there is little evidence of any structural economic imperative underlying authoritarian rule. The more concerted attempt of late to bolster the service sector, notably knowledge-intensive, industries reinforces this point. As for the middle class, its social and economic position too is established and not under any threat that requires the defence of a one-party state.

Second, although the interests of the middle class are well served by the PAP regime, this does not cancel out for it various irritations associated with authoritarian rule. The excessive paternalism of the regime in the social and cultural spheres in particular is increasingly resented by sections of the middle class. As we have seen, the PAP itself has made some gestures towards change in these areas, but internal party divisions and contradictions on these questions indicate something less than a wholehearted commitment to reform here.

Third, whereas in the earlier development phase of rapid industrialisation the PAP successfully attracted the support of the bulk of the middle and working classes, the capacity to appease both classes simultaneously is now becoming increasingly difficult. Growing material disparities and heightened consciousness thereof, processes not peculiar to Singapore but generally associated with advancing capitalist economies, invariably complicate the task of reproducing traditional levels of political support and provide a more fertile environment for opposition parties. This need not threaten the PAP as government, but it does potentially place the goal of total political dominance in jeopardy.

Fourth, clearly, the political strategies and nature of leadership by the PAP are crucial factors in the determination of the regime's future. What we have seen above is a campaign to foster more extensive consultation and participation with the ruling party in the political process. The purpose of the exercise is, however, to ensure that the definitive feature of the regime—the de facto one-party state—does not become a casualty of the development process. The

New Guard leadership recognises that the previous political formula
that supported the one-party state is losing currency, not just among
a younger, better educated and more worldly and expanding middle
class. It is now discovering that the electoral alienation with the
PAP also includes substantial sections of the working class and the
small business sector. But none of this compels the PAP to adopt a
programme of rapid liberalisation, nor does it recommend any
particular response by the leadership. So some of the points made
by O'Donnell and Schmitter (1986) have relevance for the Singapore case. Singapore's now 'developed' economic status and considerable middle class may be extremely important preconditions
for political liberalisation, but they are in themselves insufficient.
At the same time, there are also limits to the insights of O'Donnell
and Schmitter (1986) since the current strategy of political co-option
does not appear to be stemming the trend of electoral alienation.
Marx's widely quoted observation in *The Eighteenth Brumaire of
Louis Bonaparte* remains relevant: 'Men [sic] make their own
history, but they do not make it just as they please: they do not
make it under circumstances chosen by themselves, but under circumstances directly encountered, given and transmitted from the
past' (Marx & Engels 1962: 247). Whereas in the past the PAP could
draw on Singapore's relatively undeveloped economic condition,
communal violence, the threat of communism and the political
insecurity of the nation state of Singapore itself as a rationalisation
for the authoritarian regime, the changed historical conditions are
less supportive of the PAP's case for absolute political dominance.
Now the PAP's case for blunting oppositional politics appears more
conspicuously inspired by party political considerations.

Notes

1 I am grateful to Kevin Hewison, Richard Robison, James Cotton and
   Chua Beng Huat for their constructive criticisms in the development
   of this paper. Of course the responsibility for any errors rests solely
   with the author.
2 CCCs were established in 1963 in each of the then 51 electoral
   constituencies. Comprised of appointments by the Permanent Secretary in the Prime Minister's Office, CCCs had a blatant political
   purpose: to neutralise or minimise opposition to PAP policy. They
   pursued this by favourably presenting government policy at grassroots
   level and by channelling dissent through the PAP-controlled state (see
   Seah 1973; 1987).
3 The high ethnic Indian population may also have been more disposed

towards Jeyaretnam because, being born in Sri Lanka, he could appreciate some of their concerns as members of a minority group.

4 The category 'middle class' is a notoriously difficult one for theorists. In Marxist terms, it is a somewhat ambiguous concept to the extent that the fundamental social relations of class are conceived as arising out of surplus extraction. The distinctiveness of the middle class lies in its indirect involvement in this relationship. One important theme in the contemporary literature attempting to refine the category is the incorporation of some notion of domination between classes resulting from the technical division of labour, drawing on a Weberian understanding of class. The middle class 'dominates' the working class yet is itself dominated by the owners of capital (see Burris 1987). At a more concrete level, most writers agree that managers and supervisors are located in the middle class. They also see a range of non-supervisory professional and technical positions belonging to this class, with differences remaining over exactly which such positions qualify.

5 The Town Council governing committees comprise an MP who has the power to nominate a minimum of six and a maximum of thirty councillors. It is required that two-thirds of the councillors be residents of the public housing administered by the Town Council of which they are members. Identifying sufficient people within constituencies with the interest and skills to be involved has proven difficult and led to some 'outside' appointments (see *ST* 12 July 1991).

6 The two NMPs were Maurice Choo, a heart specialist and associate professor, and Leong Chee Whye, president and chief executive officer of United Industrial Corporation and chairman of Singapore Tourist Promotion Board.

7 GRCs were introduced in May 1988. According to the government, they were intended to guard against racial politics. Under this change, political parties were required to field three candidates in a GRC, but this has since been raised to four, with a diversity of ethnic composition.

8 The command of Mandarin by the SDP's Cheo Chai Chen in Nee Soon South and of Teochew by the WP's Low Thai Khiang in Hougang enabled them to reach out to their electorates more effectively than the respective PAP candidates.

9 According to one estimate, while the consumer price index rose by 3.8 per cent for the first half of 1991, costs in public transport rose by 19 per cent, health charges by 9.9 per cent and education by 6.8 per cent (*FEER* 10 October 1991).

10 He received some public encouragement in this reassessment. See, for example, the letter to the *Straits Times* by local academic Chua Beng Huat in *STWOE* 7 September 1991.

11 Ironically, surveys showed that it was the Chinese-educated who attended the Restricted (R-rated) films, notably those classified as soft

pornography and violent, in greatest numbers (see *STWOE* 2 November 1991). Though they were not mentioned, possibly the lifting of a 32-year ban on juke boxes in 1991 and the revival of Bugis Street, a tourist attraction previously notorious for transvestite activity, belonged to this category of reforms as well.

12 Five people were appointed to the Council of Presidential Advisers in late 1991, to take effect from 2 January 1992. The all-male appointees are: Lim Kin San, chairman of the Port of Singapore Authority and executive chairman of Singapore Press Holdings, who is the chairman of the Council of Presidential Advisers; Lee Seng Wee, a banker, billionaire and chairman of the Singapore International Foundation; Michael Fam, executive chairman of Fraser & Neave and chairman of the Nanyang Technological University; Ridzwan Dzafir, diplomat and director-general of the Trade Development Board; and Cheong Siew Keong, deputy chairman of the Public Service Commission.

13 The significance of the success of the WP's Teochew-speaking Low Thai Khiang in the Hougang consitituency was not lost on the PAP.

References

Amnesty International 1987, *Singapore: Detention Without Trial Under the Internal Security Act*, Amnesty International, New York

Asia Watch 1989, *Silencing All Critics: Human Rights Violations in Singapore*, Asia Watch, New York

Association of Women for Action and Research [AWARE] 1988a, *The Singapore Woman*, AWARE, Singapore

—— 1988b, *Population: An Issue of Current Concern*, AWARE Position Paper, no. 1, Singapore

Bellows, Thomas J. 1973, *The People's Action Party of Singapore: The Emergence of a Dominant Party System*, Yale University Southeast Asia Studies Monograph Series, no. 14, New Haven

Brown, David 1992, 'The Corporatist Management of Ethnicity in Contemporary Singapore', in Rodan ed., 1992

Burris, Val 1987, 'The Neo-Marxist Synthesis of Marx and Weber on Class', *The Marx–Weber Debate*, ed. N. Wiley, Sage Publications, Newbury Park

Chan Heng Chee 1978, *The Dynamics of One Party Dominance: The PAP at the Grassroots*, Singapore University Press, Singapore

Chua Beng Huat 1991a, 'Not Depoliticized but Ideologically Successful: the Public Housing Programme in Singapore', *International Journal of Urban and Regional Research*, vol. 15, no. 1, pp. 24–41

—— 1991b, 'Singapore 1990: Celebrating the End of an Era', *Southeast Asian Affairs 1991* Institute of Southeast Asian Affairs, Singapore

—— 1991c, 'Building a Democratic State in Singapore', Paper presented at the International Symposium, Institutions in Cultures: Theory and Practice, National University of Singapore, 19–22 June

Clammer, John 1992, 'Democratic Values: The Establishment of a "National

Ideology" and its Implications for Singapore's Political Future', in Rodan ed., 1992

Cotton, James 1992, 'Political Innovation in Singapore: The Presidency, the Leadership and the Party', in Rodan ed., 1992

Cumings, Bruce 1989, 'The Abortive Abertura: South Korea in the Light of Latin American Experience', *New Left Review*, no. 173, pp. 5–32

Deyo, Frederic C. 1981, *Dependent Development and Industrial Order: An Asian Case Study*, Praeger, Singapore

Economic Committee, Ministry of Trade and Industry 1986, *The Singapore Economy: New Directions*, Singapore National Printers, Singapore

Goh Chok Tong 1986, 'A Nation of Excellence', Text of a lecture at the Alumni International Singapore, 1 December, Ministry of Communications and Information, Singapore

—— 1988, 'Our National Ethic', *Speeches*, vol. 12, no. 5, p. 13

Huntington, Samuel 1965, 'Political Development and Political Decay', *World Politics*, vol. 17, no. 3, pp. 386–430

—— 1968, *Political Order in Changing Societies*, Yale University Press, New Haven

—— 1984, 'Will More Countries Become Democratic?' *Political Science Quarterly*, vol. 99, no. 2, pp. 193–218

Lodge, George & Vogel, Ezra 1987, *Ideology and National Competitiveness: a Comparison of Ten Different Countries*, Harvard Business School Press, Boston

Low, Linda & Toh Mun Heng 1989, 'The Elected Presidency as a Safeguard for Official Reserves: What is at Stake?', Institute of Policy Studies Occasional Paper No. 1, Times Academic Press, Singapore

Marx, Karl & Engels, Frederick 1962, *Selected Works: Volume 1*, Foreign Languages Publishing House, Moscow

Ng Chee Yuen 1989, 'Privatisation in Singapore: Divestment with Control', *ASEAN Economic Bulletin*, vol. 5, no. 3, pp. 290–318

O'Donnell, Guillermo & Schmitter, Philippe C. 1986, *Transitions from Authoritarian Rule: Tentative Conclusions about Uncertain Democracies*, Johns Hopkins University Press, London

Ooi Giok Ling 1990, 'Town Councils in Singapore: Self-Determination for Public Housing Estates', Institute of Policy Studies Occasional Paper No. 4, Times Academic Press, Singapore

Phua Kai Hong 1991, 'Privatization & Restructuring of Health Services in Singapore', Institute of Policy Studies Occasional Paper No. 5, Times Academic Press, Singapore

Quah, Jon S.T. ed. 1990, *In Search of Singapore's National Values*, Times Academic Press for the Institute of Policy Studies, Singapore

Robison, Richard 1988, 'Authoritarian States, Capital-Owning Classes, and the Politics of Newly Industrializing Countries: the Case of Indonesia', *World Politics*, vol. 41, no. 1, pp. 52–74

Rodan, Garry 1989, *The Political Economy of Singapore's Industrialization: National State and International Capital*, Macmillan, London

—— 1990, 'Singapore: Continuity in Change as the New Guard's Agenda Becomes Clearer', *Southeast Asian Affairs 1990*, Institute of Southeast Asian Studies, Singapore, pp. 295–316

—— 1992a, 'The Growth of Singapore's Middle Class and its Political Significance', in Rodan ed., 1992

—— 1992b, 'Singapore's Leadership Transition: Erosion or Refinement of Authoritarian Rule?', *Bulletin of Concerned Asian Scholars*, vol. 24, no. 1, pp. 3–17

Rodan, Garry ed. 1992 *Singapore Changes Guard: Social, Political and Economic Directions in the 1990s*, Longman Cheshire, Melbourne, forthcoming

Seah Chee Meow 1973, *Community Centres in Singapore: Their Political Involvement*, Singapore University Press, Singapore

—— 1987, 'Parapolitical Institutions', *Government and Politics of Singapore*, eds J.S.T. Quah et al., Oxford University Press, Singapore

SME Committee, Economic Development Board 1989, *SME Master Plan: Report on Enterprise Development*, Economic Development Board, Singapore

Tan Teng Lang 1990, 'The Singapore Press: Freedom, Responsibility and Credibility', Institute of Policy Studies Occasional Paper No. 3, Times Academic Press, Singapore

Thynne, Ian & Ariff, Mohammed eds 1988, *Privatisation: Singapore's Experience in Perspective*, Longman, Singapore

Turnbull, C.M. 1982, *A History of Singapore 1819-1975*, Oxford University Press, Kuala Lumpur

White Paper 1991, *Shared Values*, Singapore National Printers, Singapore

Wright, Erik Olin 1978, *Class, Crisis and the State*, New Left Books, London

Yeo, George Yong-Boon 1991a, 'Civic Society—Between the Family and the State', National University of Singapore Society Inaugural Lecture, 20 June, Singapore Government Press Release

—— 1991b, 'The Future: Looking Beyond', in *PAP Youth: In Action 1986–1991*, People's Action Party Youth Wing Fifth Anniversary Commemorative Volume, Singapore

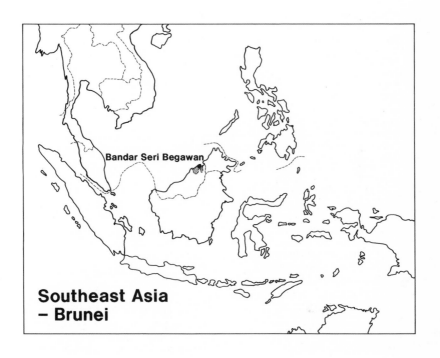

**Southeast Asia
– Brunei**

Brunei: Basic social and economic data

Population (1989)	249 000 (excl. 'transients afloat')
Population density (1989)	43.2 persons per sq. km
Average annual population growth (1982–89)	2.5%
Urban population (1990)	59%
Total labour force (1986)	86 400
Major ethnic groups	Malays, Chinese
Capital city	Bandar Seri Begawan
Population (1986)	50 500
Land area	5765 sq. km
Official language	Non-modernised Malay
Other main languages	English
Administrative division	Four districts
Education, enrolments	
Primary (1989)	40 611
Secondary (1990)	18 748
University (1990)	1145
Adult literacy rate (1990)	80.3%
Health	
Life expectancy (1990)	71 yrs
Infant mortality/1000 (1990)	11
Persons/hospital bed (1986)	267
Persons/physician (1986)	1323
Economy	
GDP at market prices (1989)	US$3.7 bn
Real GDP per capita (1989)	US$15 200
GDP growth rate (1989)	2.7%
Trade	
Exports, value (1987)	US$2.1 bn
Imports, value (1987)	US$0.8 bn
Main imports (1985)	Machinery 34.1%, manufactures 21.6%, food 14.6%
Main exports (1985)	Mineral fuels 98.5%, machinery 0.8%, manufactures 0.2%
Foreign debt as % of GDP	Nil
Foreign reserves (1990)	US$27 bn
Communications	
Rail (1990)	12 km
Roads, paved (1988)	1093 km
Religion	Islam

Sources: Far Eastern Economic Review Asia Yearbook 1991; The Far East and Australasia 1992 (Europa Publications); United Nations Economic and Social Commission for Asia and the Pacific (ESCAP) Newsletter, Statistical Yearbook for Asia and the Pacific 1989, ESCAP.

5 Rentier capitalism in Negara Brunei Darussalam

Geoffrey C. Gunn[1]

The smallest, least-populated[2], and probably the least-known state in Southeast Asia, Brunei only resumed full sovereign status from its former protecting power, the United Kingdom, in 1984. Upon independence, Negara Brunei Darussalam, as it became officially known, assumed full responsibility for its defence and foreign affairs, joined the United Nations, the Association of Southeast Asian Nations (ASEAN) and the Organisation of the Islamic Conference (OIC).

While from 1906 until 1959—with the exception of the Japanese interregnum—executive power had been in the hands of a British Resident, Brunei did not experience a complete loss of sovereignty especially in matters relating to local customs and religion. Nevertheless, as in the Borneo states and in Malaya itself, the British protectorate system laid down the fundamental administrative, legal and judicial armature. While the Sultan effectively replaced the British Resident as the source of executive power in 1959, and while representative institutions and a constitutional form of monarchy were set down in a constitution in 1959, a state of emergency imposed in the wake of an unsuccessful rebellion in 1962 has not been lifted nor have representative institutions been permitted to take root.

As a consequence of the discovery and exploitation of its oil resources, commencing in 1928, Brunei is today, in per capita terms, one of the richest states in the world (US$15 200 in 1989). Indeed, more than one observer has remarked upon parallels between Brunei and Kuwait, namely wealth, size, population density, religion, economic management, defence and security and political system, an analogy made all the more graphic by the high profile achieved by Kuwait in the Gulf War of 1990–91 (Dasse 1991). Prior to a discussion of the political economy of Brunei, a brief analysis of the Sultanate's political system will suggest this Middle Eastern analogy.

Organisation of political power in Brunei

It is a statement of fact that Brunei today remains one of a handful of absolute monarchies in the world reigned over and simultaneously ruled over by the hereditary ruler, the Sultan and Yang Di-Pertuan, Sultan Hassanan Bolkiah, who succeeded his father the late Sultan Omar Ali Saifuddin in 1967. As such, the Sultan holds the office of Prime Minister and Minister of Defence and wields full executive authority. Other immediate members of the royal family and key appointees control commanding positions in the government and in economic management. Prince Mohamed Bolkiah, the eldest of the Sultan's three younger brothers, is Minister of Foreign Affairs. The Sultan's youngest brother, Prince Jefri Bolkiah, is Minister of Finance and thus in ultimate control of the powerful Brunei Investment Agency. While notionally assisted by four constitutional councils, the Sultanate has been ruled by decree since 1962 when key provisions of the 1959 Constitution were suspended, most notably the electoral process.

As in Kuwait, the monarchical structure of government in Brunei and the concentration of power and wealth in the hands of a ruling family suggest rule by oligarchy. But unlike the situation in Kuwait, where a National Assembly provided for under a constitution inaugurated in 1962 became an increasingly vocal force in Kuwait politics prior to its dissolution in August 1976, the legislature in Brunei has never been other than a rubber stamp. Indeed, Brunei has yet to take the step adopted by Kuwait two months prior to its invasion, namely allowing the formation of a National Council or rump parliament. Where post-invasion Kuwait promises elections, there is no announced timetable for the restoration of the electoral process in Brunei nor, indeed, for the lifting of the state of emergency. Thus, whereas in Kuwait one can speak of a shadowy parliamentary opposition crystallised around political parties, the very concept of an opposition is not officially accepted in Brunei. The possibilities of the single surviving sanctioned political party in Brunei actually entering the political process looks remote at the present juncture.

Commencing in 1986, however, the cabinet system of government in Brunei was strengthened by increasing the number of ministries from seven to eleven and with the addition of deputy ministerial positions. While such an arrangement, along with a further cabinet reshuffle taking effect in January 1989, offers a more technocratic profile to the 'regime', it has become something of a pastime among observers of the Brunei scene to identify among the Ministers and advisers those who tend to ideological or Islamic solutions to the country's development and those who come down on the side of a pragmatic accommodation with modernisation and development. Usually identified as heading the 'ideologues' is the kingdom's senior religious official, the State Mufti, along with the powerful Minister of Education, Pehin Abdul Aziz. Also included in this camp are Pehin Badaruddin, Permanent Secretary to the Prime Minister (the Sultan), and with various responsibilities spanning information and religion, and the Minister of Religious Affairs, Haji Mohammad Zain. Those who are considered more pragmatic in their vision are such Western-educated confidants of the court as the Special Adviser to the Sultan in the Prime Minister's Office, Pehin Dato Isa, and the Minister of Industry and Primary Resources, Pehin Dato Haji Abdul Rahman. While the Sultan and Prince Mohamed have traditionally been perceived as pro-Western or at least pragmatic, increasingly they are obliged to straddle or play off the two camps or tendencies, an increasingly difficult act for, as few would deny, today it is the 'ideologues' who are in the ascendancy with the technocratic or pragmatic group on the defensive (Weaver 1991: 56–93).

But if official Islam is in a sense manageable in a country where the Sultan is considered the secular head of the faith, there is no doubt that the Sultan is alert to the dangers of a Nasserite-type putsch from within as much a challenge from without. From the political standpoint, the role of praetorian guard is ensured by a 1000 strong battalion of Ghurkhas recruited by and dependent upon the Sultan. But sensitivity to challenges was also shown up by a major restructuring of Brunei's armed forces in September 1991. In this move three services were effectively created where hitherto there had been one. In announcing this shakeup, which also involved a rotation of key personnel, the Sultan not only cautioned vigilance against the possible eruption of regional disputes à la Kuwait but also doubted the reliability of leadership within the otherwise professionally encadred and British-trained armed forces; in the words of the Sultan (quoted in *Borneo Bulletin* 15 October 1991) 'Senjata makan tuan' (weapons could be turned against oneself).

Rentier capitalism in contemporary Brunei

The foundation of the country's wealth, it is clear, stems from the exploitation of the country's hydrocarbon resources which began in the third decade of this century. Unlike the Asian Newly Industrialised Countries (NICs) whose economic development is based upon the manufacture and export of manufactured goods for Western markets, Brunei's economy is almost entirely dependent

(98 per cent) upon the export of oil and gas. For all intents and purposes Brunei's economy conforms to those less diversified economies of the Middle East also dependent upon high-income-earning natural resources. Such economies—at least as mediated by forms of state control—are typically beneficiaries of substantial amounts of royalties or external rentals on a regular basis. In the literature on the petroleum-based economies of the Middle East, such states have been termed rentier states supported by rentier economies. What are the acknowledged features of rentier states and rentier economies?

The rentier state concept, or the notion that states based upon external sources of income are substantially different from states based on domestic taxation, was first proposed with reference to such Middle Eastern economies as Iran by Mahdavy (1970) and Libya by Mabro (1969) and First (1974), although clearly the concept of rent (and ground rent) can be traced back to Marx and before him, Adam Smith. More recently, Colclough (1985) has proposed the relevance of the rentier state model to Brunei, albeit speculatively. In general terms, as recipients of substantial foreign rents, the economies of rentier states are extroverted in the sense that the key industry—export of oil and gas—has very little to do with the production processes of the local economy. Typically, producer states have appropriated sufficiently large shares of the rents that accrue to the oil companies as profits to embark upon large public expenditure programmes 'without resorting to taxation and without running into drastic balance of payments or expenditure problems' (First 1974: 148). In a situation of rising oil revenues, the government or at least the public sector becomes the dominant factor in the local economy. This gives rise to a special form of *etatisme*. Specifically, if most of the oil royalties or rentals are used to import consumption goods then the productive sectors of the economy will be untouched beyond that worked by foreign enterprise. In such a rentier situation there is no 'nexus between production and income distribution', since revenues accrue directly to the government not through any production but from oil taxes which come from outside the economy. Consumption patterns become geared to the use of imported commodities: 'There are no links between the proceeds of production, effort, and incentive' (First 1974: 149–50). Further, Beblawi (1987: 52) has drawn the distinction between a rentier state, rentier economy and rentier mentality. Inter alia, a rentier state is a special version of a rentier economy in which the defining feature is the 'externality' of the rent origin. But such an economy also creates a rentier mentality implying a break in the work–reward causation and where reward or wealth is not related to work and risk taking.

In theory, as Colclough has written of rentier economies in general, the state could live off the dividends by managing investment portfolios. Up against the high technology extractive industry the social base of the country remains backward; agriculture and other domestic industries tend to stand still or wither. Typical of 'enclave' economies, linkages between the oil sector and other sectors are very limited, downstream industries non-existent as the product tends to be exported in crude or refined form. Rather, in an inversion of the development process, the rentier economy supports the development of the service sector almost exclusively as the employer of an army of foreign technicians and labourers. Typically, also, the legacy of colonial education policies is a severe skill restraint. In a situation where the government is obliged to pay generous consumption benefits to nationals in the way of housing, education, medical benefits and social services, it is 'entirely rational for national workers to remain unemployed rather than take jobs outside government'. Often a situation of over-expansion of public sector employment also arises (Colclough 1985: 29–32).

In development terms, the rentier state pre-empts a shift to the producer state. The generation of wealth, albeit abundant, throws up the paradox of a state of a high technology industry in an otherwise backward economy (cf. First 1974: 150). Alongside all these features of the rentier state, additional barriers to a transformation to a producer state economy or the diversification of the economy are the inflated cost structure and an inflated currency. Almost anything can be imported more cheaply than it can be produced at home (Colclough 1985: 31). As will be discussed later, rentier states also characteristically privilege political considerations over strictly economic considerations. This has profound implications for state–society relations and the form that *etatisme* entails. How applicable, then, is the rentier state/rentier economy paradigm to the Brunei situation? What specific forms does *etatist* control over resources take in Brunei? How is the state–society relationship in Brunei mediated in an erstwhile rentier state situation?

In the following section, I shall trace the dynamic of economic development in Brunei, the making of an oil-dependent economy and the constraints this imposes upon industrial diversification, the full transition to the import-substitution stage and other indices of industrial deepening, namely domestic capital accumulation.

The dynamic of colonial economic development

One approach to modern Brunei economic history would be to

discuss the economic incorporation of the state to sub-regional, regional as well as global economic networks, according to chronological stages of both economic and political development. This broadly world-systems analysis, however, would have to be modified, to take into account the legacy of powerful local tributary forms of surplus accumulation and their culturally expressed correlates in the form of patrimonial distribution of rewards. Thus to give credence to local forms of economic activity—not inconsiderable in the case of Brunei before the Protectorate—it is important to outline such pre-colonial forms of production and exchange as the development of craft manufacture, as well as the central role of the Sultanate in mediating regional and long-distance trade and exchange. Only then can we understand the economic forms surviving into the colonial period.

A discussion of the Brunei economy under the Protectorate, then, would necessarily address not only the emergence of new forms of production, consumption and exchange but would equally account for the 'dissolution' effects of monetisation on the traditional economy, the development of a standardised currency, the imposition of new forms of taxation and the creation of colonial monopolies. Central here—and in common with other economies on the colonial periphery—is the creation under colonial auspices of 'extroverted' forms of economic activity, namely in the Brunei example the development of new extractive industries. This is not just a question of elucidating modern versus traditional economy or a restatement of economic dualism, but a question of tracing the complex evolution of, subsumption of, and coexistence of new and old forms of economic activity through time, and in response to broader regional and international political and market forces and demands.

As the British historian A.V.M. Horton has written, such was Brunei's integration or actually subsumption into a colonial economy with Singapore as sub-metropole that, by the opening years of this century, the capital city and surrounding districts were described in a British report as producing almost nothing and dependent upon imports for all necessities except for a small amount of locally produced rice. In the event, the establishment of the British Residency in Brunei in 1905–06 resulted in a reorganisation of the fiscal regime, effectively leading to the abolition of a 'feudal' system of administration, taxation and land tenure based on crown, ministerial and 'feudal' (*tulin*) lands with serf tenure. Under the new dispensation, aside from a civil list, all other revenues would go to the state. For the first decades of the century the programme of buying up *tulin* rights left the state heavily indebted. Through to the 1930s, then, Brunei was actually subsidised by the Federated Malay States and the Straits Settlements (Horton 1990: 26–32).

The first of Brunei's resources assayed by British merchant capital was coal. This resource was exploited until 1926 by the Brooke family in a special economic enclave at Brooketon in the Muara district. Another extractive industry developed under the auspices of colonial capital was cutch, a by-product of mangrove trees, processed in a plant run by the Island Trading Company in Brunei Town until closed down in the early 1950s. Cutch was actually Brunei's most valuable export between the years 1906 and 1922. In the period before oil revenues guaranteed Brunei's solvency, only the timely establishment by British capital of rubber plantations in Brunei rescued the country economically. Production fell away during the Great Depression and only recovered in the postwar period, reaching a peak in production in 1960 before being allowed to decline (Franz 1990: 243–4). But with the exploitation of oil commencing in 1932, and the realisation of super-profits through production-sharing arrangements with Royal Dutch Shell, even the vestiges of a traditional economy, paddy rice and fishing, have been permitted to run down. Not only did new oil revenues give a massive expansion to government revenue but by 1936 Brunei was able to clear its national debt (Horton 1990: 26–32). As a general statement, then, agriculture, fishing and forestry activities in the Residency period ranged from the lowest level of self-sufficient subsistence economy practised by certain tribal groups in remote areas to purely commercial farming without private consumption.

While at the outset of the Residential era the Sultan privately languished in a state of penury—consistent with the sorry state of the Sultanate at the hands of such local agents of British mercantile imperialism as the Brooke family and the North Borneo Company—by 1934, Horton (1990: 26–32) estimates, the Sultan was gaining a private income in excess of a handsome income received from the government. In the postwar period, however, Civil List expenditure rose to 35 000 pounds sterling annually, double that figure again by 1961. Together, as discussed below, the expanding revenue base along with a strengthened monarchical system served to define the nature of the evolving rentier economy.

A special form of *etatisme*

Visibly, Brunei has undergone rapid structural change in the postwar period from an overwhelmingly agrarian society to what Franz (1990: 129–31) has described as a service sector society. Thus while in 1947 more than 50 per cent of the population was employed in the primary sector, by 1971 the figure had declined to just over 10 per cent. In the same period, the tertiary—here understood as service—sector grew from around 30 per cent to over 50 per cent, while the secondary sector remained at the same level.

But even as urbanisation has progressed in Brunei, the development from an agrarian to a tertiary sector society has not followed the conventional pattern of developing countries. Rather, Brunei has moved towards a tertiary society without developing the secondary linkages. Even the growth of the secondary sector from the early 1970s onwards has been entirely due to the expansion of the construction industry and therefore does not signal any kind of industrial deepening (Franz 1990: 131). Thus today, in place of such commercial agricultural activities as rubber plantations, it is the state which supports large-scale farm projects—the Mitsubishi Corporation Macfarm or model farm is one—in the attempt to reduce dependence upon foreign imports of basic foodstuffs. But as these operations are largely uneconomic or 'showcase' operations, they should be seen more in terms of their political statements (Franz 1990: 209).

It should be clear then that Brunei's economy is almost entirely founded on its petroleum and gas resources, generating some 61 per cent of GDP, relative to 32 per cent generated by the service sector and 2–3 per cent by agriculture. Some three-fifths of Brunei's petroleum and gas resources, which, as mentioned, account for almost all export resources, are directed towards Japan. Similarly government revenue is derived primarily from its oil and gas interests and from company taxation, including that of Royal Brunei Shell. There is no income tax. There is also no trade deficit, no national debt and the balance of payments remains in surplus (Hong Kong & Shanghai Bank 1988: 8).

A special feature of the oil industry in Brunei is the 'privatised' character of ownership and operational control of the oil industry. Since 1913 the Shell Group of companies has dominated the search and exploitation of Brunei's hydrocarbon resources. Today the oil industry in Brunei is dominated by four companies belonging to Brunei Shell of which the state holds a 50 per cent share in each. Dominating the energy sector is Brunei Shell Petroleum (BSP), responsible for exploration and production of oil and natural gas as well as oil refining and crude oil trading. Second in importance is Brunei LPG, a three-way tie-up between Brunei, Shell and Mitsubishi Corporation, contracted in 1972 and which is concerned with liquefying the gas it buys from BSP. It sells the liquefied gas in turn to a third company, Brunei Coldgas (BC) which arranges its transportation and sale to Japanese customers. Central to the LPG operation was a twenty-year agreement—still in force, but coming up for renegotiation—to supply the Tokyo Electric Power Company, the Tokyo Gas Company and the Osaka Gas Company. Overall the government derives an estimated 85 per cent of all earnings of Brunei Shell Petroleum in the form of taxes and royalties (Economist Intelligence Unit 1990–91: 47).

In part as a conservation measure, the normal level of oil production has been held in recent years at 150 000 barrels per day, although this threshold was breached to take advantage of higher oil prices prevailing in late 1990 as a result of the Gulf crisis. Notably, in the period from 1986 onwards, Jasra Elf, a union of Brunei—meaning Royal family controlled—Jasra International Petroleum (Jaspet) and Elf Aquitaine Offshore Asia BV have made important offshore oil discoveries in Brunei, thus breaking into the Shell Groups' monopoly. Significant by world standards, the 1990–91 discoveries are bound to raise the threshold of known resources, albeit a closely guarded state secret. Although Brunei's large earnings from its foreign investments provide it with considerable immunity from oil price fluctuations, government spending is influenced by its hydrocarbons revenues. The construction sector in particular stands to benefit from higher state spending as do other non-oil economic activities (Economist Intelligence Unit 1991, no.1: 31).

It is of interest that Brunei has never been tempted towards nationalisation of the oil industry, as for example has Algeria, nor has it allowed a state oil industry to develop along the lines of Malaysia's Petronas or Indonesia's Pertamina, nor, indeed, has Brunei chosen to join OPEC. The reasons are basically as much political as economic. Under British tutelage, pro-Western Brunei distanced itself from OPEC's radical posturing on pricing and production policies, but as a relatively small player in the international oil stakes, Brunei was able to take advantage of the spot market when opportune. Otherwise, though, Brunei shares the basic feature of the economies of oil-rentier states, namely the way in which the state emerges as the main intermediary between the oil sector and the rest of the economy.

Another special feature of *etatisme* in oil-rentier states stemming from the accumulation of windfall profits is the massive increase in public expenditure programmes. While such infrastructural developments as housing, health and education figure in such programmes, so does spending on defence which has characteristically reached new heights.[3] Such spending and employment opportunities also constitute an important instrument of redistribution of oil revenues among various social groups, the political importance of which is obvious. This has been termed the 'internal recycling of oil wealth'. But, no less, the 'external recycling of oil rent' reinforces the rentier character of the state notably through overseas portfolio investment. Characteristically this throws up a 'tripartite

alliance' between the state (in Brunei this function is served by the
Brunei Investment Agency), the new business elite (in Brunei, the
Bumiputera merchants, contractors and financiers alongside certain
Chinese comprador interests[4]) and circles of international capital,
the subject of wide speculation on the part of finance journalists in
the case of Brunei (Abdel-Fadil 1987: 86).

The modus operandi of the Brunei Investment Agency, created in
1983 in order to manage the Sultanate's reserves and which in turn
eclipsed the British Crown Agents who had traditionally performed
this role, bears scrutiny. As explained in a recent and rare interview
by its managing director, Dato Abdul Rahman Karim, also a Permanent Secretary in the Ministry of Finance, the Agency only
handles 40 per cent of the kingdom's foreign reserves which he
estimates at US$27 billion. The remainder is divided among eight
foreign—mainly Japanese and American—institutions, including
Morgan Guaranty, Bankers Trust, Citibank, Nomura Investment and
Daiwa. From 50 to 60 per cent of the Agency's money is in bonds
and from 40 to 50 per cent is in stocks and shares (such blue-chip
companies as Mercedes, Siemens, IBM and Sony), banks and real
estate, all in all realising two billion dollars profit a year (cf. Weaver
1991: 76–7).

Besides the role of the Brunei Investment Agency in 'external
recycling' we should add QAF Holdings, 'a diversified concern with
close links to the Royal family' and the second largest business
operation in the country after Brunei Shell, and the Sultan, an active
investor in his own right (Economist Intelligence Unit 1990–91: 43).
As Beblawi (1987: 55) observes of oil rentier economies, 'the
distinction between public service and private interest is very often
blurred. There seems to be no clear cut conflict of interests between
holding public office and running private business at the same time,
and it is not infrequent to use the one to foster the other'. Clearly,
estimates of the Sultan's private wealth today turn on separating out
national reserves from those under Royal control. Bartholomew
(1989: 16) asserts that 'Brunei is a private country run like a private
possession. One is entitled to ask if the Sultan does not control the
country's reserves, who on earth does?' Further, as Dasse has written
of the switch by Brunei from sterling investments to dollars and
yen: 'The Sultanate acquired a form of direct political pressure on
the US and Japan who cannot ignore such an important investor.'

Yet another feature of the rentier state, as mentioned, is the
existence of a 'parasitic' consumer class in the absence of a producer
class. Brunei has long enjoyed the highest per capita income in
Southeast Asia, and is in the same bracket as certain of the
industrialised countries and the oil-producing countries of the
Middle East. While evidence of prosperity is highly visible, for

example Brunei boasts one of the highest car-ownership rates in the world, as Franz states, income relativities—and, by inference, income inequalities—are difficult to gauge. By any measure, however, wages are higher than in neighbouring Sabah, Sarawak and Indonesia, made more attractive by the strength of the currency, the fact that such staples as rice and sugar are fixed and subsidised, and that the state can afford not to levy tax on income. Additionally, citizens—a restrictive category in Brunei—are beneficiaries of other benefits such as subsidised education and housing. But, as Franz notes, prosperity creates demands that cannot be satisfied with a low income. Demand is thus actually stimulated by the government practice of granting loans to local Bruneians at interest-free or low-interest rates. This has had the effect, at the obvious expense of savings, of stimulating the purchase of such luxuries as television sets, video recorders and cars (Franz 1990: 135–40). Clearly, then, the Brunei consumer, not producer or risk-taker, is the apotheosis of the Brunei middle-class.[5]

Industrial diversification in the non-oil gas sectors

In what ways has the state sought to encourage industrial diversification so as to free Brunei from its erstwhile rentier state condition and push the economy along the path of domestic capital accumulation as in the free-market economies of Southeast Asia? Rhetorically, at least, Brunei has long been committed to such a course. Such was the thrust of the nation's Fifth Development Plan (1986-90). Indeed, the creation in January 1989 of the Ministry of Industry and Primary Resources was heralded as ushering in the development of productive industrialisation in the country. 1991 marks the end of the nation's fifth five-year plan and sees Brunei entering its sixth five-year plan. Although not yet formally announced, it is expected that the plan will focus on specialised infrastructural development such as industrial parks and export-oriented and capital-intensive industries, all in line with the drive to diversify the oil-based economy.

The prospects for sustained diversification of the economy in the non-oil and gas sectors are called into question by several factors. These include the inability to attract foreign investment, know-how and partners, the inability of local business to compete with the state sector, the shortage of human resources and materials, and the minuscule size of the local market for potential local manufacturers.

The inability to attract foreign investment and expertise has not necessarily been for want of trying. For example, in March 1990 a high-powered Bruneian delegation visited the UK, the first ever to

Europe, to seek UK private investment in the Sultanate. Taiwanese, Australian and Singapore businessmen have similarly been encouraged to invest in Brunei. Still the perception exists that Brunei lacks the necessary infrastructure and skilled workforce, and is otherwise only half-hearted about its commitment. This not only concerns administrative obstacles thrown up against potential investors but a public attitude that sees outside influences in terms of cultural threats. Thus the results of the diversification drive to date are meagre and include the establishment of several plants producing clothing for export, a soft-drink canning factory and a steel roofing plant, all almost wholly reliant upon the import of raw materials. Only the embryo of an industrial import substitution policy has so far been created.

Emblematic of the problem of domestic capital formation is the demonstrable inability of *bumiputera* businessmen to compete with the state sector. This was revealed in the course of a well-publicised meeting in 1990 of over 300 local businessmen in the nation's capital to discuss the problem of delayed payments by government departments to private contractors. As reported in the local press, 'the contractors were apparently not satisfied with the explanations' provided by government spokespersons (*Borneo Bulletin* cited in Economist Intelligence Unit 1990, no. 3). The result, in early 1991, was a 'funeral procession' of local civil contracting firms and a 'flood' of bankruptcies on the part of local and foreign contractors. While most of the large international consultancy companies attracted during the government building boom years have been able to leave behind a skeleton staff in the Sultanate, *bumiputera* building contractors have been victims of both 'careless cash control' and 'cash flow problems' (*Borneo Bulletin* 24 March 1991).

The labour shortage in Brunei is partly artificial, the result of cultural predilections on the part of locals, and partly real, the result of a dearth of skilled personnel. Characteristic of rentier economies, a relatively high percentage of the workforce is employed by the government. In Brunei, the public sector accounts for more than two-thirds of the indigenous labour force (57 700) and Brunei Shell Petroleum for much of the rest. Indeed, as the Minister for Industry and Primary Resources has conceded, the government's campaign to lure the local workforce into the private sector has not been successful (*Borneo Bulletin* 14 April 1990).

It is clear that the demand for labour has been sustained in the eighties by the increased level of development as laid out in the Fifth Development Plan and in various diversification policies. The increased demand for labour, both blue-collar and professional, however, has not been entirely left to market forces but is equally regulated through labour regulations, quotas and immigration controls (Thambipillai 1990: 15). In April 1990 the Minister of Industry and Primary Resources, Pehin Dato Haji Abdul Rahman, affirmed that Brunei's movement towards industrialisation will open up 40 000 new jobs as it begins to implement some 2000 industrial activities, half of which could be taken up by locals (*Borneo Bulletin* 14 April 1990). It would appear, however, that economies like Singapore, as opposed to Brunei, were poised to take advantage of these developments by exporting infrastructure engineering, professional consulting, building materials, technical support services and information technology (Biblex Supplement, *Borneo Bulletin* 8 July 1991: v).

While a small but growing local underclass of detribalised Iban migrants from Sarawak and stateless Chinese has historically existed in Brunei, labour is almost entirely imported and drawn from the labour-exporting countries of Southeast Asia, especially such sources as low-wage and labour-abundant Thailand, the Philippines and India, alongside traditional sources such as the Malaysian states of Sarawak and Sabah (Thambipillai 1990: 14–15). While Brunei is therefore a net exporter of remittances (itself an important feature of the growth economies of the region) it shares with rentier economies at large the luxury of paying no social overheads for its erstwhile dispensable, docile and imported proletariat. This comprises some 30 000 expatriate workers mostly employed in the construction, petroleum and service sectors. While union rights notionally exist in Brunei (the *Trade Union Act* of 1961) they are honoured only in the breach in the private sector, and contract labour in Brunei is exposed to the full gamut of otherwise documented risks and abuses associated with the intra-ASEAN and Middle East trade in labour.[6]

Overall, then, over-dependence upon foreign labour stems from the small number of locals entering the workforce, the insufficiency of local skilled labour and a cultural predisposition for public sector employment. Otherwise, the main constraint on expansion in the non-oil sector, and particularly in construction, is the shortage of labour rather than capital (Economist Intelligence Unit 1990, no. 2: 9).

One of the clearest statements on Brunei's commitment to the opening of the economy away from a pure rentier economy model and towards industrial diversification was made by the Sultan in July 1991. On the occasion of his 45th birthday the Sultan outlined certain of the future lines of development he wished Brunei to pursue over the next twenty years, as contained in a twenty-year master plan on Brunei's development, as well as obstacles to foreseen objectives. Indeed, the Sultan noted that while a small effort had been made by local companies in manufacturing (three compa-

nies involved in the export of clothing, a plastics factory, a plant
manufacturing roofing materials), all relied upon imported materials
and all were dependent upon foreign labour. The desired direction
for industrial diversification, he ruled, should be towards activities
that give opportunities to locals. Brunei, alone among the ASEAN
countries, he noted, does not produce consumer goods, is reliant
upon imports of all basic commodities and is entirely dependent
upon the exports of one basic commodity group, oil and gas. The
Sultan's prognosis was for Bruneians, especially the younger generation, to be *lebih cekal* (more determined) and *bersikap terbuka*
(open in their attitude) to foreign advice and training. As a panacea
he announced a new Technical and Vocational Education system to
complement existing post-secondary institutions which have already
gone far in changing attitudes and preparing a younger generation
for the workforce, especially, it might be noted, in winning acceptance for a role for women in the workplace. Matching the call for
openness in attitudes towards science and technology was an
announcement that Brunei would seek to operate a more 'open'
foreign policy in a post-Cold War situation, implying the establishment of diplomatic links with China and the Soviet Union (*Pelita
Brunei* 17 July 1991). Similar pro-development sentiments were
expressed by the Sultan on the occasion of the Fourth ASEAN
Summit in Singapore on 27 January 1992.

Transitions from authoritarianism: Changing ideology and culture

One measure of the transition from authoritarianism to a more
participatory political culture would be the emergence of a civil
society supporting such autonomous institutions as a free press,
universities, political parties, civil rights, labour rights and so on.
But, as in certain of the Gulf states, British interest in the oil-rich
Sultanate has always been proprietary; indeed Britain retained control of Brunei's external policy until 1 January 1984, the date that
Brunei became a sovereign independent country. Although the first
elections in 1962 saw an anti-Malaysia and anti-British socialist
party (the Azahari faction) swept to victory in the polls, only timely
British intervention rescued the Sultanate from widespread rebellion
mounted by the aggrieved party otherwise denied its seat in government. As mentioned, the state of emergency declared at the time
has not been lifted and security obsessions (the parallel with British
military support to the Sultanate of Oman is illustrative) have
prevented a resurfacing of the experiment in representative government.

Singh (1988: 67) writes that in fact the reverse has taken place. In 1984, the appointed State Legislative Assembly was suspended and the power of the monarchy further strengthened. A relaxation in 1985, which saw the emergence of the 'opposition' Brunei National Democratic Party and the loyalist National Alliance Party, did not prevent the subsequent banning of the former party and detention of the party's leadership following a call by its leaders (in Kuala Lumpur) for a lifting of the state of emergency, the standing down of the Sultan as prime minister and the calling of elections. Originally launched with the Sultan's blessing, the Party had attracted an estimated membership of 3000, mainly businessmen and professionals. The death in 1990 of the president of the outlawed BNDP, shortly after release from detention along with the party's secretary-general, just about put an end to this experiment in (albeit guided) representative democracy (Economist Intelligence Unit 1990, no. 3; Leake 1990).

Consonant with the language of nation-building and echoing the efforts of the other insular 'Malay' countries of Southeast Asia, Brunei has chosen to elevate the orthodoxy to the level of a national ideology. This is termed Melay Islam Beraja (MIB—Kingship) an amalgam of Islamic values grafted onto Brunei Malay culture linked with a sense of the monarchy as the 'defender of the faith and an unbroken line of independent Brunei sultans'. Unlike the more accommodative thrust of, say, Indonesia's Pancasila or even Singapore's avowed list of national values, MIB is 'emphatically not multicultural' but carries strong anti-foreign including anti-western overtones if taken too literally. As a correspondent of the *Far Eastern Economic Review* (15 November 1990) has written, by pushing the Islamic agenda, the secular course of political development has been held in abeyance (indeed secular has become a pejorative term in the context of MIB). While the MIB concept crystallised prior to independence in 1984 there is no doubt, the report continues, that the current emphasis is driven by the conservatives in the Ministries, notably those restored to influential positions following the 1988 proscription on political parties. Indeed, concern over religious dissonance is matched by concern over political dissent and social discord. In 1989 the Sultan warned that 'troublemakers' driven by jealousy and frustration were attempting to engineer a confrontation between the people and the government (Economist Intelligence Unit 1990, nos 2 & 3).

In what sense, then, is a civil society in Brunei supported by the existence of an autonomous press? Prior to the launching in 1953 of the longest running newspaper in the country, *The Borneo Bulletin*, Brunei had no tradition of a press. Originally a British-owned venture, the paper was sold in 1959 to the Singapore Straits Times

Group. Even though a part share was acquired in 1985 by QAF Holdings, Brunei's first listed company, the paper's editorial outlook as well as advertising content continued to be shaped by the Straits Times Group. QAF Holdings, otherwise under Royal family control, acquired full ownership of the paper in early 1990 and in the following year relaunched the paper as a daily (*Borneo Bulletin* 3 May 1991). Published in English and Romanised Malay the country's only local newspaper carries no editorial, one or two pages of local news, little or no analysis, and no investigative features of a political or administrative nature. Perhaps only a lively letter-to-the-editors column conveys a sense of spontaneity. Otherwise the press in Brunei is seen as an outlet for advertising media and an instrument of nation-building (cf. *Borneo Bulletin* 3 May 1991). Aside from this newspaper and certain corporate publications (such as those of the Shell Group) there have been no books or magazines published in Brunei by private or commercial concerns since 1962. All other forms of print and electronic media are under state control. Foreign publications are subject to a gamut of legislation that dates back to colonial times and has been strengthened since independence, to vet material deemed subversive of the social, political and religious order (cf. *Laws of Brunei Darussalam*).

As in other Islamic states Bruneian Muslims are torn between loyalty to nation and to the *ummat*, the Muslim community at large. National choices are, necessarily, mediated by religious affiliation. Brunei, as an active member of the OIC, politically tends to an Islamic consensus on international issues. In the tension between modernity and tradition, it is often religious priorities which take precedence in developmental decisions. As an Islamic state it is not surprising that since independence the trend in Brunei has been towards strengthening public institutions commensurate with an Islamic ideal. This holds in education, banking, public administration, the legal superstructure, as well as in morality and public conduct. While other Southeast Asian states see themselves as repositories of Asian values, model Asian-style democracies, agents of development, potential NICs or a combination of all, Brunei sees itself, first and foremost, as an exemplary Islamic Malay *negara* state in Southeast Asia. The strengthening of the official political and religious orthodoxies in the country, however, leaves no leeway from those who would dissent from the official Sunni creed and who would—as the Sultan warned in 1990—defile Brunei's way of life, including Islam and loyalty to the monarchy. The matter was made more explicit in February 1991 when a Royal decree banned a Muslim movement known as Al Arqam on the grounds that it was 'spreading teachings contrary to Islam' (Economist Intelligence Unit 1991, no. 2: 31). No crisis of authoritarianism, such as that identified by Pye (1990), has yet threatened to undermine the state. The ability of the state to co-opt, reward and silence has neutralised or at least postponed those voices that would champion the idea 'that no one has a monopoly on absolute truth'.

Conclusion

In the literature on rentier states, Mahdavy (1970) has demonstrated the case of Iran, while Mabro (1969) and First (1974) have noted the applicability of the model to Libya. As shown above, Brunei fits the pattern exactly. Colclough (1985), in highlighting the barriers to diversification of the Brunei economy away from the 'distortions' arising from a high-income-earning natural resource, sees Brunei as a potential or 'qualified' rentier nation. But the vulnerabilities described and cautioned by Colclough are in fact symptoms of the condition, namely the 'heavy dependence upon the productive activity of other people' in order to preserve consumption standards and the political and economic risk of converting capital into foreign financial assets.[7]

Whereas the phenomenon of the rise of the new middle classes has helped to define the production and consumption patterns of the populations of the NICs of Asia, no such middle class *qua* class has emerged in Brunei. That is not the same as saying that a new consuming class has not arisen in Brunei. As shown above it has, but whether this new class of consumers—in the absence of producers—is supported by the integuments of civil society matched by the emergence of truly autonomous institutions has to be answered in the negative.

It is no doubt the example of the ASEAN economies as much as Brunei's membership of ASEAN that has motivated Brunei to adopt this version of economic perestroika and the rhetoric of developmentalism.[8] But beyond the rhetoric lies the dead hand of tradition and history. In Brunei even development is mediated through the veil of cultural rationalisations. The implication for organisation development, as one management consultant concluded from a controlled study of one Brunei work unit (a university), is that a profound tension exists between 'a national policy designed to limit the extent and slow down the rate of cultural change *and* a development policy that advocates rapid educational and technological advancement' (Blunt 1988: 239). Indeed, as Abdel-Fadil (1987: 106–7) argues, the transitional path from one form of rentier economy to another, under the conditions of declining income from oil, is 'highly unstable and surrounded by many uncertainties'. He continues that it is 'impossible' to draw safe conclusions about the capability of an oil-rentier economy to steer a transitional course to a self-sustained growth path.

Similar uncertainties surround the prospects in Brunei for the transition from authoritarianism to a more representative form of government. If the models are increasingly Middle Eastern, then we may say that historically Islam has not proven to be hospitable to democracy. In Brunei, unlike the case of Malaya, the British abrogated their responsibility to bequeath democratic institutions and, unlike the experience of other Southeast Asian countries, the populist nationalist push in Brunei was belated, misdirected and botched. But neither in Brunei—anomalously perhaps—have the structural and demographic distortions wrought by developmentalism to a basically traditional polity found their corollary in demand for new political rights as in the manner of a Taiwan, a South Korea or, for that matter, a Kuwait. Brunei obviously fails to meet the basic cultural preconditions for democracy as set down by Huntington (1984). Anderson (1991: 1–15) has argued that contrary to conventional wisdom the monarchies of the Middle East are in fact particularly well suited to the requirements of state formation. Among the advantages of legitimated absolutism she cites the ability of monarchs to appeal to tradition 'to hobnob with international bankers and ride horseback with presidents'. Still, she would not refute Huntington's argument that 'the monarchy is ultimately too brittle and restrictive to accommodate the political demands of new social groups'. She would also concede that the half-hearted commitment on the part of the Middle Eastern monarchies to egalitarian values raises the question of who is to benefit from the transition.

In what way, then, does the Brunei example inform the debate on the transition to democracy? Overall the experience of Brunei would not appear to support the view that authoritarianism is a necessary and facilitating element in a country's social, economic and political transformation. As seen in the Brunei case, even alongside the ASEAN economies, the structures of authoritarianism are contradictory to the political and economic needs of an increasingly complex regional capitalist sub-system. As shown, the state in Brunei has actively sought to affect the ability of certain groups of capitalists to accumulate. For example, *bumiputera* businesspeople might be able to win contracts, but fetters have been imposed when the contracts are implemented. The overall privileging of citizens over non-citizens as a legal category has also imposed a serious obstacle to the operations of the important Chinese segment of capital. The subordination of labour, especially migrant labour, is another example of the ability of the state, under rentier capitalism, to distort the class and even demographic profile of the country. Yet another contradiction facing the Brunei state is that between a low skills base and the increasingly sophisticated information, knowledge and management needs of industry, especially in the oil sector.

What has been argued in this chapter, then, is that the limits to a full-blown transition from 'feudalism' to rentier capitalism to a mature capitalist economy are as much a function of the state in specific historical context and a country's particular subordination within the world system as of the legacy of culture *per se*. However, it is true that culture, ideology and tradition might become, under the auspices of the rentier state, a mask, a guide to action, and rationalisation of the political, economic and social status quo.

Thus, the argument has not been, after Huntington, to ascribe to culture either a determinant or independent role (Huntington 1984). Rather, after Cumings (1989), culture has been viewed as integral to the political and material levels of society, a function of time and global context. Accordingly, it has not been suggested, *pace* O'Donnell, Schmitter and Whitehead (1986), that it is necessary to separate out social, economic and cultural elements but, rather—in line with a broad political economy perspective—it has been demonstrated that it is necessary to build socio-structural factors into explanations of regime formation and the processes of transition. However, as argued by the editors of this collection, this is a very complex task. In this analysis, then, it is easier to delineate why a transition will not and cannot occur, especially in the absence of even the trappings of a bourgeois democratic culture much less raw industrial capitalism, rather than predict how or when such an event will take place.

Notes

1 The author wishes to acknowledge a critical reading of a draft of this paper by Mark Cleary, although the author alone remains responsible for matters as they stand.

2 In terms of residential status, of the country's total population of 226 329 in 1986, 67.7 per cent were Brunei citizens. A further 9.2 per cent were permanent residents, while 23.1 per cent were temporary residents, including one to two per cent transients or short-term visitors. Of the residents, the overwhelming majority were Malays. Chinese constituted the majority (61 per cent) of the permanent residents and, while all the main ethnic groups were represented in the temporary resident category, 39.7 per cent were Chinese (cf. Tong [n.d.]: 78).

3 In 1989 the UK concluded a 250 million pounds sterling arms deal with Brunei, under which Brunei is buying 16 BAe Hawk 100 fighter aircraft and three corvettes to be equipped with Exocet anti-ship

missiles. Brunei already has a Rapier air defence missile system (Economist Intelligence Unit 1990, No. 3).

4 Notorious among Chinese comprador interests in Brunei was the former National Bank of Brunei, 70 per cent owned by the Chinese tycoon, Khoo Theck Puat, and 30 per cent owned by the Sultan. This was closed in September 1986 but not before Khoo absconded with some 650 million dollars. Otherwise the 66 000 Chinese in Brunei play a dominant role in private sector activity, as shopkeepers and in the service industry. Only 6000 are thought to be citizens. Besides an anomalous legal status thus depriving a considerable percentage of the population of the country of 'rights' and citizen privileges, Brunei Chinese—erstwhile comprador capitalists—are also victims of state policy which massively favours *bumiputera* interests (cf. Economist Intelligence Unit 1990–91: 42).

5 Between 17–21 July 1991 the Brunei Malay Chamber of Commerce and Industry organised an 'International Consumer Week'. The rationale for this event was ostensibly the demand created by a more discerning Brunei consumer armed with 'oil-powered purchasing ability'. As the advertising blurb stated:

> Never before seen under one roof in Brunei. This incredible variety of consumer products ... From costume jewellery, silver tableware, furniture, home hi-fi, crystal chandeliers, exercise equipment, electrical appliances, security systems, handicraft to holy water from Medina (Consumer Week Supplement, *Borneo Bulletin* 8 July 1991, p.1).

Indeed, among Brunei's main imports are jewellery, precious metals, paintings, watches and furniture.

6 The matter was stated clearly by the Brunei Darussalam Commissioner for Labour, Awang Haji Zainal, who informed Japan's Vice-Minister of Labour in the course of a visit that the formation of trade unions is 'redundant' owing to 'the peaceful and harmonious relations between the employers and employees' in the country (*Borneo Bulletin* 7 August 1991: 1).

7 Writing in 1985 he cites the case of the US freeze on Iranian assets in 1979. The events of 1990-91 over the Gulf are no less indicative of the risks of this strategy (Colclough 1985: 29–32).

8 Illustrative of the way that Brunei is being drawn into a more technocratic superstructure via its links with ASEAN is a report alluding to an agreement signed by Brunei on behalf of ASEAN with the European Community, whereby Brunei will fund and site in Brunei a centre to develop business management skills (*Borneo Bulletin* 24 July 1991: 1).

References

Abdel-Fadil, Mahmoud 1987, 'The Macro-behaviour of Oil-rentier States in the Arab Region', *The Rentier State*, eds Hazem Beblawi & Luciani Giacomo, Croom Helm, London

Anderson, Lisa 1991, 'Absolutism and the Resilience of Monarchy in the Middle East', *Political Science Quarterly*, vol. 106, no. 1, pp. 1–15

Bartholomew, James 1989, *The Richest Man in the World: The Sultan of Brunei*, Viking, London

Beblawi, Hazem 1987, 'The Rentier State in the Arab World', in Beblawi & Giacomo eds (1987)

—— & Giacomo Luciani eds 1987, *The Rentier State*, Croom Helm, London

Blunt, Peter 1988, 'Cultural Consequences for Organisation Change in a Southeast Asian State: Brunei', *Executive* (The Academy of Management), vol. 2, no. 3, pp. 235–40

Colclough, Christopher 1985, 'Brunei: Development Problems of a Resource Rich State', *Euro-Asia Business Review*, vol. 4, no. 4, pp. 29–32

Cumings, Bruce 1989, 'The Abortive Abertura: South Korea in the Light of the Latin American Experience', *New Left Review*, no. 173, pp. 5–32

Dasse, Martial 1991, 'Brunei: the Kuwait of South-East Asia' , *Defense National*, vol. 47 (June), pp. 135–49 (in French)

Economist Intelligence Unit 1989, 1990, 1990-91, 1991, *Country Report, Malaysia, Brunei*, The Economist, London

First, Ruth 1974, *Libya: The Elusive Revolution*, Penguin, Harmondsworth

Franz, Johannes C. 1990, *The Sultanate of Brunei: Oil Wealth and Problems of Development*, Universitaet Nuernberg, trans. from German by Michael Schmitz & Alistair Sharp, Universiti Brunei Darussalam

Hong Kong & Shanghai Bank 1988, *Business Profile Series: Brunei Darussalam*, Hong Kong & Shanghai Banking Corporation, Hong Kong

Horton, A. V. M. 1990, 'Aspects of Finance in Brunei During the British Residential Era, 1906–1959', *Borneo Research Bulletin*, vol. 22, no. 1

Huntington, Samuel P. 1984, 'Will More Countries Become Democratic?', *Political Science Quarterly*, vol. 99, no. 2, pp. 193–219

Leake, Jr, David 1990, *Brunei: The Modern Southeast Asian Sultanate*, Forum, Kuala Lumpur

Mabro, Robert 1969, 'Libya: Rentier State?', *Projet*, vol. 39 (Nov), pp. 1090–101 (in French)

Mahdavy, H. 1970, 'The Patterns and Problems of Economic Development in Rentier States: The Case of Iran', *Studies in the Economic History of the Middle East from the Rise of Islam to the Present Day*, ed. M.A. Cook, Oxford University Press, Oxford

O'Donnell, Guillermo, Schmitter, Philippe C. & Whitehead, Laurence (eds) 1986, *Transitions from Authoritarian Rule: Tentative Conclusions about Uncertain Democracies*, The Johns Hopkins University Press, Baltimore

Pye, Lucien W. 1990, 'Political Science and the Crisis of Authoritarianism', *American Political Science Review*, vol. 84, no. 1, pp. 3–19

Singh, Ranjit 1988, 'Brunei Darussalam in 1987: Coming to Grips with Economic and Political Realities', *Southeast Asian Affairs 1988*, Institute of Southeast Asian Studies, Singapore

Thambipillai, Pushpa 1990, 'Foreign Workers and Development in ASEAN: The Brunei Context', Working Paper, Department of Public Policy and Administration, Universiti Brunei Darussalam, February

Tong Niew Shong (n.d.), *Demographic Trends in Negara Brunei Darussalam*, Educational Technology Centre, Universiti Brunei Darussalam, Bandar Seri Begawan

Weaver, Mary Anne 1991, 'Our Far-Flung Correspondents: In the Sultan's Palace', *The New Yorker*, 7 October, pp. 56–93

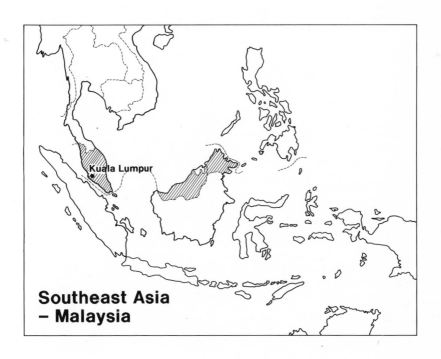

**Southeast Asia
– Malaysia**

Malaysia: Basic social and economic data

Population (1990)	17.8m
Population density (1990)	53 persons per sq. km
Average annual population growth (1982–89)	2.5%
Urban population (1989)	41.5%
Total labour force (1990)	7.6m
Major ethnic groups	Malays & indigenous groups, Chinese, Indians
Capital city	Kuala Lumpur
Population (1980 census)	919 610
Land area	329 749 sq. km
Official language	Bahasa Malaysia
Other main languages	Chinese dialects, Tamil, English
Administrative division	14 states
Education, enrolments	
Primary (1990)	2.33m
Secondary (1990)	1.35m
University (1990)	51 000
Adult literacy rate (1990)	76%
Health	
Life expectancy (1989)	70 yrs
Infant mortality/1000 (1989)	23
Persons/hospital bed (1989)	400
Persons/physician (1989)	1935
Economy	
GNP at market prices (1989)	US$37 bn
Real GNP per capita (1989)	US$2130
GDP growth rate (1990)	9.4%
Trade	
Exports, value (1989)	US$25.1 bn
Imports, value (1989)	US$22.5 bn
Main imports	Machinery & transport equipment 50.3%, manufactures 21.6%, chemicals 8.6%
Main exports	Machinery & transport equipment 36.0%, mineral fuels 17.5 %, crude materials 14.7%
Foreign debt (1989)	$US18.6 bn
Foreign reserves (1989)	$US7.9 bn
Energy consumption/capita (kg coal equiv. in 1989)	1379
Communications	
Rail (1990)	1644 km
Roads, paved (1990)	21 330 km (peninsular Malaysia only)
Religions	Islam, Buddhism, Hinduism

Sources: Far Eastern Economic Review Asia Yearbook 1991; The Far East and Australasia 1992 (Europa Publications); United Nations Economic and Social Commission for Asia and the Pacific *Newsletter, Key Indicators of Developing Asian and Pacific Countries* 1991, Asian Development Bank.

6 Malaysia: Neither authoritarian nor democratic
Harold Crouch

Much of the debate outlined in the theoretical chapter of this book has been concerned with political transition. In the 1960s and 1970s the focus was on the transition from democracy to authoritarianism but during the 1980s scholars theorised about the transition from authoritarianism to democracy. As the editors have pointed out, a key issue in the debate is whether political transitions are determined primarily by the social and economic change that accompanies capitalist economic development, or whether political change has its own dynamic separate from broader social and economic development. While both the modernisation and the neo-Marxist schools stressed in their own ways the predominance of socio-economic factors, the so-called 'transitions approach' places the main emphasis on the autonomous behaviour of political leaders.

An examination of the experience of Malaysia is interesting in this context. In contrast to much of the Third World where regime changes have been common, the Malaysian state has been marked by extraordinary continuity. At the same time, Malaysia has experienced rapid economic growth which has brought about far-reaching changes in the country's class structure. How is this political continuity despite rapid social and economic change to be explained? Does it indicate that socio-economic pressures have only minimal impact when political elites are committed to an established political order? Or has socio-economic change in fact reinforced the basic character of the state even when some political leaders may have wanted to change it? In this chapter, it will be suggested that socio-economic change is often very ambiguous in its impact, generating pressures that in some respects push the regime in an authoritarian direction while other pressures facilitate democratisation.

Any explanation of Malaysian political evolution must also take account of the communal factor. Although communal rivalries cannot be understood apart from their socio-economic and political context, they cannot be dismissed as merely disguised expressions of class interest. The political struggle in Malaysia is not only about the ownership of wealth and the distribution of material benefits but also involves ethnic identity.

The Malaysian state

The Malaysian state has always been controlled by an unequal alliance between the elites of the Malay and non-Malay (mainly Chinese) communities. British colonial rule had fostered the growth of a Malay bureaucratic class which, after independence, continued to dominate the key organs of the state—the bureaucracy, judiciary, military and police—and provided the leadership of the United Malays National Organisation (UMNO). During the colonial era those areas of commerce and industry not controlled by foreign capital had been left largely in the hands of Chinese traders and business people who later formed the backbone of the Malayan (later Malaysian) Chinese Association (MCA) which became UMNO's main, although junior, partner in the government. After racial rioting in 1969, largely in response to the Malay perception that Malays were falling further behind the Chinese in the economic field, the Malay-dominated government introduced its New Economic Policy (NEP) which was designed to bring Malays into the modern sector of the economy. Under the aegis of the NEP, direct state involvement in the economy expanded enormously and a deliberate programme was launched to create a Malay business class. As a result, the politicians and bureaucrats of the established Malay elite were joined in the 1970s and 1980s by the state-sector managers and client-business people spawned by the NEP while the influence of the Chinese business class declined (Jomo 1986: Ch. 10). Despite these shifts in composition, however, the unequal partnership between the elites of the Malay and non-Malay communities, represented mainly by UMNO and the MCA, was maintained and continued to constitute the foundation of the Malaysian state.

The political regime in Malaysia is neither fully democratic nor fully authoritarian but contains elements of both (Crouch 1992; Means 1991). Its formal structure, the essence of which has not changed greatly in the years since Malaya became independent in 1957, continues to be characterised by democratic, representative institutions. Elections have been held regularly in which the ruling coalition has been challenged by vigorous opposition parties and, at the state level at least, occasionally defeated. But, at the same time, the government has at its disposal a battery of authoritarian powers which have been employed to restrict the activities of the opposition. It is therefore difficult, although not completely impossible, to envisage the government's defeat in an election. Nevertheless, the opposition parties have mobilised substantial electoral support. In 1969, the government coalition's share of the votes in Peninsular Malaysia fell to less than half, and in subsequent elections its share of votes in the entire country ranged from a high of 60.7 per cent in 1974 to a low of 53.4 per cent in 1990.

The government has taken the form of a Malay-dominated multi-communal coalition. Initially consisting of three parties, one each for the Malay, Chinese and Indian communities, the ruling Alliance, as it was then called, expanded first to incorporate the ruling parties in Sarawak and Sabah after the inclusion of those states in the new Federation of Malaysia in 1963 and then to co-opt several opposition parties after the racial rioting of 1969. Known since 1974 as the *Barisan Nasional* (BN—National Front), it owes part of its success to its superior electoral strategy. As a multi-communal coalition, it has won substantial support from both the Malay and non-Malay communities while the main opposition parties, the predominantly non-Malay Democratic Action Party (DAP) and the essentially Malay Pan-Malaysian Islamic Party (PAS), have usually forgone multi-communal support by directing their appeal almost exclusively to either Malays or non-Malays. Malay BN candidates, therefore, have often defeated Malay opposition candidates because they have also received non-Malay votes, while in predominantly non-Malay constituencies Malay voters have helped non-Malay BN candidates to victory. Since its formation in 1974, the BN has won more than four-fifths of the seats in parliament in all elections except that of 1990 when its share fell to 71 per cent.

The BN's electoral success has also been assisted by the weighting of the electoral system to favour the Malay community. The number of voters in predominantly non-Malay urban constituencies is always much larger than in predominantly Malay rural constituencies so that, although Malays constituted only 57 per cent of the population on the peninsula in the 1980s, they made up majorities in 70 per cent of the peninsular seats, guaranteeing heavy Malay over-representation in parliament. As long as UMNO, as the dominant party in the ruling coalition, retained majority support in the Malay community, the continued success of the BN was virtually assured. In the four elections during the 1970s and 1980s, UMNO won all the seats it contested in 1974 and 1986, and lost only five out of 74 in 1978 and three out of 73 in 1982. Its worst post-1969 performance was in 1990 when it lost 14 out of 85 following a major party split.

The government has also resorted to the use of authoritarian powers to back up its political manoeuvring. It has justified its recourse to authoritarian measures as necessary to meet the danger of inter-communal conflict but at the same time authoritarian powers have also been used to restrict the activities of the opposition parties and other critics. The emergency provisions of the constitution, for example, have been used twice to overthrow state governments controlled by opposition parties—in Sarawak in 1966 and Kelantan in 1977. The *Internal Security Act* has been used to detain without trial not only communists and communalists but government critics and opposition activists (and indeed members of dissident factions within the BN parties, including UMNO). The *Sedition Act* and the *Official Secrets Act* have been used to deter public debate while the main newspapers are owned indirectly by individual BN parties, and radio and television are part of a government monopoly (except for one 'private' television channel indirectly owned by UMNO). Various restrictions have also been imposed on potential opposition groups such as trade unions, student organisations and public interest groups.

Although the BN, like the Alliance before it, routinely used authoritarian means to bolster its position, it has also been responsive, to some extent at least, to pressures from society. The key to the coalition's continuing success has been UMNO's ability to hold the support of the majority of the Malay community. This has been partly due to its control over patronage distribution at all levels. Business people wanting contracts, bureaucrats wanting promotion, peasants wanting land and parents wanting scholarships for their children have all found it helpful to be recognised as UMNO supporters. But the UMNO-dominated government has also been responsive to the broader aspirations of a large part of the Malay community. Under the NEP since 1971 the government has pursued a policy of positive discrimination in favour of Malays in business, employment and education. Major programmes of rural development, benefiting mainly Malays, have been implemented. And the government has favoured Malays in its language, cultural, religious and immigration policies.

But the BN did not ignore the interests of its non-Malay constituents. Although the government provided special benefits to Malay business, non-Malays, and especially Chinese, continued to enjoy opportunities to carry on profitable businesses. Despite quotas favouring Malay students, non-Malays continued to be well represented in tertiary education. And despite its promotion of the Malay language, Malay culture and Islam, the rights of Chinese and Indians to use their own languages, observe their own customs and follow their own religions continued to be respected.

The main reason why the government was careful to respond to the expectations of a large part of the society was because competitive elections continued to be held. UMNO could not afford to ignore the interests and aspirations of the Malay community because Malay voters could turn to the opposition parties in elections. And UMNO had to listen to the demands of its non-Malay partners in the BN because the coalition also needed non-Malay support in elections. The pressure to be responsive was reinforced by elections within the BN parties. Aspirants for party office in all the BN parties had to show that they were prepared to support the demands of their respective communities.

Competitive elections continued to be held in Malaysia, in contrast to some neighbouring countries, partly because they did not threaten the established political order. In each election, the government was returned to power with substantial majorities through a combination of genuine popularity, manipulation of the electoral system and authoritarian controls. As long as the government kept on winning, it felt no need to seek an alternative political system. But, in any case, as will be discussed later in this chapter, the interests of significant class, communal and political forces were better served by the preservation of the existing system than would be the case under a fully authoritarian regime. Even if it wanted to, therefore, it would not be an easy matter for the government to abandon established semi-democratic institutions.

It is difficult to detect a clear-cut and consistent trend in the evolution of the regime during the last three decades. Although it became more authoritarian in some respects, democratic characteristics remained important. During the 1960s public debate between government and opposition was relatively unrestricted although authoritarian emergency regulations due to communist insurgency and Indonesia's confrontation policy were in force for much of the period between independence and 1969. In response to racial rioting in 1969 a new emergency was declared and parliament suspended. Although parliament was restored in 1971, the system moved in an authoritarian direction during the 1970s as increasing restrictions were imposed on political activity. But elections continued to be held in which opposition parties obtained substantial support and, following the split in UMNO in the late 1980s, the government was faced in 1990 with a serious electoral challenge from a semi-alliance of opposition parties headed by the new *Semangat '46* formed by the UMNO dissidents. Despite authoritarian controls, the constitutional framework facilitated the opposition challenge, forcing a government no longer assured of easy victory to compete with the opposition for votes.

The political regime, therefore, could be understood neither as a form of democracy nor as a form of authoritarianism but as a distinct model combining both democratic and authoritarian elements. The democratic and authoritarian characteristics of the regime, however, were not so much in conflict with each other as integrated to constitute mutually supporting aspects of a cohesive system. On one hand vigorously contested elections were held regularly at the national and state levels as well as within individual parties. But on the other hand restrictions on political activity made it difficult for the opposition to win. A balance was achieved in which democratic institutions forced the government to be responsive to popular demands while authoritarian restrictions ensured that it remained in power.

How can we explain both the hybrid character of the Malaysian regime and its continuity? To what extent has the nature of the regime been shaped by socio-economic factors? And to what extent can its evolution be explained in terms of essentially political dynamics? In this chapter the impact on the political regime of changes in the class structure, communal relations and political competition will be examined.

Economic growth and the class structure

Economic growth has been rapid in Malaysia. During the initial post-independence period from 1957 to 1970, the economy expanded at an average annual rate of 6 per cent, rising to 7.8 per cent during the 1970s, before slowing back to 6 per cent in the 1980s when the impact of world recession caused two years of stagnation in 1985 and 1986 (Government of Malaysia 1976: 3; 1981: 9; 1991c: 20). Overall the economy doubled in size during the 1960s and tripled between 1970 and 1990 (Government of Malaysia 1976: 3; 1991b: 36). The rapid growth of the economy was accompanied by rising living standards. By 1988, Malaysia's per capita income had reached US$1940, far above neighbouring countries such as Thailand (US$1000), the Philippines (US$650) and Indonesia (US$440) although well below Singapore (US$9070) (World Bank 1990: 178–9). During the period of the NEP, from 1970 to 1990, the proportion of the peninsular population living below the poverty line was officially estimated to have declined from 49.3 per cent to 15.0 per cent (Government of Malaysia 1991b: 46).

Rapid growth was accompanied by far-reaching structural change as the industrial sector grew in importance. When Malaya became independent in 1957 its economy was organised around the export of rubber and tin, which together constituted 85 per cent of exports, while the tiny manufacturing sector contributed only 8.5 per cent of GDP in 1960 (Lim 1973: 7, 109). During the 1960s the government began to diversify the economy and launched an industrialisation programme based on import substitution. By 1970 the contribution of rubber and tin to exports had fallen to 53 per cent (calculated from Government of Malaysia 1981: 18) and the manufacturing contribution to GDP had grown to 13.9 per cent (Government of Malaysia 1991b: 41). In the late 1960s, however, the government changed the emphasis of its industrialisation strategy from import substitution to exporting. During the 1970s and 1980s the manufacturing sector grew rapidly and by 1990 contributed 27 per cent of the GDP (Government of Malaysia 1991b: 41) while the share of manufactures in total exports rose from 11.1 per cent in 1970 to 60.4 per cent in 1990 as the combined contribution of rubber and tin to exports fell to 4.9 per cent (Government of Malaysia 1991a: 23). During the 1980s the contribution of manufacturing to GDP surpassed that of agriculture and forestry which fell from 29 per cent in 1970 to 18.7 per cent in 1990 (Government of Malaysia 1991b: 41).

Rapid economic growth and structural change brought about a transformation of the class structure. At the time of independence Malayan society was dominated by a small Malay bureaucratic elite and a Chinese business class. The white-collar middle class was small and overwhelmingly non-Malay, while the majority of the people were either Malay peasants and other rural workers, Chinese tradesmen and labourers, or Indian plantation workers. But by 1990 the middle class had grown enormously, a business class had developed and the working class had expanded while the rural classes had declined.

The Malaysian class structure, therefore, had changed in a way that would lead political scientists—whether of pluralist, structuralist or Marxist persuasion—to expect, on the basis of recent political theorising, a strengthening of pressures towards liberalisation and democratisation. But in practice the impact of the changing class structure was ambiguous. Pressures toward democratisation increased but were not always especially strong and were counterbalanced by social groups with reason to be satisfied with the status quo. Further, in the Malaysian context, the evolution of the 'modern' classes did not take place simply as a consequence of economic growth but was consciously shaped by a Malay-dominated government which, especially after the racial rioting of 1969, wanted to make sure that the Malay community was not left behind as the modern economy expanded.

The middle class

The most striking change in the class structure was the growth of the middle class.[1] When Malaya became independent in 1957, the upper or solid middle-class occupational categories ('professional and technical', and 'administrative and managerial') made up only four per cent of the workforce while another 11.5 per cent were employed in the lower middle-class 'clerical' and 'sales' categories, making a broad white-collar middle class of about 15.5 per cent of the workforce. The economic growth of the 1960s resulted in the steady expansion of the upper middle-class category to 5.9 per cent and the lower middle class to 14.1 per cent by 1970, making a total of 20 per cent of the peninsular workforce. During the next twenty years the middle class continued to expand rapidly and by 1990 the upper middle-class category—for all of Malaysia and not just the peninsula—had almost doubled to 11.3 per cent and the lower middle-class category had grown to 21.3 per cent so that the middle class as a whole constituted 32.6 per cent or almost one-third of the workforce.

No less significant than the changes in the general class structure were changes in its communal composition. In the 1960s the middle class had been overwhelmingly non-Malay. Although Malays dominated the upper reaches of the civil service, they were under-represented in the middle levels of the bureaucracy and hardly represented at all in the professions and commerce. One of the goals of the NEP was to bring more Malays into the modern sector of the economy, especially the middle class. Malays were given preference in gaining access to tertiary educational institutions and in appointments to government jobs, while pressure was applied to private employers to recruit Malays to white-collar positions. In 1957 Malays had constituted only 22.0 per cent of the four middle-class occupational categories but by 1970 their participation in these occupations had risen to 33.6 per cent, and by 1990 had reached 48.1 per cent. Between 1970 and 1990 the proportion of the Malay workforce working in middle-class occupations more than doubled from 12.9 per cent to 27.0 per cent. Malays were predominant in public sector employment but their participation in private sector employment had risen rapidly.

The rapid growth of the Malay middle class had not been directly at the expense of the non-Malay middle class which continued to expand, although it certainly would have expanded faster if special measures had not been taken by the government to ensure increased Malay participation in middle-class occupations. While the non-Malay share in middle-class employment declined as the Malay share increased, the proportions of both the Chinese and Indian communities employed in middle-class occupations continued to increase. Between 1970 and 1990 the proportion of the Chinese workforce employed in middle-class occupations rose from 28.6 per cent to 43.2 per cent, while in the case of Indians it rose more slowly from 23.4 per cent to 27.3 per cent.

The middle class, to which by 1990 about one-third of the population belonged, provided a strong base of support for the government. Rapid economic growth had made it relatively easy for the government to satisfy the material aspirations of the middle class. Middle-class housing estates sprang up around all the main towns, car ownership became widespread, and middle-class families acquired the full range of consumer durables. Of particular importance was the steady expansion of the middle class as the children of peasants and labourers acquired from the education system the skills and certificates that qualified them for middle-class employment. Social mobility proceeded at an extraordinary pace within the Malay community but was also significant among Chinese and, to a lesser extent, Indians.

Middle-class support for the government, however, was not unconditional. Although the middle class provided broad, general support for the established social and political order, the numerous sectors that made up the middle class also expected that the government would respond to their particular demands. Policies in such fields as taxation, education, health, communications and urban development, for example, normally furthered general or particular middle-class interests. But the political weight of the middle class was partly dissipated because it was divided along communal lines. Members of the Malay middle class, whose social mobility had been a direct result of the government's discriminatory policies, tended to be much more strongly committed to supporting the government than middle-class non-Malays who, although recognising the material benefits and opportunities they had received, resented the discriminatory policies which were so well regarded by the Malays.

The growth of the middle class had been achieved in part through the expansion of education. While most members of the new middle class supported the government and the political system of which they were beneficiaries, education also produced dissidents and critics. In the 1970s and 1980s several non-governmental organisations—such as Aliran, the Consumers' Association of Penang, the Selangor Graduates' Association and Insan—were formed which offered a steady stream of criticism of the government. Later, relatively established bodies, such as the Malaysian Bar Council, joined the chorus of middle-class dissent. Although most members of the middle class voted for the BN in elections, a substantial number of middle-class non-Malays gave their votes to the opposition DAP while a small number of middle-class Malays aligned themselves with PAS.

The growth of the middle class, therefore, had an ambivalent impact on the nature of the regime. On one hand, it provided the government with a solid base of support as long as its interests were taken into account. On the other hand, the various groups that made up the middle class constituted significant checks on the government's power which could be activated if their interests were disregarded. The ability of the opposition parties to attract some middle-class support and the flowering of organisations representing well-educated middle-class dissent served as a constant reminder to the government that it could not take middle-class support for granted. While the members of the middle class appreciated the government's use of authoritarian powers to maintain the stability of the political and social order, they also valued the semi-democratic institutions through which they could make demands on the government for measures favourable to their particular interests.

The business class

The theoretical orientations that emphasise the importance of socio-economic change as the driving force in political change usually give much attention to the emergence and growth of the business class or bourgeoisie. As capitalist economic development proceeds, the capitalist class inevitably grows and asserts its influence on the political system. In the early stages when the business class is still small and dependent on government favours, business people tend to be pliant clients of politicians and bureaucrats but, as the economy grows and especially when the industrial sector develops, business becomes more independent and constitutes an important check on the power of the government. While some big business people benefit enormously from their close links with authoritarian regimes, the business class as a whole has an interest in making the government responsive to the requirements of business in general. It can be expected therefore that the business class will want a political system that provides business with access to the government and is responsive to its demands. Business, therefore, is often seen as a force pushing for liberalisation and democratisation.

The development of the business class in Malaysia cannot be understood without taking into account the country's colonial past and its communal composition (see Jomo 1986: Part IV; Jesudason 1989). During the immediate post-independence period, British and other foreign enterprises continued to control the 'commanding heights' of the economy—rubber plantations, tin mines, banks and the big trading companies—while Chinese business dominated much of the rest. In 1970 it was officially estimated that 63.3 per cent of share capital in limited companies in peninsular Malaysia was owned by foreigners and 34.3 per cent by 'other Malaysians', most of whom were Chinese. Only 2.4 per cent was owned by Malays, of which 1.6 per cent was held by individual Malays and 0.8 per cent by government-sponsored agencies holding shares 'on behalf of' the Malays (Government of Malaysia 1976: 86).

Apart from policies designed to bring Malays into the middle class, the NEP specifically aimed at increasing Malay participation in business. During the 1970s and 1980s special measures were taken to spawn a Malay entrepreneurial class. Malay business people were given special access to licences, loans, contracts and so on while pressure was applied to foreign and Chinese firms to 'restructure' by taking in Malay partners and shareholders. In addition, the government itself expanded its own direct role in the economy 'on behalf of' the Malays. State corporations bought into, and gradually took over, the plantations, mines, banks and trading enterprises that had given the British control of the 'commanding heights', while becoming joint venture partners with foreign and Chinese investors in new industries. In the 1980s many of the shares held by state corporations were transferred to a new body, *Permodalan Nasional Berhad* (PNB—National Equity Corporation), which established a unit trust fund through which individual Malays could acquire stakes in the PNB's massive holdings. During the 1980s UMNO itself, as a Malay entity, expanded its business interests and controlled one of the largest corporate empires (Gomez 1990).

By 1990 foreign equity ownership in the corporate sector had fallen drastically to 25.1 per cent while Malay ownership had grown to 20.3 per cent, of which, however, only 8.2 per cent was owned directly by Malay individuals, the rest being owned either through the unit trust scheme or by state agencies. Although one of the main purposes of the NEP had been to stimulate Malay participation in business, it was domestic Chinese business that held the largest share of equity capital (44.9 per cent) in 1990 (Government of Malaysia 1991b: 12, 91). Nevertheless, the 'commanding heights' had largely passed to Malay hands, either individuals or government agencies. When the NEP expired at the end of 1990, it was replaced by what was called the New Development Policy which placed more emphasis on growth of the private sector and less on ethnic restructuring, although the general thrust of the NEP was retained.

To what extent did the evolving business class constitute a check on government power and a force for democratisation? Compared to the relatively 'laissez faire' era before 1970, the state sector had grown enormously under the NEP. Corporations like *Pernas* (established in 1974 to oversee the petroleum industry), the Heavy Industries Corporation of Malaysia (set up in 1980 to manage the government's investments in heavy industries) and, later, PNB, as well as the State Economic Development Corporations—owned by the state governments—acquired shares, and sometimes control, of hundreds of plantations, mines, banks and industrial enterprises. The expansion of the state sector inevitably reduced the political weight of the private sector while many private business people became involved as joint venture partners with state corporations.

The new Malay business class was in fact a creation of the government. Malay businesspeople were not entrepreneurs who set up new enterprises but clients of politicians who were given business opportunities as rewards for political support. Foreign or non-Malay enterprises were in effect forced to allocate shares, normally at below-market prices, to Malay business in order to conform with the government's equity guidelines which required that a certain percentage of equity—usually 30 per cent—be held by Malays before the company could get the licences or contracts that it needed. Many companies appointed politically well-connected Malays to their boards for the same reason. Some prominent Malays set up their own companies which became giant conglomerates with assistance from the government. Virtually all the members of the new Malay business class had close ties to UMNO. Many were politicians or retired bureaucrats and some were members of royalty. Malay business people did not so much constitute a class determined to further its common interests but rather consisted of coteries of clients preoccupied with maintaining individual links with political patrons. Malay business people, therefore, served to strengthen the state rather than acting as a check on its powers.

Chinese business people, on the other hand, were usually entrepreneurs with commercial skills. In the 1960s Chinese business was linked to the MCA as the Chinese party in the ruling coalition. But, while Chinese business turned to the MCA for help in times of need, it was largely able to stand on its own feet. Following the launching of the NEP, however, Chinese business people increasingly found themselves at the mercy of a Malay-dominated government committed to expanding Malay participation in business. Nevertheless, although unable to prevent the implementation of a wide range of policies harmful to its interests, Chinese business continued to expand during the NEP period. Although Chinese business was forced onto the defensive, it continued to constitute a very important, indeed indispensable, part of the economy so that the expectations of Chinese business could not be simply brushed aside by the government. The Chinese business class was still strong enough to ensure the preservation of a commercial environment which allowed them to make substantial profits, even if these had to be shared increasingly with Malay partners.

Under the political circumstances after 1970, a strong and autonomous bourgeoisie could not develop in Malaysia. Rapid capitalist development saw the expansion of a dominant state sector and the emergence of a dependent Malay business community while the Chinese business class was forced on the defensive. The Chinese business class still constituted a significant bulwark against movement toward Malay-dominated authoritarianism but the business class as a whole could not play the democratising role anticipated by some theorists.

The working class

Capitalist economic development and industrialisation also led to an expansion of the working class at least in absolute numbers if not as a proportion of the workforce. The 'production, transport and other workers' occupational category, which approximates the working class, grew from 18.9 per cent of the peninsular workforce in 1957 to 27.3 per cent in 1970. By 1990, when statistics referred to the Malaysia-wide workforce, the working-class category had risen slightly to 27.6 per cent. The static overall figure, however, disguised significant changes in composition as the proportion of Malays increased sharply in response to government pressure to increase Malay employment in the modern sector. In 1957 Malays made up only 16.7 per cent of the working-class category. By 1970 this had risen to 34.2 per cent and by 1990 to 48.5 per cent. The proportion of the Malay workforce employed in working-class occupations rose from 18.0 per cent in 1970 to 23.2 per cent in 1990 in contrast to the Chinese workforce in which working-class occupations declined from 41.6 per cent to 33.8 per cent (Jomo 1986: 300, for 1957; Government of Malaysia 1981: 59, for 1970; Government of Malaysia 1991b: 118, for 1990). The proportion of women in working-class occupations also increased, especially as young Malay women from the villages were recruited in large numbers to work in the burgeoning electronics industry.

Despite its size, the working class has had very limited political influence. The trade union movement has been weak, only 17 per cent of wage earners belonging to unions in 1990 (*New Straits Times* 1 May 1991). Moreover, trade union members are divided along communal lines. The trade union movement was originally associated with Indians who made up more than two-thirds of trade union members in the early 1960s, largely through the mainly Indian members of the National Union of Plantation Workers. Industrial expansion, however, was accompanied by the recruitment of Malay workers from the rural areas with the result that Malays made up slightly more than half of union members by 1980 (Ministry of Labour 1986: 190). The political loyalties of most workers seem to be determined by communal considerations and there has been no widespread support for a non-communal political party representing the interests of labour. The leftist Labour Party, which drew nearly all its support from non-Malays, was in effect banned in the early 1970s while many of its union officials were detained under the *Internal Security Act.*

The trade union movement has been too weak to prevent the adoption of restrictive trade union and industrial relations legislation. In the late 1960s, just as the policy shift was made towards export-oriented industrialisation, the right to strike was severely restricted. Between 1962 and 1968 the number of workdays lost in strikes ranged between 152 660 and 458 720 but, following the declaration of emergency in 1969, the number dropped drastically, never exceeding 110 000 in the 1970s and never exceeding 25 000 between 1980 and 1987 (Hua Wu Yin 1983: 163; Kementrian Buruh Malaysia 1985: 55; Information Malaysia 1990: 544). In the rapidly expanding electronics industry, unions were not permitted at all until 1988 when the government agreed to the formation of 'in-house' unions for electronics workers.

Unlike some other industrialising countries where organised workers have played a major role in challenging authoritarian governments, the impact of the Malaysian working class has been very slight. Divided along communal lines, the Malaysian working class has never been united politically to fight for class interests. It has therefore been relatively easy for the government to suppress organisations like the Labour Party.

The rural classes

Economic growth has been accompanied by a drastic decline in the proportion of the workforce involved in agriculture, from 56.4 per cent in 1957 to 44.9 per cent in 1970 and 28.3 per cent in 1990. The agricultural workforce has remained overwhelmingly Malay in composition, the Malay component actually rising from 72.0 per cent in 1970 to 76.4 per cent in 1990 as non-Malays left agricultural occupations more rapidly than Malays. Nevertheless, the proportion of the Malay workforce employed in agriculture declined steadily from 62.3 per cent in 1970 to 37.4 per cent in 1990. By 1990 the proportion of the Chinese workforce involved in agriculture had dropped to 13.5 per cent, while the proportion of Indians—mainly plantation workers—had declined to 23.4 per cent (Statistics calculated from Jomo 1986: 300, for 1957; Government of Malaysia 1981: 59, for 1970; Government of Malaysia, 1991b: 118, for 1990).

Despite their decline as a proportion of the Malay community, agricultural and other rural workers continued, thanks to the weighted electoral system, to be an important vote bank for the government. The Malay-dominated government, therefore, had to be sensitive to the expectations of its rural supporters who were vulnerable to the appeals of PAS and, in 1990, the new party of UMNO dissidents, *Semangat '46*. The government therefore implemented a wide range of rural development policies which resulted, according to official statistics, in a fall in the incidence of poverty in rural areas of peninsular Malaysia from 58.7 per cent in 1970 to 19.3 per cent in 1980, while poverty among Malays declined from 65 per cent to 20.8 per cent (Government of Malaysia 1991b: 46). That rural poverty had really declined was supported by other social indicators. For example, the infant mortality rate fell from 39.4 per 1000 in 1970 to about 23 in 1990 and enrolment in primary school became virtually universal (Government of Malaysia 1991b: 44). Between 1970 and 1987 the proportion of rural households supplied with electricity rose from 29 per cent to 88 per cent and the proportion with access to piped or potable water rose from 39 per cent to 73 per cent (Government of Malaysia 1981: 43; 1986: 58–9). As part of its drive to reduce rural poverty the pre-independence government had set up the Federal Land Development Authority (FELDA) in 1956 to allocate land to smallholders to grow rubber, palm oil and some other crops. Only 20 700 families had been settled in 1970 but by 1990, 116 293 families, virtually all of whom were Malay, had been settled on 315 FELDA schemes, involving around half a million people (*Utusan Malaysia* 2 April 1990).

The government, through UMNO, also mobilised Malay rural voters by means of its elaborate patronage network. Villagers wanting to acquire land or government agricultural assistance found it to be in their interest to be members of UMNO. Village heads were almost always UMNO supporters who used their powers to benefit fellow party supporters. Referring to government assistance to farmers in rural Selangor, Shamsul wrote: 'My detailed findings show that most of the peasants who receive these aids are either immediate relatives of the village heads, or loyal UMNO supporters' (Shamsul 1986: 220; Scott 1985: especially 220–31). Villagers who wanted to be accepted into a FELDA scheme were also expected to support UMNO and could be expelled if they did not.

The government did not of course eradicate rural poverty but it made sure that it retained its political base among the rural Malays. Although PAS was never able to match UMNO at the national level, its ability to mobilise substantial rural Malay support, especially in the predominantly Malay and rural states of the north and northeast, put the government under constant pressure. Democratic elections, therefore, made UMNO, as the dominant party in the ruling coalition, sensitive and responsive to the expectations of a large part of the rural population. As long as Malay peasants and other rural workers felt that the government was heeding their basic expectations and providing gradual material improvements, they continued to give their votes to UMNO and were not too concerned about the allegations of middle-class dissidents that the government was often behaving in an authoritarian manner.

Changes in the class structure, therefore, tended to make the government responsive to pressures from important segments of society. Thus the government was sensitive to the aspirations of rural Malays. By providing them with small concessions, the government could reap big rewards in terms of votes and, due to the weighted electoral system, especially in terms of seats in parliament. The government also responded to the interests of the middle class, especially the rapidly growing Malay section of the middle class. The government's response to the interests of the non-Malay middle class and business, however, was ambivalent. By satisfying the expectations of a large part of the Malay peasantry and middle class and meeting some of the material expectations of the Chinese middle and business classes, the government was then in a stronger position to reject the demands of the working class and those demands of the Chinese business and middle classes that it deemed unacceptable. The political system, therefore, made the government relatively responsive to the expectations of a substantial part of the society.

But the changing class structure did not produce strong pressures toward full democratisation. The Malay middle class was largely satisfied with the regime while the client status of Malay business meant that the government had no need to fear a challenge from that quarter. On the non-Malay side, the middle and business classes were alienated by the government's discrimination in favour of the Malays but many still appreciated the material benefits that they enjoyed and had too much to lose from direct opposition. And without a lead from the business and middle classes, the working class, which in any case was communally divided, could not be mobilised behind the cause of democratisation while the Malay rural classes accepted the established system. The small groups of middle-class reformers calling for further liberalisation and democratisation were therefore easily isolated.

Although the government was responsive to the expectations of a substantial part of society, it retained its authoritarian powers and regularly took limited repressive action. Most often this was against its political opponents such as non-Malay trade union leaders, non-Malay and some Malay middle-class dissidents and even Muslim 'extremists' among the Malays, all groups that lacked sufficiently large mass bases to protect themselves, partly because their potential class bases were communally divided. But, precisely because it had a strong social base, the government had less need to resort to extreme authoritarian measures to maintain itself in power. At the same time, the evolution of the class structure had produced significant class interests which had a stake in the preservation of the semi-democratic institutions through which they could press their demands on the government.

The communal structure

Class pressures, as we have seen, were constantly vitiated by cross-cutting communal loyalties. By 1985 Malays and other indigenes (together known as *bumiputera*—sons of the soil) made up 56.5 per cent of the population on the peninsula, Chinese made up 32.8 per cent and Indians 10.1 per cent. For the country as a whole, including the indigenous peoples of Sabah and Sarawak, *bumiputeras* made up 60 per cent. Communal politics was inextricably linked with economic interests but it also involved fundamental perceptions of 'identity. It had, therefore, a dynamic of its own that was separate from the struggle over the distribution of economic benefits.

Most Malays believe in the principle of 'Malay Dominance' which claims precedence for the Malays, as the presumed original inhabitants of the Malay peninsula, over the non-Malays whose forebears mostly migrated to the region during the nineteenth and early twentieth centuries. Malays regard themselves as the owners of what they call *Tanah Melayu*—the Land of the Malays—and succeeded in having written into the nation's constitution the symbols of Malay dominance—a Malay sultan as head of state, Malay as the national language and Islam as the religion of the state. The constitution also permitted the gerrymandering of the electoral system, virtually ensuring a permanent Malay majority in parliament. Following the racial riots of 1969, which the government attributed to the resentment that poor Malays felt because of the economic success of non-Malays, the government launched the NEP which gave special preference to Malays and other *bumiputeras* while Malay was gradually adopted as the sole language of education and administration, and Malay culture was virtually equated with the national culture.

The discriminatory policies of the government, especially after 1969, naturally alienated non-Malays who believed that they had as much right as the Malays to belong to the country of their birth. In response to the Malay concept of 'Malay Dominance', non-Malays turned to the slogan of a 'Malaysian Malaysia', implying that all Malaysians—Malay or non-Malay—had an equal stake in their country. Non-Malays deeply resented policies that favoured Malays in almost every field, such as access to tertiary education, recruitment to the civil service and the armed forces, language and cultural policies, immigration and many more. Non-Malays, whether big business people or ordinary labourers, believed that they were being treated as 'second-class citizens'.

Communal violence has never been far from the surface in Malaysia. The widespread inter-communal killing that took place immediately after the Japanese surrender in 1945 was followed by intermittent outbreaks during the 1950s and 1960s until the conflagration in Kuala Lumpur in 1969, when nearly 200 people were killed according to official estimates and many more according to unofficial estimates. In a society where almost every political issue has communal connotations, the possibility of violent racial conflict remains a constant factor in all political calculations and provides what to many is a legitimate reason for the government to impose authoritarian controls. When, for example, the government detained over one hundred dissidents during a period of heightened communal tension in October 1987, the general public mood was one of relief rather than outrage at the violation of civil liberties.

Authoritarian controls have not, of course, been limited to measures intended to suppress communal conflict but have also strengthened the Malay-dominated state in facing non-Malays. In the 1960s repressive measures were directed against the underground Communist Party and other leftist organisations, most of which were overwhelmingly non-Malay in membership. Then, following the racial rioting of 1969, the government acquired increased authoritarian powers in order to protect the implementation of the NEP which, because it favoured Malays, inevitably met with strong non-Malay resistance. Many Malays regard the regime's authoritarian powers as necessary in order to preserve Malay political dominance and achieve Malay socio-economic goals.

On the other hand, the very division of society into communal segments in itself constitutes a built-in check on the use of authoritarian powers. Malay political leaders are aware that any attempt on their part to establish an exclusively Malay regime would meet with enormous resistance from the non-Malay part of society. Not only would they face social upheaval and the risk of civil war but would have to deal with economic disruption if Chinese skills and capital were withdrawn. The UMNO leaders, therefore, have preferred to establish a coalition regime in which they are the dominant element but which also includes parties representing the non-Malay communities.

The existing semi-democratic institutions have facilitated the preservation of social harmony by ensuring that the non-Malay partners
in the government are more than token representatives and that real
concessions are given to non-Malay interests. Thus, despite the
implementation of policies favouring the Malay community, Chinese
business, for example, still gets government contracts, the quota for
non-Malay students in universities was gradually raised to 45 per
cent during the early 1980s, Chinese- and Tamil-language primary
schools continue to operate, and Chinese and Indians are permitted
to practise their own customs and religions. Although dominated by
its Malay component, the presence in the government of parties
representing the Chinese and Indian communities, as well as the
indigenous communities of East Malaysia, means that the Malaysian
government lacks the unity of purpose of a truly authoritarian
regime. The government's need for multi-communal electoral support ensures that it is responsive to at least some of the demands
of the non-Malays who therefore have an interest in the preservation
of semi-democratic representative institutions.

Political competition

That socio-economic factors tended to support a political system
that was relatively responsive to the interests of important segments
of society, while resorting to authoritarian measures to repress
others, does not necessarily provide a full explanation of the nature
of the political system. It is also worthwhile to look at the dynamics
of political competition and its effects on the system.

Even when socio-economic factors facilitate or at least do not
obstruct the implementation of particular authoritarian measures, it
needs political leaders to implement them. Authoritarian measures
are introduced on the initiative of political leaders who are motivated at least in part—and often a very large part—by the desire to
strengthen their political position against challenges from their
opponents. Authoritarian controls are not usually introduced according to a grand design but incrementally as political leaders deal with
particular challenges to their authority. Thus, in Malaysia, the *Internal Security Act* was used to settle an internecine struggle within
UMNO in 1976 and to silence government critics in 1987; the
emergency provisions were used to oust the PAS-controlled state
government in Kelantan in 1977; the *Official Secrets Act* was
tightened in 1986 to deter the revelation of embarrassing information; limits were imposed on election campaigning at various times
in order to disadvantage the opposition parties; and constituency

boundaries were redrawn periodically in such a way as to ensure government victories in ensuing elections.

On the other hand, however, the dynamics of political competition can sometimes lead to a strengthening of democratic characteristics in the system. During the 1980s the struggle for power within UMNO reached a point where the party split and a new party of UMNO dissidents—*Semangat '46*—was founded. The UMNO split was partly a result of personal rivalries between UMNO leaders but it also took place during the severe recession of the mid-1980s when many of the Malay business people produced by the NEP were facing economic disaster as the government was forced to cut back sharply on the credit, contracts and concessions that had been the lifeblood of the client business. Rising dissatisfaction in the party was expressed in support for Dr Mahathir's challenger, Tengku Razaleigh, who, after his narrow defeat for the party leadership in 1987, eventually set up *Semangat '46* in 1989 (Crouch 1992; Shamsul 1988). It has been suggested that Razaleigh's Semangat '46 represented those, especially small and medium Malay business, who wanted to continue the state-centred policies of the NEP, while Mahathir's UMNO, supported by bigger business interests, was more inclined toward privatisation, deregulation and internationalisation (Khoo Kay Jin 1992). Others, however, regarded the two parties as ideologically indistinguishable, as indicated by the ease with which many of the dissidents were reabsorbed into UMNO in later years.

As the 1990 general election approached, the new party was able, in negotiations that lasted more than a year, to set up an opposition front with the Malay-based PAS and the non-Malay-based DAP, something that PAS and the DAP had never been able to work out for themselves in the past. As a result of these political manoeuvres, the BN was confronted for the first time with a semi-alliance of all major opposition parties in the 1990 election. Although the BN once again secured a convincing victory, the unprecedented challenge from a multi-communal opposition front forced it to chase votes in a way that had not been necessary in the past. Although many of the means used by the BN to fight off the challenge were not 'fair' by democratic standards, the government had no choice but to respond to increased pressures from society.

The dynamics of political competition, therefore, have led to shifts in both authoritarian and democratic directions. The manoeuvres and counter-manoeuvres of politicians—arrests of political opponents, declarations of emergency, restrictions on the media, party challenges and splits, and the formation of electoral alliances—were often motivated primarily by the quest for political power and were not essentially responses to social and economic pressures. The regime sometimes became more authoritarian not in order to protect the state but to safeguard the careers of individual leaders and their supporters; and it sometimes became more democratic not because of a fundamental realignment of social forces but because opposition leaders were able to put aside their longstanding rivalries in order to mount an electoral challenge to the government.

Conclusion

The class and communal structures of Malaysian society provided a setting that was supportive of a political system that was neither fully authoritarian nor fully democratic. The result was a system in which the government was fairly responsive to the demands of a substantial part of the population while ready to use authoritarian measures against the rest.

The social structure was such that it would be very difficult to establish a fully authoritarian regime. The establishment of such a regime with the support of the predominantly Malay bureaucracy and armed forces would have undoubtedly alienated the non-*bumiputera* two-fifths of the population and risked losing the support of a large part of the middle class, both Malay and non-Malay. But, in any case there was no need for the government to turn to extreme authoritarianism. As long as the government was reasonably responsive to the interests of the Malay villagers, the lopsided electoral system would continue to provide it with a solid bloc of seats in parliament, while the growth of the Malay, and to a lesser extent the non-Malay, middle class gave it another reservoir of votes. And the political stability that the government safeguarded won it the support of many non-Malays, including Chinese business people, otherwise alienated by its policies. On the other hand, the critics of the government who demanded full democratisation lacked a strong class and communal base of support.

In this context, the dynamic of political struggle also produced its own authoritarian and democratic tendencies. During the 1970s and 1980s the UMNO leaders of the government implemented a series of measures which reduced the scope for its opponents to mobilise support. Justified in terms of maintaining peace and stability in a communally divided society, these measures were often motivated primarily by the desire of government leaders to neutralise their political opponents. But, on the other hand, vigorous democratic competition for votes continued. The system was still sufficiently open to allow opposition parties to win substantial support and, when UMNO itself split in the late 1980s, the government not only became more responsive to popular pressures but it seemed for a time that it might even be defeated.

The Malaysian political system, therefore, contained both authoritarian and democratic elements. In the struggle at the political level between government and opposition, the government sometimes resorted to authoritarian measures but the opposition still had scope for mobilising popular support. At the same time, the class and communal structures of the society constituted a set of checks and balances that stood in the way of a reversion towards authoritarianism but did not provide compelling support for those who called for further democratisation.

Note

1 Statistics in the next three paragraphs are calculated from Jomo (1990: 82) for 1957, Government of Malaysia (1981: 59) for 1970, and Government of Malaysia (1991b: 118) for 1990. The categories used in the International Standard Classification of Occupations do not, of course, provide an exact measure of the 'middle class' or any other class. Some members of the 'sales' category, for example, do not live in a middle-class style while some of the generally lower-class 'services' category should be considered middle class. Nevertheless, these occupational categories provide a useful, although rough, indication of the growth of the middle class.

References

Crouch, Harold 1992, 'Authoritarian Trends, the UMNO Split and the Limits to State Power', *Fragmented Vision: Culture and Politics in Contemporary Malaysia*, eds Joel Kahn & Francis Loh, Allen & Unwin, Sydney
Gomez, Edmund Terrence 1990, *Politics in Business: UMNO's Corporate Investments*, Forum, Kuala Lumpur
Government of Malaysia 1976, *Third Malaysia Plan 1976–1980*, Kuala Lumpur
—— 1981, *Fourth Malaysia Plan 1981–1985*, Kuala Lumpur
—— 1986, *Mid-Term Review of Fifth Malaysia Plan 1986–1990*, Kuala Lumpur
—— 1991a, *Sixth Malaysia Plan 1991–1995*, Kuala Lumpur
—— 1991b, *The Second Outline Perspective Plan 1991–2000*, Kuala Lumpur
—— 1991c, *Laporan Majlis Perundingan Ekonomi Negara*, Kuala Lumpur
Hua Wu Yin 1983, *Class and Communalism in Malaysia: Politics in a Dependent Capitalist State*, Zed Books, London
Information Malaysia 1990, *Yearbook 1990–91*, Berita Publishing, Kuala Lumpur
Jesudason, James V. 1989, *Ethnicity and the Economy: The State, Chinese*

Business and Multinationals in Malaysia, Oxford University Press, Singapore

Jomo Kwame Sundaram 1986, *A Question of Class: Capital, the State, and Uneven Development in Malaysia*, Oxford University Press, Singapore

—— 1990, *Growth and Structural Change in the Malaysian Economy*, Macmillan, London

Kementrian Buruh Malaysia 1985, *Petunjuk-Petunjuk Buruh 1984*, Kuala Lumpur

Khoo Kay Jin 1992, 'The Grand Vision', *Fragmented Vision: Culture and Politics in Contemporary Malaysia*, eds Joel Kahn & Francis Loh, Allen & Unwin, Sydney

Lim, David 1973, *Economic Growth and Development in West Malaysia 1947–1970*, Oxford University Press, Kuala Lumpur

Means, Gordon P. 1991, *Malaysian Politics: The Second Generation*, Oxford University Press, Singapore

Ministry of Labour 1986, *Labour and Manpower Report 1984/5*, Kuala Lumpur

Scott, James 1985, *Weapons of the Weak: Everyday Forms of Peasant Resistance*, Yale University Press, New Haven

Shamsul Amri Baharuddin 1986, *From British to Bumiputera Rule: Local Politics and Rural Development in Peninsular Malaysia*, Institute of Southeast Asian Studies, Singapore

—— 1988, 'The "Battle Royal": The UMNO Elections of 1987', *Southeast Asian Affairs 1988*, eds Mohammed Ayoob & Ng Chee Yuen, Institute of Southeast Asian Studies, Singapore

World Bank 1990, *World Development Report 1990*, Oxford University Press, New York

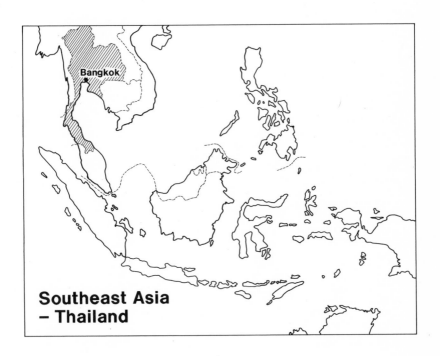

**Southeast Asia
– Thailand**

Thailand: Basic social and economic data

Population (1990)	56.3m
Population density	109 persons per sq. km
Average annual population growth (1982–89)	1.5%
Urban population (1989)	22% (official)
	20–40% (unofficial)
Total labour force (1989)	31.2m
Major ethnic groups	Thai, Lao, Malay
Capital city	Bangkok
Population (1990)	5.9m
Land area	542 273 sq. kms
Official language	Central Thai
Other main languages	Lao, other Tai dialects
Administrative division	72 provinces
Education, enrolments	
Primary (1990)	7.39m
Secondary (1990)	1.79m
University (1990)	582 250
Adult literacy rate (1990)	90%
Health	
Life expectancy (1989)	66 yrs
Infant mortality/1000 (1989)	29
Persons/hospital bed (1989)	624
Persons/physician (1989)	6294
Economy	
GNP at market prices (1989)	US$64.3 bn
Real GNP per capita (1989)	US$1160
GNP growth rate (1990)	10.0%
Trade	
Exports, value (1989)	US$20.1 bn
Imports, value (1989)	US$32.7 bn
Main imports (1989)	Machinery & transport 41.9%, manufactures 25.5%, chemicals 10.0%
Main exports (1989)	Manufactures 39.9%, food & live animals 28.2%, machinery & transport equipment 22.3%
Foreign debt (1989)	US$23.5 bn
Foreign reserves (1990)	US$14.3 bn
Energy consumption/capita (kg coal equiv. in 1989)	637
Communications	
Rail (1990)	3735 km
Roads, paved (1990)	45 000 km
Religions	Buddhism, Islam

Sources: Far Eastern Economic Review Asia Yearbook 1991; The Far East and Australasia 1992 (Europa Publication)s; United Nations Economic and Social Commission for Asia and the Pacific Newsletter, Key Indicators of Developing Asian and Pacific Countries 1991, Asian Development Bank.

7 Of regimes, state and pluralities: Thai politics enters the 1990s
Kevin Hewison[1]

At the end of the 1980s Thailand appeared to be following a number of other newly industrialised countries (NICs) and near NICs along the road of democratisation. Some political theorists have argued that increased social complexity, rapid economic growth, and the development of capitalism, with its emphasis on legal and rational procedures, gives rise to pressures for parliamentary regimes (cf. Almond 1991).

It has been a common and long-held proposition that the parliamentary regime, as a form of state power, may well be the most appropriate model of political rule for capitalist societies (Jessop 1978: 29; Marx & Engels 1973). Anderson (1990: 40), has recently argued that parliamentary democracy is the 'style of regime with which all ambitious, prosperous and self-confident bourgeoisies feel most comfortable, precisely because it maximises their power and minimizes that of their competitors'. Thailand, together with Taiwan, South Korea, and a number of Latin American countries, suggested that a transition to parliamentary forms was on the cards for those nations on the road to NIC-dom.

The Thai case appeared particularly promising for a number of reasons. First, a long period of parliamentary tutelage (often called semi- or quasi-democracy) had been experienced under the administration of General Prem Tinsulanond (1980-88). During this period, in 1981 and 1985, two attempted military coups were defeated. Second, the leading military figure of the late 1980s, General Chaovalit Yongchaiyuth, while expressing a strong interest in politics, continually reiterated that he would not have his increasingly professional military intervening in the civilian political process. Third, as the head of the largest party in the parliament following the 1988 elections, Chatichai Choonhavan became the first elected prime minister since 1976. There was tremendous initial and widespread enthusiasm for his government and its 'new broom' approach. There can be no doubt that the selection of Chatichai as prime minister was seen as a victory for democratic forces. Fourth, the Thai class structure was becoming far more complex, both in rural and urban areas. Finally, all of this took place in a context of spectacular economic growth, remembering that economic downturn had been a justification for coup-making in the past.

However, in February 1991, the military again took power, and all of the democratic progress made since Thanin Kraivixien's troglodytic regime was replaced in 1976 had apparently been cast asunder. The vandals of parliament were led by a coterie of officers who had graduated from the military academy in 1958. The coup group called itself the National Peacekeeping Council (NPKC), and quickly established its own government. At least in the short term, all questions concerning the relationship between parliamentary regimes and capitalist development seemed to be pushed aside by the military's action.

No matter how one defines it, democracy had suffered a serious setback as the military moved to entrench itself. While appointing a government led by former diplomat and businessman Anand Panyarachun, the NPKC maintained control over the political system while preparing a new constitution and establishing the framework for elections in March 1992. The new constitution meant that the NPKC nominated the Senate and gave this unelected house significant legislative and parliamentary powers. This ensured the military's parliamentary control no matter what the election produced, and meant that it would continue to direct the institutional aspects of the political process (*Bangkok Post Weekly Review* [*BPWR*] 10 January 1992). Significantly, and harking back to the Prem era, it also confirmed that the prime minister could be nominated by parliament, meaning that the post was not reserved for a member of parliament (MP).

No one could doubt that MPs and especially, and most conspicuously, their ministerial leaders did much to bring themselves undone. The popular enthusiasm for the elected regime had been replaced by generalised cynicism. By late 1990, almost everyone seemed to believe that the Chatichai government was riddled with corruption, as the primary objective of political parties was clearly to get their snouts in the trough of public power and wealth. This was confirmed after Chatichai's final reshuffle of his cabinet, which was plainly conducted to further the financial interests of the various coalition parties and their leaders.

However, some months prior to this final reshuffle, when General Chaovalit was replaced as Army commander by General Suchinda Kraprayoon, many observers were convinced that a coup was at hand. General Suchinda despised parliament, its demands, practices and trappings, on one occasion stating:

> We hope that a military officer has dignity and will not submit himself to politicians. I will not submit myself to politicians . . . I am supposed to have breakfast with the Prime Minister [Chatichai] . . . every Wednesday . . . but I do not go . . . Why should I go? I do not bow to politicians. I have dignity. If we don't [submit], they cannot do anything against us . . . [Personally] I will definitely not play politics. This is not in my character . . . I cannot go begging for votes . . . I cannot lower myself . . . (*Bangkok Post [BP]* 6 March 1990).

The General also expressed concern over the alleged corruption of civilian politicians and of the electoral system (cf. *BP* 2 October 1990). In comparison, General Suchinda contended that the military was dignified and untainted by corruption. In fact, the term he used, *borisut*, suggested more, implying that the military was pure or virginal (Thai TV Channel 7 News, 2 April 1990). It was in this context that General Suchinda and his cohorts acted to remove the claimed corruption and ineptitude of civilian and parliamentary rule. Along with them went the constitution and the aspirations of many Thais who had wanted and hoped that a parliamentary system might be made to work.

While most commentators agreed that there was general relief that Chatichai's corrupt civilian government was ousted, it is clear that many Thais did not view the military as untainted knights riding chargers to the rescue of Thai society. Indeed, history and recent events suggest there is no reason to consider that the military would be any different from civilian politicians.[2] For example, the demise of earlier generations of military rulers like Field Marshal Sarit Thanarat and, later, of his followers, Generals Thanom Kittikachorn and Prapas Charusathiarana, brought considerable public and official scrutiny of their 'unusual wealth' (cf. Thak 1979: 335–8; Girling 1981:190–2). More recently, during the periods of the Prem and Chatichai governments, there were numerous allegations of military corruption. These included reports of public monies being used secretly by the military (*Bangkok World* 5 March 1987); irregularities in arms trading (*Nation* 13 November 1987; *Matichon sutsapda* 18 April 1990); military figures reportedly involved in shady trade deals with Burma, Cambodia and Laos (*Far Eastern Economic Review [FEER]* 22 February 1990); and bribery in the military draft (*BP* 6 April 1990). More seriously, and in common with allegations made against political parties, links were made between military leaders and underworld figures (referred to as *chao pho* or *itthiphon muet*). A recent example was the attempted murder of Charoen

Pattanadamrogkit (or *Sia* Leng, Khon Kaen's 'godfather') in April 1990, which saw General Sunthorn Kongsompong, who became titular head of the NPKC, rushing to comfort him at his hospital bedside (*Nation* 16 April 1990). In return, *Sia* Leng and *Kamnan* Poh (Somchai Khunpluem, Chonburi's 'godfather') called on General Sunthorn soon after the coup to promise their support (*FEER* 18 April 1991). It is clear, then, that the military and its NPKC could not boldly claim to be squeaky clean.

But none of this explains the military coup in February 1991. In this chapter I will suggest two possible, but not necessarily mutually exclusive, perspectives which might explain the coup: a military-centred perspective and a society-focused view. This analysis also suggests a potential explanation for the popular uprising which challenged military authoritarianism and led to the Bangkok massacre in May 1992. However, my purpose is not merely to describe a coup, for I wish to reflect on the wider relationships between state, class and democratisation.

The military-centred perspective

If one was to adopt the view of political scientists who devote their energies to watching the military leadership, then a reasonably straightforward explanation of the 1991 coup is possible. Such an explanation might begin by arguing that the 'vicious cycle' of coups identified by Chai-Anan (1982a) has merely been slower this time around; instead of the usual three-year cycle, the cycle that ended with the 1990 coup required fourteen years. The reasons the military had to wait so long before making their comeback may be traced to the events of the early seventies. A brief scenario may be outlined.

In October 1973 students led a popular uprising against a military regime tainted by corruption and nepotism. One of the reasons for the success of this uprising was that the military and in particular, the Army, was seriously split. The military returned three years later, marching back to political centre-stage over the bodies of hundreds killed at the Thammasat University campus. Nevertheless, the military remained divided, with its image tarnished (Suchit 1987: 5–6). It was significant that the 1976 coup group was led by a naval officer, Admiral Sang-ad Chaloiyu, who was also Supreme Commander. The usual leader in these events, the Army, seemed unable to produce an acceptable leader, and a civilian rather than military government was initially established. Out of this division grew three groups that aimed at restoring the position of the Army specifically and the military generally. These groups were the Young Turks, the Democratic Soldiers, and the Class 5 Conservatives.

The Young Turks (or Young Military Officers') group

This group was drawn principally from graduates of Class 7 at the Chulachomklao Military Academy. It had expressed considerable dissatisfaction with the structure of political activity, and espoused a perspective that attacked corrupt politicians, big capitalists, inequality, and weak civilian and military leadership (Chai-Anan 1982a,b).

Their support assisted in bringing General Kriangsak Chomanand to power in 1977, and their switch to General Prem in 1980 saw him replace Kriangsak as prime minister. However, their involvement in the failed coups of 1981 and 1986 saw them lose much of their influence.

One of this class's best-known members was Chamlong Srimuang, who resigned his Army commission to eventually be elected governor of Bangkok. He has distanced himself from the Young Turks, but even so the enmity that existed between this group and Class 5 was most vividly portrayed in his opposition to Class 5's government in early 1992.

The Democratic Soldiers

The Democratic Soldiers were a group of self-styled intellectual officers associated with the Internal Security Operation Command, lecturers at the Military Academy and Army War College, and former Communist Party of Thailand (CPT) central committee member Prasert Sapsunthorn. This group appeared to have the support of General Chaovalit, and argued strongly for a 'democratic revolution' in Thai society, both to win the war against the CPT and to restore confidence in the capacity of the political system following the bloody events of October 1976. The now well-known Prime Ministerial Order 66/2523 has been seen as one of their successes (Suchit 1987: 15–16; Chai-Anan 1982b: Ch. 7; Democratic Soldiers [n.d.]).

Class 5 Conservatives

This group is composed of the Class 5 graduates of the Chulachomklao Academy in 1958, and has been headed by General Suchinda. With about 140 members, the group is not simply a fraternity, for Class 5 developed a cohesiveness necessary to counter the Young Turks, who they felt had been disrespectful towards senior officers (Suchit 1987: 16; *FEER* 1 August 1991). By extension, this perceived impertinence suggested that the Young Turks had stepped outside the old structures of authority and political activity, while Class 5 craved a return to more traditional values.

This group, perhaps to a greater extent than the other two, reflected the traditional military view that a government relying on parliamentary support was inherently unstable. Consequently, such governments were seen as a threat to national security (Chai-Anan 1990: 185).

In addition, it appears that elements within Class 5 had been unhappy with aspects of General Chaovalit's efforts to modernise and professionalise the military. In an era where both internal and external threats had been greatly reduced, Chaovalit opted for a 'leaner, meaner' military force. Some saw this policy as signifying less political influence for the military, and more parliamentary control over the military budget and its activities.

Thus while each of these groups aimed to restore the military to its respected position in Thai society, the methods they chose and the various ideologies adopted pitted them against each other (Suchit 1987: 17–31). Their competition provides the backdrop to Thai politics in the 1980s, while the eventual supremacy of Class 5 sets the stage for the 1990s. The major events may be summarised here.

The Young Turks appeared defeated after their failed coup attempt in 1981, with General Arthit Kamlang-ek, who played an important role in defeating the coup, having a rapid rise to the top, supported by Class 5. However, when he agreed to reinstate a number of cashiered Young Turks in 1984, Class 5 switched their allegiance to General Prem, whom Arthit had been challenging for the prime ministership. At the same time, Class 5 supported Chaovalit, who was also opposed to the Young Turks and, together with Suchinda, had publicly chastised and embarrassed Young Turk leaders Colonel Manoon Roopkachorn and Colonel Prajak Sawangjit (Suchit 1987: 29, 42). With Class 5 support, Prem was eventually able to sack Arthit and promote General Chaovalit to Army leadership.

Later, as Chaovalit prepared to move into civilian politics in the late 1980s, Class 5 orchestrated an effective campaign to discredit the Democratic Soldiers and Prasert Sapsunthorn, consolidating a link of convenience between Chaovalit and Suchinda. The former's position came to rest heavily upon Class 5 and, by the time he resigned, this group had gained control over virtually all the important command positions within the military and police (*FEER* 1 October 1987; *BP* 16 April 1990). This meant that, for the first time since 1973, the military and especially the Army, while not free of factionalism, was effectively under the control of one group.

During the period of the Chatichai government, members of Class 5 regularly charged that the military's honour was under attack, and continually flexed their political muscles and rattled their swords. Many of these perceived attacks may be interpreted as a conservative response to civilians meddling in policy-making arenas previously considered to be the preserve of military and civil bureaucrats (*FEER* 19 January 1989). Perhaps the most significant of these arenas was in foreign policy, especially concerning Indochina. In foreign affairs, Chatichai, his relatively young advisers and politicians, elbowed aside a whole range of military and bureaucratic policies and perquisites. This was deeply resented (Surin & Suparra 1991: 3–4), and the result was a military-orchestrated campaign against prime ministerial adviser Sukhumbhand Paribatra, who was forced to resign in 1989 (*Nation* 10 August 1989).

The last straw, and the catalyst for the coup, was again related to the Young Turks. Young Turk leader, Colonel Manoon, in disgrace following the second failed coup in 1986, again had his career resurrected under Chatichai. Not only was he reinstated, which incensed conservative military leaders, but he was promoted and given a position close to Chatichai. When it appeared that Chatichai was about to install General Arthit (who had reinstated Manoon following the 1981 coup attempt) as Deputy Defence Minister, it must have appeared that Class 5's position was being further eroded. However, before Arthit could be appointed the Class 5 Conservatives effected their coup (*FEER* 7 March 1991). The events that followed, leading to the brutal use of military force to defeat an unarmed opposition to Suchinda's prime ministership, indicated Class 5's determination to maintain military and civil bureaucratic dominance over policy-making.

This represents a reasonably straightforward explanation for military intervention in politics based on inter-clique rivalry, and there can be no doubt that this rivalry did motivate many of those involved. However, as indicated above, there is another perspective.

The society-focused perspective

As was outlined in the introduction to this volume, political actions are not illuminated from merely instrumental explanations, but should be considered in the context of structural imperatives and constraints upon the state and social classes. In addressing these issues it is necessary to first acknowledge that Thailand is undergoing an extensive capitalist revolution which is irreversibly changing the face of Thai society. These changes are apparently occurring at an ever-accelerating rate, and class relations and politics both reflect these transformations and are part of them.

Capitalists, who make up only a few per cent of the population, are firmly in control of the Thai economy (Hewison 1989a). The economy they dominate is increasingly oriented to the commercial and industrial sectors, as the following figures illustrate:

- agricultural employment was projected to fall from 55 per cent of total employment under the Fifth Plan to 33 per cent during the Sixth Plan (National Economic and Social Development Board [NESDB] n.d.: 213);
- manufacturing's share of GNP has increased from 12 per cent in 1960, to 20 per cent in 1975, and up to 25 per cent by 1988 (*National Income of Thailand*, various issues);
- manufacturing exports have risen from 32 per cent of total exports in 1980 to 63 per cent in 1987 (Somsak & Suthiphand 1990: 201).

As the economic base has expanded, economic activity has become far more diverse, demanding a greater range of human resource skills and a more complex division of labour. For example, there is a critical shortage of some professional skills: demand for engineers is far greater than universities can graduate them (*Nation* 12 May 1989), while for computer engineers demand was estimated to increase by more than 2700 per cent between 1987 and 1997 (*Nation* 12 September 1988).

Thailand is now an economy and society immeasurably more diverse and complex than it was even a decade ago. It is sometimes difficult to fully comprehend the rapidity of these changes. For example, in 1955, Blake (1955) reported an automobile journey of great difficulty through the country, only rarely encountering other private vehicles. Three decades later an extensive road network, making virtually every village accessible, means it is difficult to even conceive of the difficulties of transport in earlier decades. Other examples of rapid change are listed in Table 7.1.

These data suggest an increased complexity and affluence of civil society. As Rodan has noted in his chapter on Singapore, these changes are not just nationally focused, for there has been considerable exposure to international lifestyles and political styles. This has been especially acute as Thailand's international economic position has been reoriented from that of primary commodity exporter to manufacturing base.

These changes have also had a marked impact on politics and the state.[3] However, this rapidly increased complexity has not been reflected in its entirety in the state. There is no doubt that the Thai economy and state may be characterised as capitalist (Hewison 1989a), but the state has yet to be transformed to a thoroughly bourgeois one as the capitalist class has not been able to fully establish its control over the state's apparatus or its cultural and legal hegemony.[4]

In suggesting modifications to my (Hewison 1985) earlier instrumental position on the state, Andrew Turton (1984: 29) has cogently argued that in Thailand:

Table 7.1 Complexity and change in Thai society

Population	38m (1970)	57m (1990)
Population growth rate	3.3% (1970)	1.5% (1990)
Tourists	0.8m (1972)	5.3m (1990)
Per capita income	16 000 bht (1982)	22 500 bht (1987)
Newspapers	22 (1968)	51 (1990)
Magazines	na	380 (1990)
Radio stations	105 (1970)	381 (1990)
TV stations	5 (1968)	11 (1990)
Hospitals	203 (1970)	362 (1986)
Reg'd motor vehicles	692 738 (1970)	6 138 114 (1988)
Km of paved road	10 100 (1970)	45 000 (1990)
Tertiary students	55 315 (1970)	582 250 (1990)
Universities	8 (1970)	39 (1989)
Registered unions	~200 (1978)	713 (1990)

Sources: *The Investor* (November 1977); Brown & Frenkel (1992); Ogilvy & Mather (1991); Family Health Division (1984); Ministry of Public Health (1988); *Statistical Yearbook Thailand* (various issues); *BP* 1 May 1990; Board of Investment (1990; 1991)

. . . the bourgeoisie as a class does not effectively or adequately control the state and its apparatuses . . . Nor does the state exist primarily to serve the interests of the bourgeoisie. To some extent it exists to serve the interests of the various elements which formally comprise its ruling and governing classes, among which the military is dominant.

This is important, suggesting that the state is constituted of an amalgam of social, political, ideological and economic elements organised in a particular manner. Additionally, a distinction between state apparatus, regime, and civil society is implied.

James Petras (1989: 26), noting considerable confusion over these terms, advanced the following useful distinction:

The state refers to the *permanent* institution of *government* and the concomitant *ensemble of class relations* which have been embedded in these same institutions. The permanent institutions include those which exercise a *monopoly over the means of coercion* . . . as well as those that control the *economic levers* of the accumulation process. . . The 'government' refers to those political officials that occupy the *executive* and *legislative* branches . . . There are various types of government classified along several dimensions. For example there are civilian and military regimes . . . [emphasis in original].

In line with this, the state apparatus comprises the coercive, judicial and bureaucratic arms of the state, while a regime can be said to represent particular forms of organisation of these, and includes, for example, liberal democracy, parliamentary democracy and authoritarian forms. Thus a regime is a political and legal arrangement of control over government and the state apparatus.

In this context then, the overthrow of the Chatichai government did *not* represent an attack on the state, for the state exists behind the government and regime, and its basic elements were not threatened by the military; the bureaucracy, its arrangement, law and judiciary, and the national symbols of Nation, Religion and Monarchy were not challenged. However the coup *did* represent an attack on the parliamentary regime, for the constitution, parliament, MPs and the manner in which the regime operated were targeted. Significantly, however, there was not an assault on capitalists or capitalist values, as had occurred, for example, during the 1981 Young Turks' failed coup (*Prachammit* 30 May 1981).

Rather, the civilian government, and the regime it represented, was overthrown because *it* threatened the amalgam that constituted the state. It did this by unleashing societal forces that may be perceived as moving the Thai state towards a more thoroughly bourgeois one. In other words, the state remains intact, but the civilian government and the parliamentary regime were bundled out, and a new government, drawn from military and civilian managers and business was constituted, and a military regime established (*FEER* 21 March 1991; *Matichon sutsapda* 17 March 1991).

How was it that Chatichai's government and its parliamentary regime challenged the Thai state? This elected government, the parliamentary form, and the logic of its operations, represented the spirit of the capitalist revolution and embodied the spirit of change in society. While this government precipitated many changes, it was itself a government born of momentous changes already underway. With the flowering of the parliamentary regime, coinciding with a propitious time for the economy, and the advent of a parliamentary government, headed by an elected prime minister, accelerated the whole process of change. As Anderson (1990: 40) has commented, the period since 1973 may be seen as '. . . the struggle of the bourgeoisie to develop and sustain its new political power . . . against threats from the left and right. . .'.[5]

In suggesting how this challenged the state, attention may be usefully directed to the increasing plurality of Thai politics. This is significant, for such pluralities directly challenge the way the state is constituted and the manner in which senior military and civil officials have defined legitimate political activity (cf. Chai-Anan 1990: 186). As Girling (1981: 147–8) has noted, officials of the Thai state have tended to define *their interests* as national interests, and have not been willing to account for democratic interests (that is, the interests of the 'common people'). Concepts such as order, stability, tradition, hierarchy and knowing one's place in it, and unity, symbolically entwined in the national shibboleth, 'Nation, Religion, Monarchy', have defined the exercise of legitimate power.

This has recently been strikingly demonstrated: following the 1991 coup, General Suchinda made it clear that any opposition to the NPKC amounted to an attack on the nation—perhaps 'state' is a better term—and would be met with force (cited in Bandhit 1991: 235).

A discussion of a few, selected, emergent groups that have had an impact on political activity during the past decade will illustrate how these groups contest this amalgam of the Thai state. The groups chosen are environmental, organised labour, intellectuals, business, and Buddhist sects.[6]

Environmental groups

The political potential of environmental issues became focused in early 1973. Then, a student-led campaign against military and other influential figures involved in illegal hunting in the Thung Yai national park was undertaken, and became a part of a wider action against the then military regime. Following that regime's overthrow, the 1973–76 period of parliamentary government saw a number of other environmental issues elevated to the national political stage. Following the 1976 coup, this activity ceased (Hirsch & Lohmann 1989: 442–3).

The renaissance of environmental politics came in 1982 with the Prem government's proposal for the construction of the Nam Choan Dam in upper Kanchanaburi and lower Tak provinces (Hirsch 1986), ironically in the same area as the 1973 hunting scandal. The campaign against the proposed dam gradually gained momentum, bringing together students, urban environmentalists, popular entertainers, monks, local villagers including minorities, business organisations, women's groups, MPs, and even some officials (Nation 1988; Hirsch & Lohmann 1989: 445–8).

Following this success, a range of environmental questions emerged as political issues. These included: opposition to the Doi Suthep cable car near Chiangmai; deforestation; flooding; salt farming and resultant pollution of local water; shrimp farming and the destruction of mangroves; dams in Phayao, Ubonratchathani and Suratthani Provinces; pollution of rivers, coastal areas and Bangkok; and expressway development (from various issues of *Thai Rath*, *Bangkok Post*, *Nation*, *Matichon*).

The success on the Nam Choan issue demonstrated that citizens could publicly challenge state environmental policy. The idea that policy could be debated and opposed by various groups was threatening to many, especially state managers. This was emphasised by popular opposition to the expansion of commercial eucalyptus plantations.

Between 1985 and mid-1988 there were at least a dozen anti-eucalyptus actions by local people in the northeast alone (*Nation* 30 March 1989). Not only did peasants join with monks and students to oppose commercial plantations replacing forest areas, but some of their protests involved violent attacks on state property. The Chatichai regime apparently took these protests seriously, and attempted to incorporate greater participation in the development of a National Forest Master Plan (*Nation* 2 June 1989). Still, protests continued. More seriously, villagers, supported by monks, non-governmental organisations (NGOs) and students, began to forge district- and province-level alliances against state officials and forestry firms, leading local officials to threaten and harass villagers (*BP* 25 June 1990). Villagers remained defiant, however, and in many cases the military was used to enforce state policy. Increasingly, too, the military claimed that local 'influential persons' were taking advantage of villagers and organising them to occupy forest land, which the 'influentials' could then take or buy for themselves (*BP* 5 July 1990).

More significantly, however, environmentalists saw state forest policy increasingly oriented towards business interests. For example, despite the Chatichai government's ban on logging, evidence suggested that villagers—long blamed for forest encroachment—were being displaced from forest areas by commercial plantation operations (cf. Hirsch 1990; Shalardchai 1989).

The military has been forceful in its response to villagers identified as encroaching on forest areas. It obviously feels threatened by NGO–peasant alliances, for the military has considered rural areas their political and economic territory, especially since the demise of the CPT. For example, the military's leadership has been accused of involvement in forestry along the borders. While the military has denied any illegality, military interests in forestry along the borders with Laos, Cambodia, and especially Burma has been widely reported (*BP* 12 March 1990; 29 July 1990; *FEER* 22 February 1990).

Following the February 1991 coup the NPKC began the implementation of a draconian programme, aimed at resettling millions of villagers out of forests to make way for commercial reafforestation. Environmental groups, and even some commercial groups, have been outspoken in their opposition to the programme (*BPWR* 21 February 1992).

More significantly, in October 1991 a coalition of NGOs, led by environmental groups, organised a People's Forum to coincide with the World Bank–International Monetary Fund Meeting in Bangkok. This Forum challenged many of the assumptions and principles of the government, and state practices (Project for Ecological Recovery

1991). The fact that this was an international event further sharpened its impact.

Environmentalists represent a potent challenge to the concept of power embodied in the Thai state. More challenging are the coalitions they build between activist monks, villagers, NGOs, students, academics, and urban activists (*Nation* 30 August 1989). It was these groups that formed the backbone of the movement opposing General Suchinda's premiership and the 1991 constitution. One interesting and challenging aspect of the environmental movement is that it may not be defined as a merely middle-class movement, for it brings middle-class activists into alliances with peasants. Coalitions such as these are redefining legitimate political power.

Organised labour

Labour has been something of a barometer of political participation in Thailand, emerging as a significant force in times of relative political openness (1932–34, 1944–47, 1955–57, 1972–76), but being repressed for almost all of the modern period (see Brown & Frenkel 1993; Hewison 1985: 284–6). Under Prem organised labour emerged again, in spite of repression, and experienced unprecedented political influence under the Chatichai government, but has again faced curbs under the NPKC (Brown 1991b).

Throughout the 1980s unions agitated for the recognition of basic union rights, social security provisions, employer compliance, and against privatisation. The tactics adopted included tripartite meetings, political lobbying, public protests, strikes, and the use of existing labour legislation (Brown & Frenkel 1993). Even so, labour found its political influence limited by state policy and the Prem government's reliance on reasonably strict legalistic interpretations of dispute resolution. Few union leaders were satisfied with the Prem government's relationship with labour, and this was emphasised by the support provided by some of them to the Young Turks.

In 1988, as anti-Prem political coalitions were formed, a number of political parties courted labour, promising to support a social security bill, protect the right to strike, and oppose privatisation.[7] Party representatives argued that workers should vote for parties supporting labour (*Nation* 4 July 1988). More than forty labour leaders stood for election, representing a range of parties, and campaigning against low wages, poor conditions and laws that impeded labour organisation (*Nation* 22 June 1988).

Indeed, pressure from labour groups helped to bring Chatichai to the prime ministership, and he recognised this by having his son, Kraisak Choonhavan, who had well-established ties with labour organisations, act as his confidant on labour issues. Chatichai met with labour leaders and recognised the right to strike, specifically involving state enterprise unions which had been excluded under Prem (*Nation* 8 February 1989). Chatichai presided over both the 1989 and 1990 May Day celebrations, and gave undertakings to pursue social welfare legislation and to upgrade the Labour Department to a ministry (*Matichon* 1 May 1989; 2 May 1990). In fact, the 1990 event was televised live nationwide (*BP* 1 May 1990). While the Chatichai government attempted to deal with labour, this did not amount to a desertion of capitalists. Rather, Chatichai and his advisers apparently regarded an accommodation with labour to be both politically and economically correct. Chatichai's advisers were well aware of the growing political and especially electoral significance of labour. As one explained: 'We need labour on our side, . . . [a]nd that means better wages and benefits' (*FEER* 27 July 1989). At the same time, better capital–labour relations would maintain Thailand's attractiveness to investors.

It appears that Chatichai's approach was successful, for information available indicates that in 1989 there were only five official work stoppages, the lowest figure for twenty years (*BP* 23 March 1990). Even so, labour disputes remained common, with 30 per cent of all cases sent to the Supreme Court in 1988 being labour disputes (*Nation* 30 December 1988). Despite this the general trend has been for a decrease in disputation as unionisation has expanded (Brown & Frenkel 1993).

It might be argued that Chatichai and his advisers were seeking to develop a corporatist relationship with peak labour organisations. Whatever the case, there is no doubt that the inclusion of labour unions in policy dialogue greatly increased labour's prestige and political role, and increased the initial popularity of the government. Equally, some employers and state managers had become aware of the economic importance of labour, especially as Thailand attempted to move beyond its low-wage and low-skill labour base (Brown & Frenkel 1993).

This increased role was rejected by many employer groups and, significantly, by Class 5 leaders. General Suchinda led a spirited rejection of the Social Security Bill in the appointed Senate, after it had been passed by the lower house, claiming it was a mere vote-winning strategy (*BP* 8 May 1990; 11 July 1990). Despite setbacks, Chatichai continued to receive the qualified support of the major unions until just prior to the coup (*BP* 16 October 1990), when his government lost the backing of major state unions because of its push for state enterprise privatisation, which the unions opposed (Brown 1991a,b).

As noted above, however, the coup leaders were not so keen on maintaining labour as a political force. As Brown (1991a: 1–2) has reported, a number of NPKC actions were meant to reduce the influence of labour. These included the exclusion of state enterprise unions from the provisions of the 1975 *Labour Act*, removing their right to strike, and restricting their activities to 'welfare' issues.[8] State enterprise unions had been the backbone of the labour movement, so the NPKC's strong actions were meant as a threat to other workers, and they began to desert their unions. This was reinforced by the disappearance of a senior union leader in confused circumstances. Heavy penalties were also to apply to any workers deemed to instigate strikes or stoppages. In addition, labour's role in the NPKC's Assembly was greatly reduced from its representation in Chatichai's parliament. For example, while Prime Minister Anand met with many business leaders, he did not have a single meeting with labour leaders during his first term (*BP* 1 January 1992).

However, labour was not willing to retreat fully. For example, despite intimidation, unions, including those representing state enterprise workers, demanded significant pay rises in early 1992. More threatening to the NPKC, however, were statements by labour leaders that they would be inviting political parties that supported labour to their meetings. The argument was that labour may give its support to a party or even form a labour party.

While the middle-class nature of the opposition to General Suchinda and Class 5 has been emphasised in many reports (*FEER*, 21 May 1992), it should not be forgotten that labour was also prominent in the opposition movement. It remains to be seen, however, if the working-class movement will be able to create its own 'political elbow-room. . . [or will take] . . . the position of extreme wing of the middle class radicals' (Engels 1973: 62).

Intellectuals

Intellectuals have long held a significant social position in Thailand, but it has only been in modern times that some members of this group have distinguished themselves from the ruling classes.[9] As Anderson (1977: 16) notes, the traditional education system '. . . helped to conserve its constituents in their existing social and economic positions. Western-style higher education gave polish to those already born to rule'.

In part, the passing of this system had to do with the increasing complexity of the society. Education, particularly at the secondary and tertiary levels, expanded at a remarkable rate during the sixties, with tertiary enrolments up from about 15 000 in five universities in 1961 to 100 000 in seventeen universities in 1972. This meant increased expectations of social mobility, but because of the numbers involved, for the first time the future for students was no longer guaranteed (Anderson 1977: 16–17). Political activity was heightened at this time, with attacks on the military regime, and students and intellectuals provided a solid core of activists and critics. This activism and the history of its rise, decline and destruction, as repression caused intellectuals to flee to the jungles and overseas, is chronicled by Morell and Chai-Anan (1981) and Sulak Sivaraksa (1980).

Under the premierships of Kriangsak and Prem, a reintegration of academics and students took place. Many who had fled to the jungles in 1976 and 1977 returned, suitably chastened by the implosion of the CPT, and were reintegrated within the mainstream of politics. Nonetheless, there was still ample reason for discontent and activism. For example, some gave their support to the Young Turks, and many felt that General Chaovalit was an inspiration, seeing him as a 'thinking soldier' because he drew on intellectuals for advice. In appreciating Chaovalit, Prem was increasingly seen as a weak and indecisive leader.

It was under pressure from these groups that Prem decided not to stay on as prime minister, and which brought Chatichai to power. When it appeared that Prem, who refused to face a popular vote, might again be prime minister after the 1988 election, students and academics spearheaded a campaign for an elected premier. A coalition of 99 academics petitioned the King requesting that he only appoint an elected prime minister, a position strongly supported by the respected elder politician and writer Kukrit Pramoj. Likewise, students joined the campaign, demanding an elected prime minister (see *Nation* and *Matichon* July issues, 1988).

Chatichai appeared to acknowledge the significant role these groups played in his elevation to the position of prime minister by establishing an Advisory Council composed of relatively young academics. This Council was to provide him with independent policy advice and was brought together by Kraisak Choonhavan, then an academic at Kasetsart University, and Pansak Vinyaratn, a journalist and social and political activist. It was composed of academics who had generally been outside the established policy-making circles (*Nation* 15 August 1988). Although drawn into the maelstrom of political intrigue that marked the end of the Chatichai government, and losing much of the support it previously had enjoyed from academics, whether for or against Chatichai, intellectuals continued to have a significant voice in policy-making and, it must be added, criticism.

Even the Class 5 Conservatives came to see that it was not unreasonable for intellectuals to become publicly involved in policy-making, for they too have attempted to develop support from students and academics. For example, a group of academics who opposed Chatichai's Indochina policy, in favour of the Ministry of Foreign Affairs and the military position of support for the Chinese-backed Khmer Rouge, were vociferous in their attacks on the government. Similarly, small student groups were formed in a number of universities in support of Class 5 positions.

After the coup, and despite threats against some, academics and students remained critical of the military regime, and were in the vanguard of opposition to Suchinda's prime ministership. While most attention has been given to Chamlong's leadership of the opposition, academics and especially students played major roles in the May 1992 uprising. However, prior to this it was intellectuals, in alliance with NGOs, who maintained pressure on the NPKC. Examples include a petition by 99 academics opposing the coup (*Journal of Contemporary Asia* 1991: vol. 21, no. 4), and a state-ment by the president of the Student's Federation of Thailand arguing that the main obstacle to democracy was not vote-buying as alleged by the NPKC, but military coups (*BP* 23 June 1991). And, consistent with the line adopted in 1988, student groups were loud in their calls for an elected prime minister following the 1992 election (*BPWR* 14 February 1992).

Business

In the 1960s, Riggs characterised Thailand as a 'bureaucratic polity' which included a theory of the relationship between business and government. In summary, Riggs (1961: 97–8) believed that business could have little influence upon the government and that business people are reduced to positions of 'pariah entrepreneurs'. He argued that the political elite:

> is not politically responsible to the business community, [and] *there is no reason to think that it would want to adopt or enforce any general rules protecting the business interests of the businessmen* (Riggs 1966: 252, emphasis in original).

The theoretical position embodied in this perspective has been criticised elsewhere (Hewison 1989b: Ch. 2), but the view that Thailand is a bureaucratic polity has remained a popular character-isation. In spite of the fact that pariah entrepreneurship was a central concept in Riggs's bureaucratic polity, it has fallen from the lexicon of Thai studies. The reason is that it increasingly appears as an unrealistic description of actuality.

A number of publications have indicated the increasing signifi-cance of capitalists in Thailand's political economy (cf. Hewison 1989b). In the political arena, it has been shown that, in terms of

direct participation in government, business representation has
increased greatly. For example, Anek (1988: 454–5) notes that, since
Kriangsak's time, business persons have made up just less than
one-half of the Cabinet.

In the sphere of interest-based lobbying, business has apparently
become a significant player. In 1987 there were more than 200
Bangkok-based trade associations and chambers of commerce. Perhaps more significant, however, has been the rapid expansion of
provincial chambers. In 1979 there were four of these, but by 1987
there were 72 (Anek 1988: 456–9). But the increased prevalence of
such associations does not, *ipso facto*, mean political influence. At
least publicly, all of these associations adopt standardised lobbying
techniques, and express satisfaction with the results they obtain in
dealing with the government and state (Anek 1988: 457, 461). Even
so, it should be noted that the formation of these chambers had
government support, and there is a stated determination to make
them independent associations (Anek 1988: 459).

A formal mechanism of business–government relations has been
established in recent years in the form of the Joint Public–Private
Consultative Committee (JPPCC). This Committee was formed in
1981, after years of attempts to formalise the relationship between
the bureaucracy, government and business (Kraiyudht 1990: 117).
The JPPCC included the prime minister, the ministers responsible
for economic matters, and representatives of banking, industries and
commerce associations, and was provided with a secretariat within
the NESDB. Similar provincial Committees are also being encouraged, and all of this has had the financial support of the USAID
(Anek 1988: 460).

The emphasis on private interest lobbies by Anek (1988) and
Kraiyudht (1990) represents the instrumentalist approach to capital–
state relations characteristic of recent pluralist and corporatist
theory. While such relations are important, significant structural
constraints and imperatives should not be overlooked (cf. Hewison
1989a: Ch. 2). For example, the fact that the economy is now
unambiguously capitalist means that state officials must be increasingly cognisant of the general interests of capital, for these interests
are increasingly those of the fiscal agencies of the state.

Less formal, and arguably as significant, arrangements tend to
pervade the relationship between business people and state officials
especially, but not exclusively, in the countryside. This is the phenomenon of 'dark influences' (*chao pho* or *itthiphon muet*), important local business people whose leverage is based on both their
businesses and their control of the not-so-legal aspects of business
(prostitution, gaming, murder, drugs, logging, land encroachment,
weapons trade, smuggling, and protection rackets). Both Turton

(1984: 56–9) and Anderson (1990) note the increased political significance of these persons in recent decades, but neither says much about their role in business. Indeed, the history of such groups is not well known, and literature exhibits a reluctance to examine links between 'dark influences', business and officials.[10] Here it is only possible to suggest some lines of inquiry.

First, these groups have developed at a crucial economic conjuncture. No further discussion of rapid economic development is required here, except to note that regional GDP growth has also been rapid, and that agricultural diversification has created considerable scope for surplus extraction in the countryside. This has created many opportunities for the development of wealth in regional towns and cities. Anderson (1990: 39–40) has noted the rapid expansion of provincial business ('small-town entrepreneurs') generally. These people have developed lifestyles that are 'competitive with those of locally stationed state officials . . . [and] put down strong local roots, social as well as commercial', in contrast to officials, who are regularly transferred, and who rarely develop such ties. Many of these local 'godfather' capitalists have become immensely wealthy, with no area of economic activity outside their influence (*FEER* 18 April 1991).

Second, rural areas have become more politically significant in recent years. The sub-district development plans and funding launched by Kukrit Pramoj's government in 1975 and later policies on decentralisation have had a significant impact on regional development. In addition, parliamentary representation has meant that rural areas have become important political bases. For example, the Northeast region has the largest number of potential voters in the country. Hence, General Chaovalit emphasised the economic and social development of the Northeast (the Green Isarn Project) when establishing his party political base in the late eighties and early nineties. Middlemen (and most are men) who have become so significant in business and trade are also middlemen in politics (*FEER* 23 April 1987). Money is now central to electoral politics, and the pattern of seeking financial support from business has meant that 'influential persons' have been legitimised, even when their money has been derived from illegal activities.

Third, the combination of these political and economic conjunctures means that these 'godfathers' are often all-powerful in their areas. Thus, when *Sia* Leng was shot, and some criticised General Sunthorn's visit to wish him well, the Supreme Command Headquarters responded that the visit was justified because *Sia* Leng had assisted the Army's Green Isarn Project (*BP* 18 April 1990). Others have been elected to parliament or had their puppet MPs elected (*FEER* 18 April 1991).[11]

The upshot of all of this is that the pariah entrepreneurs, if they ever existed, are now of the past. Business is not merely an interest group, however. In its relations with state officials, through its economic power, and by its formal and informal organisations, capital has become a predominant power. State officials may not like it, but they now understand that capitalists have aggregated tremendous power for their class. State economic policy clearly and unambiguously reflects this (cf. Hewison 1989a,b). Hence, the Thai state may accurately be described as a capitalist state.

In the 1991 coup, state officials, and especially the military, have made a last ditch effort to conserve their state against the capitalist class's movement to make the state more bourgeois. It appears as if this effort may have been in vain. The many links that tie the modern state to capitalist accumulation were well illustrated when Narong Wongwan was nominated as prime minister following the March 1992 election. Narong, accused by the US government of links with drug dealing, offered to stand down *only if trade was likely to be affected* (*BPWR* 10 April 1992). When Suchinda was nominated to replace Narong, most major business groups refused to support him, with the significant exception being the huge CP conglomerate, which had received big contracts during the NPKC period (for details on CP see Hewison 1989b: Ch. 5).

Buddhist sects

Buddhism is Thailand's state religion, and is a powerful element of both nationalist rhetoric and of social and political control (Ishii 1968). Indeed, many argue that being Buddhist is an essential part of being 'Thai' (Kukrit 1983: 203–4). Even so, this state dominance of religion has not gone unchallenged. The emergence of sects contesting official religious interpretations has been a common phenomenon. For example, Jackson (1988:136–9) and Chatthip (1984) list a range of millenarian rebellions dating back several centuries. Often these challenges have coincided with rapid social, economic and political change. Examples include the Holy Men's Rebellions throughout Laos and Northeastern Siam at the turn of the century as both French colonialists and the Siamese monarchy expanded their activities in the region (Gunn 1990: Ch. 5; Chatthip: 1984). Similarly, in the late 1920s and early 1930s, and again during Sarit's premiership in the late 1950s, both periods of great political and economic change, official Buddhism was challenged (see, for example, *Bangkok Times* 2 July 1928; and *Siam Rath Weekly Review*, issues of June–July 1959). In the contemporary period these challenges have re-emerged in the guise of the 'middle class' ascetic

Santi Asoke and the more capitalist and materialist oriented Thammakai sects.[12]

Santi Asoke in particular represented a serious challenge to state Buddhism, a significant symbol of the state. In addition, Santi Asoke has been overtly political, supporting former Young Turk and retired governor of Bangkok, Chamlong and his Palang Dhamma (Dhammic Force) Party.[13] As Taylor (1990: 139) notes, these sects drew 'antipathy from conservative institutions (secular and religious)'. While one might argue, as Suwanna (1990: 397) does, that these movements attempt to meet the spiritual needs of Buddhists in a rapidly changing society, they also challenge the establishment and one element of the triumvirate of state ideology.

During the period of Chatichai's premiership a remarkable series of scandals involving the monkhood came to light. To name but a few, monks were found to be selling religious artefacts (*Nation* 13 January 1989), falsifying temple records (*BP* 8 January 1992), and of having relations with women, including the infamous cases of *Phra* Nikorn (*BP* 23 July 1990) and *Phrakhru* Jiab. The latter was also accused of bribing other senior monks and of being involved in deceiving or drugging a very senior monk (*Nation* 19 July 1989; *Nation Afternoon Extra* 6 July 1989).

Combined, these events and the challenges posed by the sects suggested that the tenets of official Buddhism were in danger of being subverted (see *FEER* 4 July 1991). By 1989 there were already calls for the monastic laws, which dated from Sarit's time, to be updated (*Nation* 6 October 1989). Whatever an individual's position on any particular case, it is reasonable to assume that conservatives viewed this malaise with trepidation. Certainly the press called for a cleansing of Buddhism so that it could be reinstated as a true symbol of the nation (state). Unlike other groups, these sects do not necessarily threaten privilege, but undercut an important element of state ideology. More than this, the continual cycle of 'problems' and scandals has tended to reinforce conservatives in their view that traditional values and order are under threat.

Conclusion

It was noted above that the military-centred and society-focused perspectives are not necessarily mutually exclusive. How might they be brought together? The following is an approach to this question.

Basically, Thai social and political life has reached a watershed. In a period of rapid change a new 'logic', a new amalgam, of social and political forces is emerging to reshape the Thai state. This logic is one more closely aligned to the capitalist structure of economic relations. These changes have produced new ways of thinking and organising in all areas of Thai life. As if to illustrate this outlook, the statement by academic petitioners against the military coup contended:

> In recent years Thailand's economy has become larger, more complex, and more closely linked to the world economy. Such an economic system can progress further only within a liberal economic and political framework, which permits everyone the freedom to participate and to organise to claim their economic rights . . . Modern Thailand has become a complex, plural society. The democratic system . . . provides every individual an equal opportunity to voice opinions and to participate in determining the future course of the country without domination by any one privileged group . . . (cited in *Journal of Contemporary Asia* 1991: vol. 21, no. 4).

Such changes have also produced a reaction, and it is the Class 5 Conservatives who best exemplify this. Their victory over other cliques within the Army, and the support they have received from senior bureaucrats, represents the triumph, if momentary, of an old guard. They object to what they perceive as a relentless chipping away at the edifice that is the Thai state, the national interest, and, not coincidentally, their privileges, perquisites and status. Their 1991 coup represents many things, including inter-clique rivalry, but also a last ditch bid to shore up their increasingly anachronistic position against the charge of a new group of 'Young Turks', not in the military this time, but in business. The events of May 1992 illustrate the vicious lengths the conservatives were prepared to go to maintain the existing but crumbling state.

Capitalists may not necessarily be recognised as a natural enemy of the state or the conservatives. Indeed, they may well be considered as an ally—in the past capitalists have entered into numerous political and economic alliances with the monarchy, aristocracy, military and bureaucrats—but enemies they are. As Marx and Engels (1973: 72–9) noted almost 150 years ago, the history of the bourgeoisie is one of alliance and coalition as it emerges to eventually become a truly revolutionary force.

Business, as noted above, is not merely an interest group for, as capital, it is now in the process of entrenching its class rule. An important element of this process is to firmly establish its political rule and prove its capacity to rule. Where this challenges the existing state, and the conservatives who assign to themselves the task of protecting the state, is in the need to reshape the state. No class can merely take hold of the existing state; as Marx and Engels (in Engels 1973: 66) argued for the proletariat following the defeat of the Paris

Commune, it was not sufficient to merely '. . . lay hold of the ready-made state machinery, and wield it for its own purposes'. In Thailand, the bourgeoisie must now continue its active reform of the state, its apparatus, the logic of its operations, and its ideology. By its nature this process will continue to pose a threat to conservative values, the old order and institutions, and entrenched interests.

This capitalist revolution receives part of its momentum from an alliance with the middle class, most vividly demonstrated in the opposition to Suchinda in May 1992 (*FEER*, 21 May 1992). The alliance grows out of a coincidence of interests—at this time both capitalist and middle-class interests are served by increased political representation and, more importantly, greater influence over policy-making. Hence, a continuing conservative response from various increasingly anachronistic interests is to be anticipated.

The coup, then, may not be the last for Thailand, but coup-making becomes increasingly reactionary and is seen as such. Indeed, Dr Pramote Nakhonthap's description of the coup as the 'action of barbarians' (*BP* 23 June 1991) was tragically confirmed by the murder of perhaps a hundred peaceful protesters in Bangkok between 17 and 20 May 1992. Equally, as both Democrat MP Surin Pitsuwan and former prime ministerial adviser Kraisak Choonhavan predicted (Australian Broadcasting Corporation, Radio National, 2 November 1991), the contrast between a civilian regime, where people had the right to call on MPs for support and to make public political points, and the authoritarian military regime became ever more conspicuous.

Yet prior to the Bangkok massacre even the NPKC had come grudgingly to recognise this. Its inability to completely regain control of the political agenda or to redirect civil society was indicated soon after the coup by the fact that even its hand-picked prime minister showed himself to be not wholly acceptable to the NPKC as he would not do all his master's bidding. And, even though effectively 'fixed', as the March 1992 election approached, the NPKC found itself facing a range of significant challenges.

For example, a coalition of groups, led by NGOs and intellectuals, mounted a concerted campaign against the NPKC's constitution, effectively forcing revisions, following the monarchy's intervention to demand compromise (*BPWR* 13, 20 December 1991). Following this, the NPKC was forced to compromise and accept the creation of a panel that was to act as a watchdog for electoral fraud. Interestingly, this panel was made up of a number of opponents of the NPKC, and included representatives of labour, academics, NGOs, the media and students (*BP* 9 January 1992). In the past it might have been expected that such groups would have been effectively censored; this time, in spite of threats, they have remained vocal. It was too much for one NPKC leader (*BPWR* 21 February 1992), who seemed to feel that his group should have been appreciated rather than denigrated for running the coup: 'This is a lesson for the NPKC in staging a coup. It's full of bitterness.'

Even if the constitutional changes were not major and the electoral watchdog panel lacked power and was an attempt to quieten opposition, the concessions required from the military were significant and symbolic. However, the military conservatives retained control of the new parliament, and eventually nominated Suchinda as prime minister, unleashing a further round of ever-larger protests in Bangkok and the provinces.

The negotiated settlement, belatedly brokered by the King, *does not* suggest an unambiguous victory for the democratic forces of the bourgeois revolution. Suchinda resigned, but was effectively pardoned of any responsibility for the massacre by the King. The constitution was changed, but by a parliament put in place by the NPKC. Class 5 has not been destroyed and, most importantly, the King's intervention represents another attempt to save military conservatism. With perhaps up to a hundred slaughtered, the King only intervened when it appeared that the military was about to turn on itself (see *Asian Wall Street Journal*, 21 May 1992). In preventing this he has ensured that the struggle between the military and civilian politicians will continue. This was clearly seen in the campaign for the September 1992 election, where the military continued to destabilise the political situation and threaten its critics. The next elected government, like its predecessors, will face challenges from a conservative military.

Notes

1 This chapter draws on a paper originally presented at the first Thailand Update Conference, at the Australian National University, in November 1991, and published as Working Paper No. 4 of Murdoch University's Asia Research Centre (January 1992). In that paper it was suggested that political conflict was likely to intensify, and the tragic events of May 1992 have verified that prediction. This chapter was written to explain how the military coup of 1991 might be understood, and while the basic theoretical points remain valid, I have attempted to also take account of the events until late May 1992. The chapter is dedicated to those who fell under the guns commanded by General Suchinda Kraprayoon and his Class 5 cohorts during the Bangkok Massacre. The author acknowledges the useful criticisms provided by Andrew Brown, Suchai Treerat, Dick Robison and Garry Rodan.

2 It is difficult to know how the public views these allegations and whether they compare them with the alleged corruption of civilian politicians. One reason for this is that the need to make money has become all-pervasive, causing some social critics to question the impact of 'radical baht-ism' on Thai and Buddhist values. In the early 1970s, two social scientists stated: 'Money is the most crucial factor determining the behavior of the Thai people. . .' (Morell & Chai-Anan 1981: 21). More recently, a pithy letter to the *Bangkok Post* (1 August 1990) claimed that 'money is God' and that there is a new Triple Gem for Bangkokians: the Benz, the condo, and the mobile phone; Nirvana is the golf course and the temple is the Stock Exchange of Thailand.

3 A trite example of this might be to note that the NPKC's 1991 constitution is the first to be faxed to and from the King (*FEER*, 14 March 1991).

4 Max Weber once made a similar point concerning the German bourgeoisie, in noting that while it was economically powerful, the bourgeoisie had not clearly demonstrated a capacity for political rule (Bottomore 1989: 130).

5 Anderson views the October 1973 student-led uprising as Thailand's 1789, but such a perspective does not pay due regard to the overthrow of the absolute monarchy in 1932. Certainly, though, Thailand still awaits its equivalent of the June 1848 revolution, which Engels (1973: 62) described as 'the first great battle between proletariat and bourgeoisie'.

6 For lack of space some significant groups have been excluded from this discussion. For example, a range of non-governmental development organisations, which have emerged since the mid-seventies, are not discussed (cf. Gohlert 1990). Significant, but also omitted, are political parties, women's groups, local government, and the mass media.

7 Social security has been under discussion at least since the overthrow of the absolute monarchy in 1932, when Pridi Phanomyong proposed a national system, but this was eventually rejected by the King and the People's Party (see Thak 1978: 108–237). Other proposals were presented in 1954, 1957 and 1970, but all failed to materialise (*Bangkok Bank Monthly Review* June 1970: 139–40).

8 They would continue to be called unions, however, in order to comply with international labour conventions. It is worth noting that nine of the country's ten largest unions were Bangkok-based state enterprise unions (Brown & Frenkel 1993).

9 It is recognised that there was a strong relationship between Pridi Phanomyong and students at Thammasat University (cf. Prizzia & Narong 1974: Ch. 2).

10 Chakrit & Hagensick (1973) do not mention crime even though their discussion of local elites includes notes concerning entertainment,

massage parlours, logging and construction, all areas where 'dark influences' have been at work. The conclusion is that either these local 'mafia' are recent phenomena or the authors' methods deliberately ignored such elements (e.g. the lucrative drug trade is not mentioned). However, in a later study Chakrit (1981: 45, 72–6, 119) does suggest at least an awareness of the significance of these factors, especially in eastern Thailand. Nevertheless, he does not analyse the significance of the phenomenon.

11 A useful example of legitimacy being bestowed on the wealthy, no matter what the source of money, was recently provided when gambling mogul and 'influential person' Soh Thanavisut, formerly an adviser to Pramarn Adireksarn when he was Minister of the Interior under Chatichai, was pictured with the 'legitimate' wealth of department store tycoon Suthikiat Chirathivat celebrating new year (*Nation* 6 January 1992). To emphasise that this is not only an issue for civilians, the military-dominated coalition, established after the 1992 election, initially selected a 'godfather' for prime minister. The nominee was rumoured to have a doubtful background, having been refused a visa to the US because of alleged connections with the drug trade (*BPWR*, issues of April 1992).

12 Thammakai's Abbot, Phra Thammachayo, is reported to wear robes of Swiss cloth, to have a number of luxury vehicles, including a Rolls Royce, and uses a Mercedes for his alms-round (Taylor 1990: 141). Thammakai has also attempted to integrate symbols of the Thai state (Zehner 1990: 424–5). This appears to be in stark contrast with Santi Asoke's rejection of materialism and national symbolism.

13 Class 5 can be assumed to have opposed this sect because of Chamlong's role in it.

References

Almond, Gabriel A. 1991, 'Capitalism and Democracy', *PS: Political Science & Politics*, vol. 24, no. 3, pp. 467–74

Anderson, Ben 1977, 'Withdrawal Symptoms: Social and Cultural Aspects of the October 6 Coup', *Bulletin of Concerned Asian Scholars*, vol. 9, no. 3, pp. 13–30

—— 1990, 'Murder and Progress in Modern Siam', *New Left Review*, no. 181, pp. 33–48

Anek Laothamatas 1988, 'Business and Politics in Thailand: New Patterns of Influence', *Asian Survey*, vol. 28 no. 4, pp. 451–70

Bandhit Thammatreerat 1991, 'Chiwit khabuan kan sahaphap raengngan thai phaidai rabop ro so cho', *Chomna raengngan thai*, ed. Bandhit Thammatreerat, Arom Phongphangan Foundation, Bangkok

Blake, W.T. 1955, *Thailand Journey*, The Travel Book Club, London

Board of Investment 1990, *The Investment Environment in Thailand*, Office of the Prime Minister, Bangkok
—— 1991, *Key Investment Indicators of Thailand*, Office of the Prime Minister, Bangkok
Bottomore, Tom 1989, 'Max Weber and the Capitalist State', *Democracy and the Capitalist State*, ed. Graeme Duncan, Cambridge University Press, Cambridge
Brown, Andrew 1991a, 'Thai Unions Since the Overthrow of the Chartchai Government', *Thai-Yunnan Project Newsletter*, no. 14, pp. 1–2
—— 1991b, 'History of Thai Unions', *Thai-Yunnan Project Newsletter*, no. 15, pp. 2–7
—— & Frenkel, Stephen 1993, 'Union Unevenness and Insecurity in Thailand', *Organized Labor in the Asia–Pacific Region: A Comparative Study of Trade Unionism in Nine Countries*, ed. Stephen Frenkel, ILR Press, Ithaca, forthcoming
Chai-Anan Samudavanija 1982a, *The Thai Young Turks*, Institute of Southeast Asian Studies, Singapore
—— 1982b, *Yang toek kap thahan prachatippatai: kan wikhro botbat thahan nai kanmuang thai*, Bankit, Bangkok
—— 1990, 'The Military and Modern Thai Political System', *Development, Modernization, and Tradition in Southeast Asia: Lessons from Thailand*, eds Pinit Ratanakul & U Kyaw Than, Mahidol University, Bangkok
Chakrit Noranitipadungkarn 1981, *Elites, Power Structure and Politics in Thai Communities*, National Institute of Development Administration, Bangkok
—— & Hagensick, A. Clarke 1973, *Modernizing Chiangmai: A Study of Community Elites in Urban Development*, National Institute of Development Administration, Bangkok
Chatthip Nartsupha 1984, 'The Ideology of "Holy Men" Revolts in North East Thailand', *History and Peasant Consciousness in South East Asia*, eds Andrew Turton & Shigeharu Tanabe, National Museum of Ethnology, Osaka, pp. 111–34
Democratic Soldiers (n.d.), *Khosaeno naewthang kae banha khong chat*, Chutima kanphim, Bangkok
Engels, Frederick ed. 1973, 'Preface to the English Edition [of the "Manifesto of the Communist Party"] of 1888', *Karl Marx: The Revolutions of 1848*, ed. D. Fernbach, Penguin, London, pp. 62–6
Family Health Division 1984, *Basic Facts in Family Health in Thailand*, Department of Health, Ministry of Health, Bangkok
Girling, John L.S. 1981, *Thailand: Society and Politics*, Cornell University Press, Ithaca
Gohlert, Ernst W. 1990, *Power and Culture: The Struggle Against Poverty in Thailand*, White Orchid, Bangkok
Gunn, Geoffrey C. 1990, *Rebellion in Laos: Peasant and Politics in a Colonial Backwater*, Westview Press, Boulder
Hewison, Kevin 1985, 'The State and Capitalist Development in Thailand', *Southeast Asia: Essays in the Political Economy of Structural Change*, eds Richard Higgott & Richard Robison, Routledge & Kegan Paul, London

—— 1989a, *Bankers and Bureaucrats: Capital and the Role of the State in Thailand*, Yale University Southeast Asia Monograph No. 34, New Haven

—— 1989b, *Politics and Power in Thailand*, Journal of Contemporary Asia Publishers, Manila

Hirsch, Philip 1986, 'Dam on the River Kwai', *Inside Asia*, November-December, pp. 45–6

—— 1990, *Development Dilemmas in Rural Thailand*, Oxford University Press, Singapore

—— & Lohmann, Larry 1989, 'Contemporary Politics of Environment in Thailand', *Asian Survey*, vol. 29, no. 4, pp. 439–51

Ishii, Yoneo 1968, 'Church and State in Thailand', *Asian Survey*, vol. 8, no. 10, pp. 864–71

Jackson, Peter A. 1988, 'The Hupphaasawan Movement: Millenarian Buddhism among the Thai Political Elite', *Sojourn*, vol. 3, no. 2, pp. 134–70

Jessop, Bob 1978, 'Capitalism and Democracy: The Best Possible Shell?' *Power and the State*, eds G. Littlejohn, et al., Croom Helm, London

Kraiyudht Dhiratayakinant 1990, 'Role of the Private Sector in the Thai Economy: Now and in the Future', *Thailand on the Move: Stumbling Blocks and Breakthroughs*, ed. Suchart Prasith-rathsint, Thai University Research Association, Bangkok

Kukrit Pramoj 1983, *Kukrit Pramoj: His Wit and Wisdom*, Duang Kamol Books, Bangkok

Marx, Karl & Engels, Frederick eds 1973, 'Manifesto of the Communist Party', *Karl Marx: The Revolutions of 1848*, ed. D. Fernbach, Penguin, Harmondsworth

Morell, David & Chai-Anan Samudavanija 1981, *Political Conflict in Thailand: Reform, Reaction, Conflict*, Oelgeschlager, Gunn & Hain, Cambridge

Ministry of Public Health 1988, *Thailand Mini Health Profile 1988*, Bangkok

Nation 1988, *Nam Choan Inquiry: The Environmental Dilemma of the Decade*, Nation Publishing, Bangkok

National Economic and Social Development Board (n.d.), *The Sixth National Economic and Social Development Plan (1987–1991)*, Office of the Prime Minister, Bangkok

Ogilvy & Mather 1991, *Pocket Guide to Media in Thailand 1991*, Ogilvy & Mather, Bangkok

Petras, James 1989, 'State, Regime and the Democratization Muddle', *Journal of Contemporary Asia*, vol. 19, no. 1, pp. 26–32

Prizzia, Ross & Narong Sinsawasdi 1974, *Thailand: Student Activism and Political Change*, Duang Kamol, Bangkok

Project for Ecological Recovery 1991, 'The People's Forum', Bangkok, 13–17 October

Riggs, Fred W. 1961, 'A Model for the Study of Thai Society', *Thai Journal of Public Administration*, vol. 1, no. 4, pp. 83–125

—— 1966, *Thailand: The Modernization of a Bureaucratic Polity*, East-West Center Press, Honolulu

Shalardchai Ramitanondh 1989, 'Forests and Deforestation in Thailand: A Pandisciplinary Approach', *Culture and Environment in Thailand*, eds Siam Society, The Siam Society, Bangkok

Somsak Tambunlertchai & Suthiphand Chirathivat 1990, 'Management of Thailand's International Economic and Trade Relations', *Thailand on the Move: Stumbling Blocks and Breakthroughs*, ed. Suchart Prasith-rathsint, Thai University Research Association, Bangkok

Suchit Bunbongkarn 1987, *The Military in Thai Politics 1981–86*, Institute of Southeast Asian Studies, Singapore

Sulak Sivaraksa 1980, *Siam in Crisis*, Komol Keemthong Foundation, Bangkok

Surin Maisrikrod & Suparra Limsong 1991, 'Thailand: Deconstructing the Coup', *Pacific Research*, vol. 4, no. 3, pp. 3–4, 8

Suwanna Satha-Anand 1990, 'Religious Movements in Contemporary Thailand: Buddhist Struggles for Modern Relevance', *Asian Survey*, vol. 30, no. 4, pp. 395–408

Taylor, J.L. 1990, 'New Buddhist Movements in Thailand: An "Individualistic Revolution", Reform and Political Dissonance', *Journal of Southeast Asian Studies*, vol. 21, no. 1, pp. 135–54

Thak Chaloemtiarana (ed.) 1978, *Thai Politics: Extracts and Documents 1932–1957*, Social Science Association of Thailand, Bangkok

—— 1979, *Thailand: The Politics of Despotic Paternalism*, Thai Khadi & Social Science Association of Thailand, Bangkok

Turton, Andrew 1984, 'Limits of Ideological Domination and the Formation of Social Consciousness', *History and Peasant Consciousness in South East Asia*, eds Andrew Turton & Shigeharu Tanabe, National Museum of Ethnology, Osaka

Zehner, Edwin 1990, 'Reform Symbolism of a Thai Middle-Class Sect: The Growth and Appeal of the Thammakai Sect', *Journal of Southeast Asian Studies*, vol. 21, no. 2, pp. 402–26

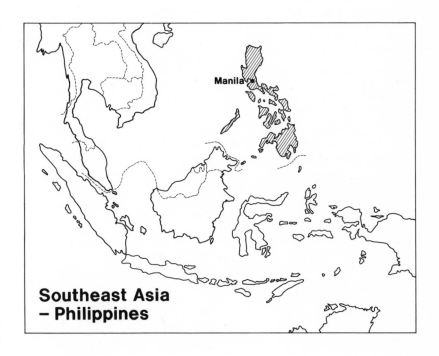

**Southeast Asia
– Philippines**

Manila

Philippines: Basic social and economic data

Population (1990)	60.7m
Population density (1990)	208 persons per sq. km
Average annual population growth	2.6%
Urban population (1990)	41.8%
Total labour force (1990)	24.5m
Major ethnic groups	Indo-Malay, Mestizo, Chinese
Capital city	Manila
Population (1991 est.)	7.9m (Metro Manila)
Land area	300 000 sq. km
Official language	Tagalog
Other main languages	English; 87 local dialects
Administrative division	14 regions
Education, enrolments	
Primary (1990)	9.6m
Secondary (1990)	3.49m
University (1990)	1.46m
Adult literacy rate (1989)	86%
Health	
Life expectancy (1989)	64 yrs
Infant mortality/1000 (1989)	43
Persons/hospital bed (1989)	600
Persons/physician (1989)	6700
Economy	
GNP at market prices (1989)	US$42.7 bn
Real GNP per capita (1989)	US$700 .
GNP growth rate (1990)	2.5%
Trade	
Exports, value (1990)	US$8.2 bn
Imports, value (1990)	US$13.0 bn
Main imports (1990)	Machinery & transport equipment 25.9%, manufactures 17.3%, unclassified goods 15.8%
Main exports (1990)	Unclassified goods 31.3%, manufactures 25.7%, food & live animals 13.1%
Foreign debt (1990)	US$28.9 bn
Foreign reserves (1990)	US$2.0 bn
Energy consumption/capita	
(kg coal equiv. in 1989)	295
Communications	
Rail (1990)	539 km
Roads, paved (1988)	159 069 km
Religions	Christian, Muslim

Sources: Far Eastern Economic Review Asia Yearbook 1991; The Far East and Australasia 1992 (Europa Publications); United Nations Economic and Social Commission for Asia and the Pacific Newsletter; Doing Business in the Philippines, 1991 Supplement, Price Waterhouse; Key Indicators of Developing Asian and Pacific Countries 1991, Asian Development Bank.

8 Class and state power in the Philippines
Jane Hutchison[1]

When Corazon Aquino came to power in 1986 on a wave of popular support, she restored the institutions of democratic government to the Philippines, thereby ending fourteen years of authoritarian rule under Ferdinand Marcos. Partly because her government's initial support was so great, expectations were high. However, at the end of her term, most assessments have considered Aquino's rule a disappointment. It has been argued in the Philippine press and in the academic literature that change at the political level has not produced more fundamental social and economic transformations. Often cited examples of this include: land reform under Aquino has been inconsequential (cf. Hayami, Quisumbing & Adriano 1990; Adriano 1992); the state still is not able to effectively tax the rich[2]; and half of the population continues to live below the poverty line in conditions of gross inequality.

The Aquino government's democratic reforms have managed to do little more than reinvigorate a class structure that, in the last years of the Marcos administration, was threatened by economic crisis and social unrest. In political terms, the wealthy families that dominated electoral processes in the pre-martial law era have been returned to prominence in the restored Congress. This chapter considers the relationship between class interests and state power which lies behind 'the restoration of elite democracy' (Bello & Gershman 1990) in the Philippines.

In much of the writing on state and society in Southeast Asia, including the Philippines, political and economic power has been understood in personalistic terms. The dominant social relations are considered to be those of kinship and clientelism. Accordingly, patronage is taken to be both the principal source and motive of political power and the most important means of economic accumulation and redistribution. This discussion does not discount the importance of clientelist politics in the Philippines situation, but attempts to place personalism within a structural context. Specifically, the personal power base of the authoritarian regime of Marcos is situated in longer term processes of class formation and state power (Rosenberg 1974; Doronila 1985; Wolters 1989) and, from this perspective, the significance of regime change under Aquino is considered.

The chapter begins with a brief historical overview of the relationship between class interests and state power in the colonial and post-colonial eras of this century, focusing on the electoral successes of the dominant economic class. It is argued that the break in the pattern of political contestation, which occurred with the switch to authoritarian rule in 1972, occurred within the context of social transformation and conflict associated with capitalist development and industrialisation, resulting in an increase in state power. Under Aquino, it is suggested, the restoration of democracy has consolidated class forces and weakened state power. In the final section of the chapter, the relationship between class interests and state power is further highlighted in a discussion of state intervention in relations between capital and labour. Here, continuities in the role of the state indicate the class base of the Aquino regime.

Before Marcos: Colonialism and electoral politics

Early this century, the United States' colonial administration introduced the institutions and processes of democratic government without regard for social and economic reform (Abueva 1988). During the period of Spanish rule, the legal precepts of land ownership and commercialisation of agriculture through foreign trade had intensified socio-economic inequalities in the Philippines.

The American period did little to alter this situation, further entrenching a landed class. The private ownership of land was secured with the introduction of government-recognised title deeds (Kerkvliet 1979: 22) while proposals for land reform were not implemented. Similarly, economic policy was directed at the expansion and 'modernisation' of agricultural production rather than structural change and the redistribution of profits through taxation (Owen 1971). In the absence of reform, members of the dominant economic class were able to use their wealth and influence to win political office. Initially at a local, but soon also at a national level, land owners were able to consolidate their economic interests through the use of state power (Doronila 1985: 101). Thus, in the American period, the processes of democratisation reproduced a class structure consisting of powerful landowners, an educated, but economically dependent, urban middle class, poor tenant farmers and wage workers in agriculture and the small commercial and industrial sector.

Industrialisation

In the postwar period, a free-trade agreement with the United States allowed agricultural products to be exported and manufactured goods to be imported duty free. Within a few years, this resulted in a serious balance of payments problem as the cost of imports outweighed the income from exports. Prompted by the threat to class and state power from the Hukbalahap movement, the immediate interests of agricultural exporters were subordinated to a greater class interest and, in 1949, import and exchange controls were introduced (Doronila 1986: 41). These changes provided a stimulus to the local manufacturing sector. As previously imported consumer goods were assembled or made locally, the contribution of industry to gross domestic production (GDP) doubled between 1950 and 1960, while the contribution from agriculture fell almost 40 per cent. The strength of manufacturing growth is demonstrated by its 150 per cent leap in contribution to GDP for the same period (Jayasuriya 1987: 85). There were, of course, important social and political consequences from this era of rapid industrialisation. In particular, the configuration of class forces underwent change with the emergence of a domestic industrial class dependent upon state protection, and an expanded urban middle and working class (Doronila 1986: 41).

Despite social change associated with industrialisation, the Philippines continued to be governed by narrow class interests in the post-colonial era. Democracy failed to institutionalise the fundamental divisions in society in the arena of political contest as parties formed around personalities rather than sectional or ideological differences (Abueva 1988: 41). Elections became the vehicle for the transfer of political power between members of the dominant economic class[3]. However, this form of state and class power did not go unchallenged, for in the immediate postwar period both were threatened by the peasant-based Hukbalahap rebellion in Central Luzon (Kerkvliet 1979) and, in the late 1960s, by a resurgence of radical forces in urban Manila. The student-led 'politics of street protest' produced a split in the Filipino left and, in 1968, a new Communist Party of the Philippines (CPP) which, inspired by the Cultural Revolution in China and the war in Vietnam, condemned 'parliamentary revisionism' (Magno 1989: 373–4). There was, in the new generation of radical politics in the Philippines, 'the predisposition towards treating technology and material conditions as being of secondary importance to subjective will' (Magno 1988: 79). Eventually, in the mid-1980s, this ideological perspective contrib-

uted to the polarisation of forces opposed to Marcos and, after the
flight of the dictator, to the political isolation of the radical left.

Marcos and martial law

When elected to the Presidency in 1965, Marcos was faced with the
serious economic problem of a large balance of payments deficit.
Contractionary policies were introduced but could not be sustained
politically, and in the lead-up to the 1969 election, the Marcos
administration stepped up its strategy of financing the country's
capital shortfall through foreign loans (Jayasuriya 1987: 90). Unable
to stave off underlying economic difficulties and increasing social
conflict, Marcos also faced a personal political crisis, for the 1935
Constitution barred him from a third term in office. In September
1972, this conjunction of economic and political circumstances saw
the familiar pattern of postwar politics end with the declaration of
martial law (Abueva 1988: 53–5; Wurfel 1988: 18–21).

Concomitant with this declaration, Marcos dismantled the institutions and processes of democratic rule. The constitution was abandoned, the legislature shut-down, political parties banned, elections
postponed and various limitations on civil and media freedoms
imposed (de Guzman 1988: 269). The traditional political and
economic elite was left without a political base in the institutions
of government under martial law. Significantly, the regime was able
to exercise a greater degree of control over violence through the
confiscation of private armies and increased funding for the military.
When, in 1978, Marcos re-established the legislature and subsequently held national and local elections, he did not give up his
powers of decree nor did he meet any institutional opposition to his
authority. Although the Batasang Pambansa (National Assembly)
officially had powers to curb the President, it was dominated by his
Kilusang Bagong Lipunan (KBL) party and power remained concentrated in the executive and in the office of the President (Infante
1980: 14–15; Catilo & Tapaples 1988).

Under Marcos, state power was strengthened and centralised, but
its social base narrowed. His personal hold over political institutions
was reinforced by giving relatives and supporters control over
strategic sectors of the economy. As Koike (1989: 127–9) points
out, very few of the so-called cronies were members of the traditional economic and political elite. They were largely 'newcomers'
to business who derived their wealth and power from personal links
with the Palace.

Nevertheless, opposition to the regime from the non-crony business sector was, Hawes (1992: 158) argues, 'slow to develop'. While

some families were squeezed by state-backed monopolies in the agricultural sector, particularly in the sugar and coconut industries (cf. Hawes 1989), and others lost companies and contracts to cronies, the social and economic base of class rule was not undermined during martial law (Eviota 1990: 39). The state continued to protect private property (Hawes 1992: 154) and, as will be discussed in the final section of this chapter, the regime acted in the general interests of the dominant class through its repression of organised labour. Moreover, large land holdings were exempted from land reform and government protection of industry remained largely in place. It was not until the economic consequences of crony capitalism and the associated debt crisis threatened class interests that opposition to the Marcos regime from within the dominant economic class was mounted (Wurfel 1988: 238).

Marcos's strategy of extravagant borrowing in the face of economic problems and, increasingly, political difficulties, delayed, but ultimately magnified, the crisis facing his regime and the country (Jayasuriya 1987: 87–8). In the long term, the economy could not support such borrowing and, with changed conditions in the international capital market, crony capitalism was a recipe for economic and political disaster. Against the background of rising interest rates and an earlier attempt by Mexico to default on its international debt, the August 1983 assassination of political opposition figure, Benigno Aquino, saw sources of foreign loans for the Philippines dwindle. In late 1983, the inevitable happened when the IMF held back a US$630 million loan and the net transfer of funds became negative (Boyce 1990: 5–17).

With his ability to borrow severely curtailed, Marcos lost an important bulwark of political power. In the deepening crisis, moderates joined radicals in opposing the dictator. As Villegas (1988: 100) described it, 'People of different and even conflicting persuasions, from Communists, clerics and the big bourgeoisie to bored rich matrons, united to protest the Marcos dictatorship in rallies, symposia, teach-ins and other forms of mass action'. The emergence of 'coalition politics' after Benigno Aquino's assassination was, according to Lane (1990: 9), a new development in Philippine politics. Not surprisingly, the organised alliances between business, labour, students, professionals and the traditional opposition figures were short-lived[4]. Indeed, by the end of 1985, anti-Marcos coalition groups had splintered along lines that reflected deeper class divisions. Lane (1990: 20) argues that, by the final months of the Marcos regime, the movement was divided, leaving significant sections of the popular opposition unorganised.

A new regime: Corazon Aquino and democratic politics

The broad-based opposition to Marcos did not survive the transition from street politics to government. The diversity of the opposition that converged to see Aquino elected in early 1986, and the demonstration of popular and military support that finally saw Marcos ousted, had suggested fresh opportunities for socio-economic reform. However, in the lead-up to the Presidential election and in the months after it, the organised forces behind Aquino narrowed and moved to 'the social and ideological centre of Philippine society' (McCoy 1987: 18; Anderson 1988: 23–5).

The objectives of key players in the electoral campaign were always limited, and Aquino's promise to deliver democratic government did not include any serious attempt to carry out socio-economic reform (cf. Lapitan 1989: 236–7). This was, at least in part, due to the new President's search for political consolidation and the restoration of constitutional democracy. Aquino abandoned the constitutional and institutional basis of authoritarian rule by disbanding the Batasang Pambansa, replacing officials in local areas associated with the KBL party of Marcos with appointees from the new regime, and by setting up a Commission to draw up the formal framework of democratic government. These political moves tended to push socio-economic reform to the back-burner. At the same time, powerful interests were keen to stymie radical reformers.

Although excluded from the new administration, the radical opposition was not the initial target in attempts at political consolidation. While there was a release of political prisoners, promised reform of industrial legislation and ceasefire talks with representatives of the New People's Army (NPA), the so-called 'democratic space' was soon closed (Lane 1990: 21–92).

The movement that had brought Aquino to power had also unleashed forces that many near to her found threatening. Peasant and labour movements called for radical reforms which threatened entrenched class interests. Aquino responded by moving closer to the conservative elements in her coalition. In January 1987, the military opened fire on and killed more than twenty people protesting outside the Palace against delays in land reform. Several weeks later, ceasefire negotiations with the NPA broke down and the regime adopted a strategy of 'low intensity conflict' against counterinsurgency forces. Finally, after an October speech to the business sector, in which Aquino promised to toughen her stand against organised labour, police acted against striking workers and the offices of the trade union centre, Kilusang Mayo Uno (First of May Movement), were raided (Lane 1990: 87).

Meanwhile, left-supported candidates had done badly in the May 1987 Congressional elections. Bello and Gershman (1990: 42-3) argue that, 'the combination of money, high media visibility, leftist ambivalence [with electoral politics], and the continuing strong influence of patron-client relations won the day'[5]. When the votes were counted, the majority of seats in Congress were returned to wealthy landowners and big business interests. Moreover, most of those elected were members of the same 'traditional political families' that dominated the legislature in the pre-martial law years (Anderson 1988: 169).

Perspectives on power: Personal politics

Two important regime changes in the post-colonial era have not brought fundamental reorganisation to the Philippine class structure. Much of the literature that attempts to explain the continuities in state and society, despite political change, draws a connection between economic and political power based on personal relations. This can be seen in debates over the extent and nature of conflict within the dominant economic class following industrialisation and the political consequences of this conflict. According to one view, the growth of a domestic industrial class under state protection diversified the economic base of the ruling class. This caused divisions to emerge between exporters in agribusiness and import-substituting industrialists over policies in the areas of trade liberalisation and currency valuation which spilled into nationalist conflicts in the late 1950s and 1960s (Snow 1983: 18–32; Doronila 1986)[6]. On this basis, the introduction of authoritarian rule by Marcos is interpreted as a political response to resistance mounted against a more open economy, international competition and foreign investment (Stauffer 1979; Bello, Kinley & Elinson 1982: 127–39; Hawes 1989: 34–7).

Another perspective holds that, because many of the new industrialists came from old landed and commercial families (Nowak & Snyder 1974: 1148), kinship bonds muted economic divisions within the ruling class (Wurfel 1988: 57; Eviota 1990: 17). In this view, the lines of conflict in Philippine society are based on kinship—wealthy families compete with each other for political and economic power (see also Anderson 1988). Accordingly, Marcos's objectives in declaring martial law were largely personal, and his principal targets, Hutchcroft (1991: 425) argues, were not particular fractions of capital but, 'those rival clans who threatened his household'.

In a recent re-assessment of his earlier position, Hawes (1992: 153) considers that Marcos's intentions in introducing authoritarian

rule were indeed 'fundamentally political and aimed at [self] preservation rather than [economic] transformation' from import substitution to export-oriented development. In other words, the
pronouncements of the dictator on the direction of national economic development belied his more personal design for power.
Hawes (1992: 159) argues, however, that the political economy of
authoritarian rule under Marcos is not reducible to the avarice of
the President, his First Lady, family or followers. He finds instead
crony capitalism has deeper roots in Philippine political culture, one
in which the nexus between economic and political power is established by a tradition that values personal, rather than institutional
or sectional, loyalties. As such, notwithstanding the introduction of
martial law, personal politics under Marcos was 'an exaggeration
of, and not a deviation from, existing relationships between economic and political power' (see also Hutchcroft 1991).

Hawes' assessment of the Marcos regime draws on a dominant
theme in writing on state and society in the Philippines, one that
has been applied to the political and economic power of 'dominant
elites'—their particularistic demands upon the state and their relationship with other social groups. In the case of the latter, the
classical model of patron-client relations holds that individuals of
different economic status are bonded together by cultural sentiments
of obligation, gratitude and shame generated by the exchange of
goods and services. Political power at a local level is held to derive
from the *support* a patron receives from a client in return for favours
granted. It is, therefore, essentially a model of consensual politics
which, McCoy (1991: 106) argues, 'excludes considerations of
coercion and exploitation in favour of an imagined symbiosis'
between unequal individuals. Further, it is a view that generally
emerges from modernisation perspectives which juxtapose personalism with class relations. Because patron–client relations and kinship are associated with the persistence of tradition, they are held
to militate against class formation (see Wurfel 1988: 34).
Importantly, the understanding of class relations is limited to notions
of class consciousness and organised conflict along ideological
lines. In brief, it is a perspective that overlooks the structural
dimensions of power (see Rothstein 1979).

State formation

A number of writers have attempted to trace personal politics at a
national level to the processes of socio-economic change that have
accompanied capitalist development (Nowak & Snyder 1974;
Doronila 1985: 100; Wolters 1989: 55). Doronila, for example,

describes the process by which clientelist relations at a local level were transformed by the commercialisation of agriculture and gradually, with the growth of the state, incorporated into the national political arena. As patron-client relations between landlord and peasant broke down and the franchise was extended, landowners could no longer rely on a personal following to win electoral support. The personalised nature of political parties, however, required that electoral support be won through patronage rather than policies directed at competing social and economic interests (see Crouch 1984: 43). The linking of local and national level politics with the introduction of the institutions and processes of democratic government, created 'a conduit' through which public resources could be traded for political support (Nowak & Snyder 1974: 1148).

Doronila (1985: 109) argues that the increased dependence of local elites on the resources of national government served to strengthen the powers of the state. Therefore, long before Marcos declared martial law in 1972, 'authoritarian tendencies' had already emerged. This trend towards increased state power was furthered by the administration of the instruments of economic policy (such as import and exchange controls, export licences and tax exemptions) and by the exercise of military force against threats to state and class power.

During the 1960s, the role of the state in economic development was expanded. The 'green revolution' in agriculture saw a growth in public infrastructure investment and the extension of credit to farmers for the purchase of fertiliser and pesticides, essential to the growing of new, high-yield rice strains (Wolters 1989: 66–7). Administrative reforms carried out under Marcos centralised political responsibility for economic development (Nawawi 1982). Importantly, the state was increasingly the dispenser of foreign funds in the form of aid and loans.

Under Aquino, the institutional arrangements that concentrated power and resources in the hands of the office and the personage of the President were reversed. The 1987 Constitution decentralised political power from the executive to the restored bicameral legislature and increased the powers, responsibilities and resources of local government (de Guzman 1988: 280–1). At the same time, many of the functions normally taken on by the state have been picked up by groups in the private sector. Non-government organisations (NGOs) have, for example, shouldered a good deal of the responsibility for the provision and delivery of basic social services (Nemenzo 1989). The breakdown of the role of the state in these areas has been compounded by the legacy of international debt. In 1985, debt repayments ate into 24.3 per cent of the government's budget, but this proportion grew to almost 50.3 per cent two years later. In 1991, the debt service was greater than the budget for social services, general services and defence, yet still the debt continued to grow (Limqueco 1992). At the end of the same year, the dispersal of state powers entered a significant stage with the passing of the Local Government Code. Under this piece of legislation, a long list of services in the areas of agricultural extension, health, education, public works infrastructure and social welfare have been devolved to local government. Moreover, the same Code has provisions for the greater incorporation of NGOs in the institutional processes of local government (Brilliantes 1992).

The 'pull back' of state functions and powers that has occurred under Aquino suggests some opportunities for political engagement and empowerment at a 'grassroots' level (see Brilliantes 1992: 8–13). However, the configuration of class interests supporting the restoration of democracy have offered few concessions to the popular forces that helped to bring about a change of regime. As will be indicated in the final section of this chapter, a less interventionist role for the state in the arena of industrial relations has been of little benefit to organised labour. Further, in the following case study of state–labour relations in the colonial and post-colonial eras, it will be demonstrated that economic and political power in the Philippines cannot only be understood in terms of personal politics. Here the role of the state in the reproduction of class interests is emphasised. As Irwan (1989) points out in the case of South Korea, Indonesia and Thailand, political patronage cannot be isolated from broader social and political processes. He argues that, in each of these countries, the removal of patronage in relations between state and business has not occurred without popular struggle. In other words, the exercise of particularistic economic interests in politics has a base in class power.

State and labour

The labour movement in the Philippines has a long history but levels of unionisation remain low. The factors in this are socio-economic and political—they relate to the processes of capitalist development and industrialisation and the role of the state. With the rise of wage labour in agriculture and industry, the colonial and post-colonial state this century has intervened in the social relations of production to limit the possibilities of collective resistance which come with structural change.

Under Aquino, the legislative framework of industrial relations developed during the Marcos era has not been significantly reformed. Regime change in the mode of political representation did not extend to state intervention in the reproduction of class relations. The new regime did, however, respond to the militancy of the mid-1980s by moving to de-politicise industrial disputation through the enforcement of enterprise-based bargaining and the introduction of wage setting on a regional basis. As a result, without concomitant improvements in the labour market and structural change through industrial deepening (see Limqueco, McFarlane & Odhnoff 1989: 70–92), the political strength of organised labour has been checked.

Legal recognition

Since the American period, the Philippine state has sought to control the organisation of labour by granting it legal status but only under certain specific conditions. Unions first started to form in industries like printing and cigarette making in Manila in 1899. Three years later, the first federation of unions was established with 150 affiliates. In response to the resulting upsurge in strike activity, the United States colonial administration set up a Bureau of Labor in 1908 to, among other things, grant recognition to mutual benefit associations of workers in the largely agricultural workforce (Carroll 1961: 227).

In 1936, the newly formed Commonwealth government endeavoured to break the growing influence of the Communist Party (Partido Komunista ng Pilipinas) in a labour movement that had grown as industry and trade expanded in the decade after World War I. To oppose this, the Department of Labor was granted broad discretionary powers in the registration and de-registration of unions. Organised workers suspected of having radical political links could be investigated by the police and denied legal status and protection (Carroll 1961: 234–7). However, this strategy of discretionary recognition backfired as the extra-legal labour movement expanded so that, by 1940, the number of unregistered unions was greater than the registered (Wurfel 1959: 237).

During the Japanese occupation (1941–45), all forms of labour organisation were banned, but following the war, the rights of labour organisation were restored. However, the now independent state acted on old discretionary powers with renewed vigour (Wurfel 1959: 589–90).

In 1945, the newly formed Congress of Labor Organisation (CLO) was effective in uniting the labour movement and in the pursuit of labour interests. As Marcos would do in the 1970s, in 1949 the state sought to increase control over the labour movement by direct official sponsorship of a trade union federation, the National Confederation of Trade Unions. Attempts were then made to weaken rival federations through the withdrawal of legal recognition. Between 1950 and 1951, when state action against the Hukbalahap peasant movement came to a head, the CLO was caught up in the repression, being declared a Communist front and outlawed, with key leaders arrested and affiliates deregistered (Infante 1980: 110; Villegas 1988: 42).

In the early 1950s, the Philippine state came under increased external and internal pressures to alter significantly the legislative framework of industrial relations. The United States-sponsored Bell Report on the social and economic crisis facing the Philippines recommended the requirement of union registration be abolished. There was resistance on the part of the state, but with elections looming in 1953, the labour movement was sufficiently strong to see a compromise *Industrial Peace Act* passed where the Department of Labor retained the requirement of conditional registration, but the discretionary and investigatory powers were removed.

In the three years after the Act was passed, the number of registered unions grew more than one and a half times. As much as anything, Wurfel argues, this was due to a decline in the number of deregistrations, rather than the formation of new unions (Wurfel 1959: 593–7). Although the state had granted greater 'freedom' from political interference, other factors converged to limit labour organisation. Industrialisation had swelled the small urban working class, but did not ameliorate unemployment, and conditions in the labour market and 'the dull compulsion of economic relations' limited organisation, with an estimated 20 per cent of unions being dominated by management (Carroll 1961: 244–6).

Disputation

During the first years of the Commonwealth, the state moved to control labour militancy in agriculture and industry by setting up, in 1936, a Court of Industrial Relations, with extensive powers of compulsory arbitration in all disputes in the agricultural and industrial sectors involving 30 or more employees, including wage workers and tenants. A record number of strikes and lockouts two years earlier had shown how limited the powers of the state were under a Department of Labor administered voluntary conciliation and arbitration system (Wurfel 1959: 586; Infante 1980: 108–9). But the Court proved to be a laggard instrument of dispute resolution and control, and the Bell Report recommendation that compulsory arbitration be replaced by a system of enterprise-based collective bargaining received a degree of support within the labour movement. Although retained, the Court of Industrial Relations was made 'subordinate and supplemental to collective bargaining' (Infante 1980: 111).

A close study by Snyder and Nowak (1982: 48–53) found that, between 1953 and 1970, only a small number of unions (34 per cent) had a collective bargaining agreement (lasting 3 years) and only 12 per cent had more than one. Some 84 per cent of unions had no record of strike action and only 2.4 per cent struck more than once. The majority of collective bargaining agreements in this period provided only what was covered by labour legislation and many did not include all provisions. Further, strike action was most often a response to union harassment rather than a show of bargaining strength. With the introduction of enterprise-based bargaining, issues of union recognition and the harassment of union members were transferred from the state to the employers at a time of significant social and economic change. Within the framework of state legislation, circumstances in the labour market and the structural conditions of wage employment ensured the reproduction of class relations at the point of production.

Protective legislation

The post-colonial state has passed various pieces of legislation designed to palliate social conflict. In 1936, under a 'social justice programme', laws covering working hours, workers' compensation, a government insurance scheme and minimum wages were put in place (Carroll 1961: 234). In the postwar period, similar laws to regulate the employment of women and children, provide for termination pay and protect Sunday as a rest day were enacted. During the late 1930s, the state twice set a minimum wage for sectors of the workforce; however, it was not until 1951 that threats to class interests and state power persuaded the legislature to enact the minimum wage-setting policy for agricultural and industrial workers previously recommended by the Bell Report. But, as with laws covering the right to organise and collective bargaining, legislation protecting working conditions and wage setting were unevenly implemented and weakly enforced by state agencies (Villegas 1988: 42). The majority of workers were effectively excluded from protective legislation because they were not in regular wage employment or because they lacked the opportunities to organise for their industrial 'rights'. Nevertheless, wage setting became something of a political football, and subsequent adjustments often coincided with an election and were designed to placate the organised sections of the workforce (Ramos 1990: 137).

Despite the efforts of labour, by the early 1970s, twenty years of

industrial development and consolidation of capitalism in agriculture
had increased the concentration of power and wealth in Philippine
society and had done little for the working class. Despite an increase
in the productivity of labour, wages were kept permanently low by
labour surplus and enterprise bargaining at the same time as profits
grew under state protection. Between 1949 and 1960, real wages
fluctuated with increases in the minimum wage and inflation, but
declined over the long term (Carroll 1961: 249–50). In the following
decade, the proportion of families whose main income was derived
from wage labour rose some 20 per cent yet, in the same period,
the share of wages to total value added fell from 38.6 to 30 per
cent (Doronila 1986: 42). On the eve of martial law, real wages
were just below their level of twenty years earlier (Wurfel 1988:
54) and levels of industrial disputation were up (Snyder & Nowak
1982: 60).

Martial law

During the Marcos era, the intensification and centralisation of state
power saw the role of the state in the arena of industrial conflict
increased. With the declaration of martial law, a total strike ban was
declared. When subsequently amended to cover strikes in industries
considered 'vital' to national development, discretionary powers in
the definition of 'vital' ensured the powers of state intervention were
undiminished. These powers were also reflected in the area of
industrial disputation. With the setting up of the National Relations
Commission under the jurisdiction of the Department (later Ministry) of Labor, in place of the Court of Industrial Relations, compulsory arbitration was reintroduced as an adjunct to grievance
procedures and voluntary arbitration, and there was an important
shift from the judicial to the administrative arms of the state (Ramos
1990: 53).

In 1974, the new *Labor Code* put further technical and procedural
barriers in the way of strike action, including a compulsory 'cooling-off' period. With the partial lifting of martial law in 1981, the
right to strike was restored but the Labor Minister retained the
discretion to intervene in the 'national interest' and the use of
previously state-sanctioned force against striking workers was made
legal (Villegas 1988: 94).

Consistent with the argument that the introduction of authoritarian
rule was directed at removing political obstacles to export-oriented
industrialisation, a number of writers have asserted that state repression of organised labour under Marcos was principally in the interests of foreign investors and the international market (see Villegas

1988: 53–78). Harsh labour laws did not, however, differentiate between workers in firms of different nationality and often they were introduced in response to strike action in locally owned enterprises. As Bello, Kinley and Elinson (1982: 147) point out, it was 'against the workers of a home-market firm, La Tondena Distillery, that the regime decided to test its hard no-strike policy in 1975 by arresting 500 striking workers' (see also Infante 1980: 136–7).

During the 1980s, militancy in the labour movement took on new, extra-legal forms. Frustrations with the enterprise-based system of industrial bargaining saw various industry and region-based alliances of local unions organised in and around Manila. Although not registrable under the existing *Labor Code* and therefore lacking the legal status to negotiate and bargain, these alliances were able to intensify pressure on employers through collective action. In the mid-1980s, they contributed to a surge of strikes in Manila which added to the destabilisation of the Marcos regime. It is the case, however, that a good many of these strikes stemmed from economic collapse as much as from political protest. As the economic crisis deepened, the workforces of establishments facing closure had little to lose (or gain) from strike action. Most of the strikes were therefore unsuccessful as factories continued to close and violence against union officials and workers increased.

The state of the labour movement during the Marcos regime reflected the failures of economic development as much as it did political repression. A large section of the Philippine workforce simply remained unorganisable (Ofreneo 1989). To begin with, one half of the workforce was not in wage employment, most of the remainder being unpaid family workers or petty producers and traders in the informal economy. In agribusiness and industry, the prevalence of seasonal, temporary and casual forms of employment reduced the number of organisable wage workers. Moreover, labour surplus, reflected in high levels of unemployment and underemployment, reduced the bargaining power of unions. In spite of a significant restructuring of exports, there was little shift in sectoral employment during the Marcos era. The percentages of persons working in agriculture, industry and services remained virtually unchanged between 1971 and 1985 (Villegas 1988: 90). Over the same period, there was a 30 per cent increase in the number of wage workers (to just under 50 per cent of the workforce) and a comparable decline in the proportion of unpaid family workers (Ramos 1990: 26). Indications are, however, that this shift was largely confined to the agricultural sector and that much of this changed form of employment was seasonal or contractual in nature (Villegas 1988: 91).

Labour under Aquino

Under Aquino, the legislative framework of industrial relations remained essentially unchanged but, consistent with the 'pull back' of state powers, the regime has sought to return industrial disputation and wage-setting to 'market forces' at the enterprise level. Policy has been directed at the promotion of collective bargaining and voluntary arbitration is encouraged over compulsory arbitration, except in cases involving the national interest (NEDA 1986: 161). Initial decrees did extend rights of unionisation to public sector employees and eased the cooling-off requirement for strike action; however, more generally, Department of Labor and Employment policy and 1989 amendments to the *Labor Code* were directed at putting procedural and technical difficulties in the way of labour militancy.

During the Marcos era, adjustments to the legislated minimum wage did not become an instrument of policy, but remained a largely political exercise. As Limqueco, McFarlane and Odhnoff (1989: 150) put it, being 'the personification of the state, President Marcos also had to maintain some legitimacy with workers and his Presidential Decrees did give regular wage rises and cost of living adjustments to those working in the formal sector'. With a change of regime, the powers of wage setting were transferred from the executive to the legislature, and then out of the political arena to regional wage boards. Between 1987 and 1989, organised labour had successfully pressured the government into increases in the minimum wage. Lacking a base in the regime, radical sections of the labour movement had launched a series of general strikes to push for wage hikes and price controls. However, with the setting up of regional wage boards, the strategy of a general strike lost its political target.

Conclusion

Organised labour was an important force in the popular movement that brought Aquino to power in 1986. The class interests that finally consolidated behind the new regime did not, however, include those of labour. Thus, the powers of the state have not been directed at the reform of fundamental socio-economic structures. Notwithstanding movements in the legislated minimum wage, real incomes continue to sit below the poverty line and the harassment and dismissal of union officials and violations of labour standards continue to be the main causes of industrial disputation (Ramos 1990: 149). From a case study of state–labour relations in the colonial and post-colonial eras, continuities in the structural relationship between class interests and state power emerge. It is from this standpoint that change at the political level must be understood.

Notes

1 The author wishes to express her gratitude to Peter Limqueco for his assistance in completing this chapter. Not only did he make data and unpublished materials available, but his draft paper, listed below, was an important stimulus for the arguments in this chapter. The author also wishes to thank Michael Pinches for his generous assistance with sources, and the editors for their patience.

2 The World Bank estimates that only 53 per cent of potential income taxes and 65 per cent of potential corporate tax is collected by the state (Limqueco 1992). The Philippines continues to have the lowest tax to GDP ratio in Southeast Asia (*Far Eastern Economic Review* 13 June 1991).

3 When the Democratic Alliance, formed by the Communist Party of the Philippines (PKP) in 1945, had six of its members elected to the House of Representatives a year later, President Roxas and their opponents in Congress prevented them from taking their seats (Kerkvliet 1979: 150).

4 McCoy (1991: 122) describes how, on the island of Negros between June and September 1985, the opposition to Marcos created an unlikely, but brief, political alliance between planters, traditional politicians and the radical leadership of the National Federation of Sugar Workers.

5 For critical discussion of the patron–client relations in electoral processes under Aquino, see Kerkvliet and Mojares (1991).

6 The relationship between import-substitution interests and nationalism is complex. As Snow (1983: 22–5) points out, during the late 1950s and in the 1960s, most ISI industries were joint ventures, that is, not wholly Filipino owned. In the face of attempts to liberalise the economy, this group moved closer to the nationalist camp (Bello, Kinley & Elinson 1982: 131), but failed to make any real cross-class alliances (Doronila 1986).

References

Abueva, Jose V. 1988, 'Philippine Ideologies and National Development', in de Guzman & Reforma eds, 1988, pp. 18–73

Adriano, Lourdes S. 1992, 'Agrarian Reform in the Philippines: Past, Present and Future Prospects', Paper, Fourth International Philippine Studies Conference, Australian National University, Canberra

Anderson, Benedict 1988, 'Cacique Democracy in the Philippines: Origins and Dreams', *New Left Review*, no. 169, pp. 3–31

Bello, Walden & Gershman, John 1990, 'Democratization and Stabilization in the Philippines', *Critical Sociology* , vol. 17, no. 1, pp. 35–56

——, Kinley, David & Elinson, Elaine 1982, *Development Debacle: The World Bank in the Philippines*, Institute for Food and Development Policy, San Francisco

Boyce, James K. 1990, *The Political Economy of External Indebtedness: A Case Study of the Philippines*, Philippine Institute for Development Studies, Manila

Brilliantes, Alex B. 1992, 'Local Governments and NGOs in the Philippines', Paper, Fourth International Philippine Studies Conference, Australian National University, Canberra

Carroll, John J. 1961, 'Philippine Labor Unions', *Philippine Studies*, vol. 9, no. 2, pp. 220–54

Catilo, Aurora C. & Tapaples, Proserpina D. 1988, 'The Legislature', in de Guzman & Reforma eds, 1988

Crouch, Harold 1984, *Domestic Political Structures and Regional Development*, Institute of Southeast Asian Studies, Singapore

de Guzman, Raul P. 1988, 'Towards Redemocratization of the Political System', in de Guzman & Reforma eds, 1988

—— & Mila A. Reforma 1988, *Government and Politics of the Philippines*, Oxford University Press, Singapore

Doronila, Amando 1985, 'The Transformation of Patron–Client Relations and its Political Consequences in Postwar Philippines, *Journal of Southeast Asian Studies*, vol.16, pp. 99–116

—— 1986, 'Class Formation and Filipino Nationalism: 1950–1970' *Kasarinlan* , vol. 2, no. 2, pp. 39–52

Eviota, Elizabeth U. 1990, 'Class, State and Development in the Philippines, 1946–1989', unpublished paper

Hawes, Gary 1989, *The Philippine State and the Marcos Regime: The Politics of Export*, Cornell University Press, Ithaca

—— 1992, 'Marcos, His Cronies, and the Philippines' Failure to Develop', ed Ruth McVey, *Southeast Asian Capitalists*, Southeast Asia Program, Cornell University, New York, pp. 145–60

Hayami, Y., Quisumbing, M. & Adriano, L. 1990, *Toward An Alternative Land Reform Paradigm: A Philippine Perspective*, Ateneo de Manila University Press, Quezon City

Hutchcroft, Paul D. 1991, 'Oligarchs and Cronies in the Philippine State: The Politics of Patrimonial Plunder', *World Politics*, vol 43, pp. 414–50

Infante, Jaime 1980, *The Political, Economic, and Labor Climate in the Philippines*, Industrial Research Unit, University of Pennsylvania

Irwan, Alexander 1989, 'Business Patronage, Class Struggle, and the Manufacturing Sector in South Korea, Indonesia, and Thailand', *Journal of Contemporary Asia*, vol. 19, no. 4, pp. 398–433

Jayasuriya, S. K. 1987, The politics of economic policy in the Philippines during the Marcos era', *Southeast Asia in the 1980s: The Politics of Economic Crisis*, eds Richard Robison, Kevin Hewison & Richard Higgott, Allen & Unwin, Sydney

Kerkvliet, Benedict J. 1979, *The Huk Rebellion: A Study of Peasant Revolt in the Philippines*, New Day Publishers, Quezon City

—— & Mojares, Resil 1991, 'Themes in the Transition from Marcos to Aquino: An Introduction' in *From Marcos to Aquino: Local Perspectives on Political Transition in the Philippines*, eds. Benedict Kerkvliet & Resil Mojares, Ateneo de Manila University Press, Manila, pp. 1–12

Koike, Kenji 1989, 'The Reorganization of Zaibatsu Groups under the Marcos and Aquino Regimes', *East Asian Cultural Studies*, vol. 28, no. 1–4, pp. 127–43

Lane, Max R. 1990, *The Urban Mass Movement in the Philippines, 1983-87*, Department of Political and Social Change, Australian National University, Canberra

Lapitan, A. E. 1989 'The Re-Democratization of the Philippines: Old Wine in a New Bottle', *Asian Profile*, vol. 17, no. 3, pp. 235–42

Limqueco, Peter 1992, 'Crisis of the Philippine State', unpublished paper

——, McFarlane, Bruce & Odhnoff, Jan 1989, *Labour and Industry in ASEAN*, Journal of Contemporary Asia Publishers, Manila

Magno, Alexander R. 1988, 'The Filipino Left at the Crossroads: Current Debates on Strategy and Revolution', *Marxism in the Philippines*, ed Third World Studies Center, University of the Philippines, Manila

—— 1989, 'Is the Revolution Dead?' *Partisan Scholarship: Essays in Honour of Renato Constantino*, ed Peter Limqueco, Journal of Contemporary Asia Publishers, Manila, pp. 369–81

McCoy, Alfred W. 1987, 'After the Yellow Revolution: Filipino elite factions and the struggle for power', *The Philippines Under Aquino*, ed. Peter Krinks, Australian Development Studies Network, Canberra, pp. 9–33

—— 1991, 'The Restoration of Planter Power in La Carlota City', eds Benedict Kerkvliet & Resil Mojares, *From Marcos to Aquino: Local Perspectives on Political Transition in the Philippines*, Ateneo de Manila University Press, Manila, pp. 105–42

National Economic and Development Authority (NEDA) 1986, *Medium-Term Philippine Development Plan: 1987–92*, Manila

Nawawi, Mohd A. 1982, 'Political Participation during the First Five Years of the New Society in the Philippines', *Journal of Southeast Asian Studies*, vol. 13, No. 2, pp. 270–8

Nemenzo, Francisco 1989, 'The Withering Away of the Philippine State', Paper, Asian Studies Association of Australia Conference, Singapore, February

Nowak, Thomas C. & Snyder, Kay A. 1974, 'Clientelist Politics in the Philippines: Integration or Instability?', *The American Political Science Review*, vol. 68, pp. 1147–70

Ofreneo, Rene 1989, 'Labor Force and Labor Movement', *Philippine Currents*, July, pp. 15–8

Owen, Norman G. 1971, 'Philippine Economic Development and American Policy: A Reappraisal', *Compadre Colonialism: Studies on the Philippines under American Rule*, ed Norman G. Owen, Michigan Papers on South and Southeast Asia No. 3, University of Michigan, Ann Arbor, pp.103–28

Ramos, Elias T. 1990, *Dualistic Unionism and Industrial Relations*, New Day Publishers, Quezon City

Rosenberg, David A.1974, 'Remonitions of Martial Law', *Political Change in the Philippines: Studies of Local Politics Preceding Martial Law*, ed. Benedict J. Kerkvliet, University Press of Hawaii, Hawaii, pp. 242–58

Rothstein, Frances 1979, 'The Class Basis of Patron–Client Relations', *Latin American Perspectives*, vol. 6, no. 2, pp. 25–35

Snyder, Kay A. & Nowak, Thomas C. 1982, 'Philippine Labor Before Martial Law: Threat or Nonthreat?', *Studies in Comparative International Development*, vol. 17, no. 3–4, pp. 44–72

Stauffer, Robert 1979, 'The Political Economy of Refeudalization', *Marcos and Martial Law in the Philippines*, ed. David A. Rosenberg, Cornell University Press, Ithaca, pp. 180–218

Snow, Robert T. 1983, *The Bourgeois Opposition to Export-Orientated Industrialization in the Philippines*, Third World Center Papers no. 39, University of the Philippines, Quezon City

Villegas, Edberto M. 1988, *The Political Economy of Philippine Labor Laws*, Foundation for Nationalist Studies, Quezon City

Wolters, W. G. 1989, 'Rise and Fall of Provincial Elites in the Philippines: Nueva Ecija from the 1880s to the Present Day', *Sojourn*, vol. 4, no. 1, pp. 54–74

Wurfel, David 1959, 'Trade Union Development and Labor Relations Policy in the Philippines', *Industrial and Labor Relations Review*, vol. 12, no. 4, pp. 582–608

——— 1988, *Filipino Politics: Development and Decay*, Ateneo de Manila University Press, Quezon City

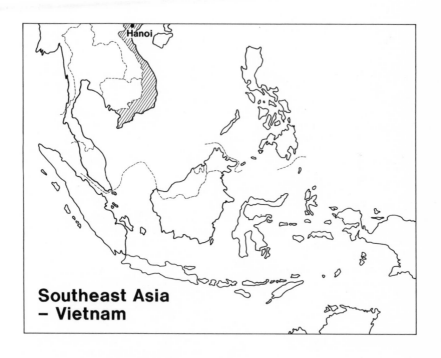

**Southeast Asia
– Vietnam**

Vietnam: Basic social and economic data

Population (1990)	67.2m
Population density (1990)	204 persons per sq. km
Average annual population growth (1979–89)	2.1%
Urban population (1989)	21.1%
Total labour force (1990 est)	32m
Major ethnic groups	Vietnamese, Chinese, various hill groups
Capital city	Hanoi
Population (1989)	1.1m
Land area	329 556 sq. km
Official language	Vietnamese
Other main languages	Various local dialects, French
Administrative division	43 provinces
Education, enrolments	
Primary (1990)	12m
Secondary (1990)	934 000
University (1990)	152 000
Adult literacy rate (1988)	90%
Health	
Life expectancy (1989)	66 yrs
Infant mortality/1000 (1989)	43
Persons/hospital bed (1989)	271
Persons/physician (1989)	963
Economy	
GNP at market prices (1989)	US$130m
Real GNP per capita (1989 est)	US$200
GDP growth rate (1989 est)	8.2%
Trade	
Exports, value (1989)	US$1.5 bn
Imports, value (1989)	US$3.1 bn
Main imports (1990)	Raw materials/food (including energy) 48.4%, Plant/capital equipment 33%
Main exports (1990)	Food & products 45%, Manufactures 37%, Metals/minerals 9%
Foreign debt (1988)	US$12.04m
Foreign reserves (1988)	US$14.6m
Energy consumption/capita (kg coal equiv. in 1989)	110
Communications	
Rail (1990)	2500 km
Road, paved (1990)	13 000 km
Religions	Buddhism, Confucianism, Christian

Sources: Far Eastern Economic Review Asia Yearbook 1991; The Far East and Australasia 1992 (Europa Publications); United Nations Economic and Social Commission for Asia and the Pacific *Newsletter; Key Indicators of Developing Asian and Pacific Countries 1991*, Asian Development Bank

9

The political economy of dismantling the 'bureaucratic centralism and subsidy system' in Vietnam

Melanie Beresford

The foundations of the present transformation of the Vietnamese political economy lie in the period during which North and South Vietnam followed divergent development paths; that is, between 1955 and 1975.[1] While in the Democratic Republic of Vietnam (DRV), construction of a socialist economy was pursued, implementation of these policies was hampered in the South by the exigencies of war and American occupation of the main urban centres. In the Mekong delta rice bowl, for example, land reforms carried out by the National Liberation Front (NLF) in the early 1960s were followed up, not by collectivisation, but by an extended period of market economy. Development of this market economy was boosted by rural redistribution of income brought about through the land reform and by the widespread availability of US-subsidised imported farm inputs and consumer goods. Mechanisation, though not as advanced as in some other capitalist Southeast Asian countries, was encouraged by rural labour shortages in some areas, while in others, the use of high-yielding varieties and associated chemical inputs became common. These things changed not only the rural economy and class structure, but ultimately defused the political pressures (for agrarian reform) which had given the Communists their major support base in the countryside.

By the end of the war, therefore, the vast majority of peasants in southern Vietnam probably had quite different aspirations from those that had inspired the struggle in the first place. In spite of widespread popular exhaustion from years of war, the corruption and venality of the Saigon regime ensured that this change of mood did not translate into wholesale desertions from the NLF cause before 1975. But with the achievement of that other great inspirational objective, national independence, the disjunction between altered peasant aspirations and unchanged Party policies came to the fore. The 'transformation of the South' under the new regime in fact

215

proceeded according to the model previously established for the DRV in the 1950s, although it was accompanied by passive resistance from both southern Party officials and peasants.[2] The attempt to collectivise southern agriculture in the late 1970s was a complete failure. Moreover, other measures taken to create a centrally planned economy in the South came unstuck as output and state grain procurement faltered. Coming on top of war along the western border with Cambodia, these developments threatened the political stability of the South in the late 1970s.

Irrespective of what was happening in the DRV then, the attempt to transform southern Vietnam, under conditions where the prevailing class structure and economic system called for a different set of policies, was a failure, and reform was necessary. Whether the stagnation also affecting the northern 'bureaucratic centralism and subsidy system' would in itself have led to the transformation of Vietnamese economic policy which has emerged since 1979 is difficult to say. But what is clear is that the refusal of the southerners to take that system to their hearts has been a crucial element in creating what is now the most reformed economy in the rapidly diminishing socialist world. I have argued in several earlier publications that it was essentially the entrenchment of a market economy and its associated bourgeois and petty bourgeois classes in the South that determined that the extension of the non-commodity, administratively planned economy of northern Vietnam was impossible in the reunified country (Beresford 1987; 1989). Moreover, the nature of southern society was important in determining the course of reforms once they were implemented. Whereas in the North the process has been difficult, hampered by resistance from bureaucrats and others who stand to lose power in the changes, it has proceeded much more smoothly in the South where most of the renewed economic growth has been generated.

These economic reforms have in turn created new social conditions. An underlying theme of this chapter is that changes in the political system are taking place in response to these transformations of the socio-economic system. New social classes are slowly emerging as a result of the economic reforms, as well as new concentrations of economic power within the existing social groups, and these changes are linked to shifts in the locus of political power. This can be illustrated by giving a brief outline of the manner in which the traditional 'socialist' system operated and showing how the economic changes of the 1980s have increasingly destroyed traditional bases of power.

The system that evolved in northern Vietnam between 1954 and 1975 was one in which there was a highly egalitarian distribution of private and social income, but a very unequal distribution of economic and political power. The political system was dominated by the Communist Party which, through the strategic location of its cadres throughout the state apparatus, also maintained control over the allocation of economic resources. Under what has now been dubbed the 'bureaucratic centralism and subsidy system', the lower echelons only had to follow orders from above.[3] Basically it encouraged a vertical, rather than horizontal, integration of society in which semi-autarchic production units, districts and regions were subjected to demands for resources (taxes, compulsory sales quotas) from higher levels and received in return an administratively determined quantity of necessary inputs, consumer goods, investment funds, etc. At each level of the hierarchy, control over collection and distribution of these resources was political. Of course, the system never functioned quite like this. It contained a lot of contradictory incentives, so that the lower levels often concealed their real activities or simply avoided work in order to minimise transfer of resources to higher levels, at the same time attempting to garner more resources from the levels below them. Nevertheless, a large bureaucracy evolved which, because of the real power conferred on it, had a vested interest in maintenance of the system.

Economic reform was introduced for two basic reasons. First, the attempt to extract resources from a largely agricultural economy to promote rapid industrialisation ran into physical limitations as farm productivity stagnated. Conflicts between peasants and the bureaucracy sharpened as the former increasingly avoided the official collective and state-run economy. Meanwhile the difficulty in obtaining agricultural surpluses led to shortages of food in the cities so that urban workers also became disaffected and productivity in industry fell. Second, the industrialisation programme, the very *raison d'etre* of the Communist regime, itself was in jeopardy. Reform, or the shift towards a market economy, was thus a process that began from below and, when it was seen to produce results, was encouraged from above as well.

The substantial transformation of the economic system which has taken place since the early 1980s has begun the processes of horizontal integration and breaking down of vertical political control over resource allocation. Inequalities of income are becoming more marked and, in the longer run, this will also lead to concentrations of economic power outside the Party and bureaucracy. As will be seen in the following sections, the social structure of Vietnam is becoming more diversified with new classes, new interest groups and new coalitions emerging.

Naturally, the changes have encountered resistance from those who derived benefits from the previous system, but, as I argued above, there are some features of the Vietnamese political economy that have weakened this resistance. One such feature has been the inability to entrench the 'bureaucratic centralism' system in the South. Ultimately, however, the reason lies in the fact that through five decades of war and crisis, the Vietnamese state had neither the opportunity nor the desire to set itself in opposition to the population. Instead the Communist Party regime relied on popular mobilisation to achieve its goal of national independence. To sustain popular support it needed a decentralised mode of operation and to maintain flexibility and responsiveness to pressure from below (Beresford 1988). While the high level of legitimacy earned by the Party during its decades of independence struggle has given it a certain amount of freedom to pursue its traditional goals, it cannot afford to ignore the demands for change and for democratisation coming from different sectors of society in the longer run.

The task of this chapter is to outline the main changes to the Vietnamese political economy brought about by economic reform and to suggest some directions that the political system is likely to take as a result. It will do this under four headings dealing first with agrarian reforms, second with the renewed growth of a capitalist sector and, third with the changes in the state sector. The final section looks at the implications for the political sphere of these changes.

Agrarian reform

The main achievement of the first phase of reform of the agricultural sector, from 1979 to 1983, was to establish, in the collective sector, a product contract system (*khoan san pham*). Individual households were allocated portions of the collectively owned land and took on responsibility for most of the labour-intensive parts of the production process (transplanting, cultivation, harvesting) on their portion. Cooperatives retained responsibility for ploughing (where mechanised), irrigation services and input supplies. These supplies and services were exchanged for contracted outputs at an exchange rate fixed by the state. Any surpluses over consumption and contract requirements could be disposed of by the households either at prices negotiated with the state or on the free market. The new system replaced work-point allocation and compulsory quota deliveries. It was designed, *inter alia*, to ensure a better match between state-supplied inputs (notoriously scarce) and deliveries to the state which had earlier provoked frequent complaints that cooperative rice farming was highly unprofitable (White 1985: 104). The reforms were partly a response to widespread peasant dissatisfaction, partly due

to recognition by Party leaders that agricultural stagnation constituted a major bottleneck for economic growth.

Khoan san pham did have a positive impact on state grain procurement as well as increasing output (Beresford 1989: 118). If the
extraction of a marketed surplus from agriculture is one of the key
aims of a socialist regime, then it is worth stressing that the
devolution of production responsibilities was more successful in this
respect than the compulsory delivery system. But continuing shortages of consumer goods and farm inputs which peasants could
exchange with their output ensured the growth would not last. This
was particularly true of the North. Moreover, the initial success of
reforms led Party leaders in 1983 to renew the drive towards
complete collectivisation of the South, to impose heavy taxes on
the private sector and towards a disastrous currency reform in
October 1985. These moves appear to have been prompted by fears
of renewed class divisions and were designed to eliminate private
accumulations of wealth. But, perhaps because they shattered newly
earned confidence in the government's commitment to raising living
standards, they caused renewed popular discontent and a further
crisis of the economy instead.

A second phase of reform began after the December 1986 Sixth
Party Congress. This phase has been characterised by adjustments
to the product contract system as well as more thoroughgoing
reforms affecting industrial management and the wider macro-econ-
omy. In agriculture, the goal of rapid collectivisation was once again
abandoned in favour of a prolonged period in which different
institutional forms would coexist. Although most of the South had
been formally collectivised by the end of 1985, the operational
effectiveness of these collectives and cooperatives was very limited
(Beresford 1989: 121). In practice, the household sector continued
to provide peasants' main source of income.

During the first half of 1988, the responsibility of households in
the collective sector was strengthened further by the Politburo's
Resolution 10. Allocations of land under the contract system were
extended to 15 years or more and were made inheritable in a move
to encourage investment in land improvements. Farmer contractors
are now given responsibility for the entire production process,
instead of only the more labour-intensive ones. They can obtain
inputs and services from the cooperative or the private sector, and
exchange or hire seasonal labour on a negotiated basis. Cooperatives
are permitted to retain ownership only of those means of production
necessary to ensure all members have access to them: the rest must
be sold to households. All prices of inputs, services and outputs
supplied by and to the cooperative are 'negotiated' (that is, market)
prices (Council of Ministers 1988: 21–5).

More prosperous farmers are favoured by the new regulations. Those who produce the greatest marketed surplus are to be allocated additional land. Tradespeople and cadres, on the other hand, are urged to give up farming.

However, the resulting social differentiation is causing some problems. For example, in 1988, shortly after implementation of the Resolution, serious disputes over land distribution broke out in the Mekong delta. Farmers demonstrated in Ho Chi Minh City over abuses by cadres who had allocated themselves the lion's share of land under the new rules and, in one case, destroyed collectively built irrigation systems (Le Manh Tuan 1988: 28). Intervention by no less than the Party Secretariat was needed to resolve the problem. Some anecdotal evidence has also emerged of the existence of illegal markets in land, enabling those with access to capital (often provincial and district cadres) to acquire effective ownership of large holdings. At the same time, increased distribution to farmers and correspondingly reduced collective funds have led to 'worries about the implementation of welfare policies. . . [while] cultural and social activities are greatly affected' (*Vietnam Courier* no. 2, 1989). There is clearly a potential for dissatisfaction with the new system from peasants who have become used to having a welfare net within the cooperative structure.

Offsetting these worries about the new system, however, are the results of a sociological survey carried out during 1989 of 6457 rural households in five regions of the country. These showed a widely held perception of improvement in standards of living during the 1980s (*Vietnam Courier* 20 June 1991).

As a result of the inbuilt disincentives of collective production, North Vietnamese agriculture had long been characterised by widespread diversion of peasants' labour into the 'five per cent plots' which each household received from the cooperative for its own use. These were far more productive than the collective fields owing to the direct relationship between labour expended and income derived. There was also a lot of illegal 'lending' of cooperative land and other assets to households, a system that often allowed Party and management cadres to favour themselves, their families and other clients (Fforde 1982: 130–4, 189). Thus the product contract system was an attempt to head off this *de facto* reversion to private property in land by linking remuneration from *collective* land more closely to productivity.

In the early stage of the reform, the government also sought to retain cooperative ownership over modern means of production and the use of the production team system. However, farmers continued to suffer from delayed and inadequate provision of machinery and inputs, while conflicts of interest also arose between householders and collective management over priorities in the allocation of collective services, opening the way to corruption.

The latest phase of reform has therefore seen the sale of most collective assets. Although the collective's property rights over land are protected, the outcome of these changes will be a dramatic weakening of the cooperative's role in agricultural production (already apparent in the South) as it becomes more of a 'safety net', providing minimum subsistence requirements of peasants unable to find employment elsewhere (in an economy with about 20 per cent unemployment).[4] The *economic* role of the cooperatives may be more confined to establishment of local industries, provision of credit, storage, processing, transport, marketing and extension services to farmers (although this in turn will depend on the cooperatives' ability to compete with other providers of these services).

As of 1987, just before the passage of Resolution 10, 88 per cent of rural households in the southern provinces and 97 per cent of those in the North were formally incorporated into cooperatives (Tong Cuc Thong Ke 1989: 138–9). Many of the cooperative structures in the South may not have survived, but for most of the country it would seem that what has emerged is a system of essentially private production enterprises (petty bourgeois farmers), dependent for their survival on access to collectively owned land and also to some extent cushioned against adversity by membership of the cooperative. It is conceivable that, as in China, cooperatives could become centres of rural capital accumulation if their business activities are able to thrive.

The private sector

Two changes have led to a big increase in the size of the private sector outside agriculture: the passage of a new foreign investment law in December 1987, and new regulations on ownership announced early the following year. Six types of ownership are now recognised,[5] and a deliberate policy has been enunciated of creating a mixed economy in which a renovated state sector would still play the leading role. The six types are state, joint state–private, collective, private, individual and domestic economy. The definition of some of these sectors has changed compared with the pre-reform years: for example, joint state–private enterprises may now have a majority private shareholding and be treated in the same way as other private enterprises; under the previous rules, they were effectively state-controlled. Private (capitalist) enterprise is now clearly distinguished from individual (family and other small) enterprises, a reflection of the new regulations removing limits on the size of private capital investments and employment of wage labour. The passage of the new Foreign Investment Law also clearly encouraged private investment. The new category of 'domestic' economy encompasses those individuals employed in other sectors who take on subsidiary income-earning occupations, usually in the informal sector.

Since the new laws were introduced, at least some of the growth in the capitalist sector has come from re-privatisation of enterprises nationalised in the late 1970s (*Indochina Dossier* 20 September 1991). After two years of operation, however, the growth of capitalism remained restricted. Employment in capitalist enterprises amounted to only 0.8 per cent of industrial employment, compared with 37.2 per cent in the individual, 31 per cent in the cooperative and 31 per cent in the state sector (Tong Cuc Thong Ke 1991: 58, 66). A major expansion of the individual and 'domestic' sectors— evident everywhere in the streets—has taken place in retail trade and the provision of services.

It should be stressed that in southern Vietnam, the state and collective sectors had never achieved a dominant position prior to the reforms. In 1980, after the termination of the push towards socialisation of the late 1970s, about half of the industrial employment in Ho Chi Minh City was still in the private and 'semi-private' sectors (97 per cent of all units) (Ho Duc Hung 1984: 33–4). Semi-private refers to those enterprises that had achieved a low level of collectivisation but were effectively operating as private enterprises. By the end of the second campaign, formal socialisation had increased, although officials admitted the high levels were not reflected in practice (Beresford 1989: 110).

Differences between the North and South are still marked. During 1987, for example, over 40 per cent of southern industrial workers were employed in the individual sector, compared with 18 per cent in the North. One-third of northern workers were in the state sector compared with a quarter in the South (Tong Cuc Thong Ke 1989, pp. 187-8). In southern Vietnam in 1988, 50 per cent of industrial output was produced in the non-state sector (including collective) compared with 31.9 per cent in the North (Tong Cuc Thong Ke 1991: 36–7). The South has 42 per cent of all industrial workers, but produces 60 per cent of total industrial output.

It is widely accepted that the new Foreign Investment Law is no more 'nationalist' in tone than the foreign investment laws of its capitalist ASEAN neighbours (Vo Nhan Tri 1990: 218). The law allows up to 100 per cent ownership by the foreign investor (compared with 49 per cent under the 1977 law), remittance of profits and other income accruing and repatriation of capital upon sale or dissolution (subject to a small tax). Company tax rates are low (15–25 per cent) with generous provisions for tax holidays (BBC SWB FE/0820, 19 July 1990: B/2) and carry-over of losses for tax purposes. Incentives for firms to reinvest profits are contained in a provision for tax exemption on the portion reinvested. Conditions set out in the law are that imports should be covered by export earnings. Firms must also provide social insurance for their workers and set wages in accordance with 'collective labour agreements', subject to a minimum set by the Ministry of Labour.[6] The exact procedures involved in reaching these agreements were not clear at the time of writing. Many other conditions are specifically left open to negotiation with individual investors (Government of Vietnam 1987).

As in China, when it first opened up to foreign investment, many firms have reportedly been able to ignore the Foreign Investment Law altogether, negotiating their own deal with the government (*Bangkok Post* 8 October 1988; *Far Eastern Economic Review [FEER]* 5 September 1991). Since 1990 the law has been opened up to allow joint ventures between foreigners and private Vietnamese companies as well as the previously eligible state companies (*Asian Wall Street Journal [AWSJ]* 18 July 1990). The idea here is to encourage overseas Vietnamese to inject capital into joint ventures with family members or former associates who have remained in the country and has already been quite successful in attracting Taiwanese investors who have contacts among the ethnic Chinese in Cholon.

Industrial development remains uppermost in the aims of the government in seeking foreign investment. The objective is to acquire Western technology for the development of light industries, chiefly consumer goods for the domestic market and export products, using domestically produced raw materials. Foreign investment policy specifically discourages the sort of investment that took place, albeit in a very limited way, under the US-backed southern regime, in which production for the domestic market was based on remarkably high imported content of raw materials and equipment (Beresford 1989: 70).[7] It is not intended that foreigners should invest mainly in development of primary resources for export.

Nevertheless, considerable foreign investment in primary resource development has taken place, especially in oil exploration and production which remained a priority area for investment during the 1986–90 plan period. It is largely as a result of this investment that the South's share of foreign investment during the first 18 months of operation of the new foreign investment law was 80 per cent (BBC SWB FE/W0086, 19 July 1989: A/8). Approval has also reportedly been given for foreign investment in another priority area, rice production in the Mekong delta, which is a truly remarkable development considering the importance of the Communist Party's land reform programme in sustaining revolutionary momentum during the years of war (FBIS–EAS–90–203, 19 October 1990: 81). Tourism is the other major investment area (BBC SWB FE/W0161, 9 January 1991: A/15). However, by mid-1991 manufacturing had begun to take off and accounted for a fifth of licensed investments (*AWSJ* 19–20 July 1991).

During 1990 construction was begun on Vietnam's first Export Processing Zone near Ho Chi Minh City. The zone is intended to attract foreign investment and joint ventures in light, pollution-free industries. Interest in the zone has mainly come from East Asian NICs (FBIS–EAS–90–211, 31 October 1990: 69).

By mid-1991, approved foreign investment amounted to some US$2.1 billion, although the realised amount was only a third of this (BBC SWB FE/W0161, 9 January 1991: A/15; *FEER* 1 August 1991). Vietnam's investment climate is a difficult one. The country remains one of the poorest in the world, with an estimated GNP per capita of US$210 in 1989 (*AWSJ* 29 November 1990), and its infrastructure, though improving, is in a poor state. It is not a highly attractive location for foreign investors in spite of its cheap, relatively skilled labour force.

Comparing Vietnam with China, it is possible to observe that, where overseas Chinese have been a major source of capital inflow ahead of much tardier Westerners and provided a major boost to the economic growth of China's coastal regions, there has been no directly comparable response from overseas Vietnamese. By mid-1991 the investment by overseas Vietnamese stood at a mere US$9.5 million (BBC SWB FE/W0184, 19 June 1991: A/13). However, the 960 000 overseas Chinese living in Vietnam have possibly played a more important role. Over a third of them live in the Ho Chi Minh City area where they dominated commercial life under the previous regime. While they have little capital of their own left after the various 'socialisation' measures of the late 1970s, they have numerous family and friends based in Taiwan or Hong Kong. These contacts can supply capital for joint ventures in which the Vietnam-based partner's primary role is to negotiate the local bureaucratic maze.

Like China a decade ago, Vietnam has been able to take advantage of the fact that it is resource rich, a potentially large market and, in a changing international political climate, foreign investors are anxious to have first foot in the door in a market that is beginning to open up. There has been a lot of talk about Vietnam as 'virgin territory' in Southeast Asia or, as a Japanese businessman described it, a 'mountain of treasures' (*AWSJ* 28–9 December 1990). This has helped increase investment which might otherwise have stayed away.

In some respects, the passage of the Foreign Investment Law has served less as an attraction to potential investors, than as a gesture of goodwill by the Vietnamese government towards the West. When Vietnam passed its first Law (in 1977) in an earlier attempt to open its doors to the West, it was largely ignored. Vietnam was then in a deepening economic crisis, while deteriorating relations with China and the US were pushing it closer to the Soviet Union. By 1988, on the other hand, its agricultural and industrial production had begun to recover, the impending withdrawal of troops from Cambodia had been announced, and the Cold War was ending.

Altogether, the progress of the private sector (capitalist and individual) has been quite rapid since 1987. Its share in output value rose from 16.9 per cent to 27.2 per cent in the two years to 1989 (Tong Cuc Thong Ke 1991: 31), offsetting the serious decline in collective and locally managed state enterprises whose subsidies were withdrawn. However, several factors continue to restrict its further expansion. For one thing the rate of inflation, though much moderated compared with 1988, remains high (about 70 per cent p.a.). This makes the business climate difficult for would-be private investors and encourages investment in non-productive assets. Second, the lack of significant accumulations of capital in the private sector slows the growth of this sector and forces most 'entrepreneurs' to exist in the low-productivity 'individual' sector. Third, there is still a lot of bureaucratic interference which means that private investors have to be very patient and persistent. Fourth, uncertainty about future political developments may encourage many private firms to remain small.

Ownership and control in the state sector

The reforms introduced in this sector have been designed to render enterprises financially autonomous. In industry, the former system of central planning via material balancing and 'commandism' is being replaced by a system in which all production, investment and marketing decisions are left up to the enterprise itself. Where, previously, enterprises were allocated inputs and equipment, lacked control over the sourcing (and therefore the quality) of these inputs, were given output targets and were required to sell their output to a specified customer (the state trading network), they are now expected to trade directly with suppliers, to seek tenders, to decide their own input and output mixes, to carry out market research and sign direct contracts with customers. Enterprises are also able to make their own investment decisions.[8] Instead of a series of compulsory financial targets combined with a legal obligation to deposit all revenue with the state bank, to rely on the state bank for allocations of working capital (allocations that were often delivered too late for the production schedule), enterprises may now have retained profits and cash holdings, use a wider range of institutions to obtain credit and have control over financial decisions. The only formal targets now set are contributions to the state budget (*Nhan Dan* 16 December 1987). These rules apply to all but a few 'key' industries such as those in the energy and transport sectors.

The functions of the State Planning Commission (SPC) are not completely eliminated, however. Instead plans have taken on a more indicative character, drawn up by enterprise managers in consultation with the SPC. The element of compulsion that remains is via the central government's use of 'economic levers' to achieve a macro-economic framework conducive to its goals for the structure and level of activity. These plans are also required to be discussed and ratified by the Workers' Congress, theoretically the highest authority within the enterprise. But within the framework of the enterprise plan, the manager has complete authority, which includes the right to hire and fire, and to determine wage rates subject to a government-imposed subsistence minimum calculated to provide a minimum of 2000 calories per day.

This is the framework being established for the management of state-owned enterprises in Vietnam. It is envisaged by the Party leadership that, while foreign investors and the private sector will be encouraged to expand and help create a mixed economy, the 'commanding heights'[9] will continue to be dominated by this reformed state sector. Thus 'society as a whole' (and the Party as society's leading element) will continue to determine the main direction of social and economic development. However, the changes raise some interesting questions concerning their implications for actual ownership and control of the means of production. It is often assumed by Western commentators, for example, that a capitalist economy is in the process of creation and that privatisation is a necessary concomitant of these market reforms.

On the surface this seems plausible. The state-owned enterprises in Vietnam are now in principle managed along very similar lines to those in a capitalist economy, notwithstanding the fact that this has, as yet, been only partially achieved and many managers and bureaucrats have resisted the change or are simply unable to adjust. Of course there are some obvious differences: the fact that the Workers' Congress fulfils a role analogous to the Board of Directors in a capitalist enterprise is one that may have implications for the way in which the new enterprise functions in practice.

The reforms have created a clear separation between legal ownership (vested in the State) and control (vested in the enterprise, partly in its Workers' Congress and partly in its manager). The extent to which the Workers' Congress will be able to function as a genuine locus of control is not yet clear. Yugoslav experience suggests that this will be variable at best. The manager, on the other hand, has clearly enhanced powers which are likely to be reflected in the pattern of what might be called 'effective ownership' in the future.

In the West there has been an extensive debate about the separation of ownership and control of private enterprises, notably around Galbraith's idea that the growing importance of the 'technostructure' whose interests would prevail over those of the increasingly inconsequential shareholders. Galbraith and others argued that the growing monopoly over technical knowledge by technicians and managers would ensure that 'effective ownership' passed into the hands of this group while the power of the legal owners would wither away (Galbraith 1969). In the course of this debate it became clear that the major shareholders do retain a crucial element of control over the corporation, even if the 'technostructure' is capable of developing independent. interests which may be expressed in medium-term growth plans. In other words, legal ownership of means of production under capitalism confers rights which, in a major conflict with the managerial group, will ensure that the interests of the owners will prevail (de Vroey 1974; Miliband 1968).

The case of state-owned enterprises in socialist Vietnam raises the possibility of a different interpretation of 'effective ownership', however. What we have already seen develop to some extent, and are likely to see more of in the future through restructuring of the financial system and establishment of a stock market, is the growth of state-owned conglomerates in which one part of the group *effectively* owns the others. Since early 1989 the existence of joint ventures, in which profits are distributed according to shares in the capital of enterprises, has been accorded legal recognition (Fforde 1990: 18). The Bank of Industry and Trade, established in Ho Chi Minh City during 1987, is the first example of such a shareholders' company being given approval. The major shareholders were a group of state-owned companies.

Such ownership seems unlikely to be very important as long as enterprises have not outgrown the stage when new investments can be financed from retained earnings. But large-scale investments usually require access to lines of credit or other outside infusions of capital, and it is here that a process of concentration and centralisation of control might make effective ownership a reality.

The financial system has already begun to be reformed in a way to facilitate this. Banks are offering interest rates designed to attract depositors and try to ensure an adequate return on the loan (*FEER* 26 October 1989; Wood 1990), although subsidies via cheap credit are still applied to many enterprises in the centrally managed state sector. The official reason given for not rigorously applying the new credit policy is the necessity to avoid further increases in unemployment (Interview, State Planning Commission official, 6 January 1992). However, the real employment effects are not so clear cut since state sector workers usually already have second jobs. Under the impact of further reforms to the financial system planned for 1992, capital will tend to flow to the most profitable sectors in the economy—in fact, the same competitive mechanism for equalising the rate of profit should operate as exists under capitalism.[10] Bankruptcy is allowed in Vietnam and has been occurring since 1989 in the sense that enterprises have simply ceased to operate (*FEER* 26 September 1991), although the planned legislation (International Monetary Fund 1990: 22), necessary to resolve the problems created by widespread indebtedness, is not in place at the time of writing. The threat of closure puts definite constraints on the behaviour of enterprises and, at the same time, leads to a process of concentration and centralisation of control over the capital stock in the hands of banks and other financial institutions. As in capitalist societies, however, the process is being accompanied by hardship for small investors, private and otherwise. Under the impact of high interest rates and an unregulated financial environment, a number of private credit institutions which had been engaged in borrowing short and lending long, crashed during April 1990, leading to a wider crisis of public confidence (*AWSJ* 10 May 1990).

We can expect similar developments to occur with the emergence of the stock market, announced in late 1990 (*Indochina Dossier* 17–26 November 1990). Since there are no very large private accumulations of capital in socialist countries, retained earnings of enterprises are likely to provide the main source of funds for the purchase of shares in other enterprises. The stock market is therefore likely to lead to considerable cross-ownership, with state-owned enterprises owning shares in other state-owned enterprises. This sort of development raises possibilities for the growth of large agglomerations of capital, with interlocking directorates, which are capable of exercising considerable influence over state economic policies.

Does this mean that introduction of a market system necessarily leads to privatisation? It seems fairly clear that privatisation is not a *precondition* for the introduction of markets: many state and collective enterprises are still capable of competing and producing efficiently. But if the logic of the market is followed through to the point where concentrations of productive capital arise which are so large that their interests cannot be ignored by government decision-makers, we may be able to speak of the *effective* privatisation of the means of production. It would seem fairly difficult to achieve democratic (that is, social) control over the economy when faced with such concentrations of economic power.[11] This would be particularly so if state-owned enterprises were permitted to establish overseas connections (for example, through foreign investment).

On the other hand, perhaps it is unrealistic to think of democratic control other than as constrained and limited by the actual development of the economy. In a market economy what may be achievable through democratic measures could be a regulated market which allows for the creation of welfare institutions, a more equitable distribution of social income, better protection of health and the environment than is apparent in the capitalist world. What Vietnam may be able to avoid is the creation of a culture in which it is accepted that accumulation of capital is brought about by the individual efforts and 'sacrifice' of the 'captains of industry', who therefore deserve to privatise the benefits. Where the major means of production are seen as private rather than social property, it is all too easy to argue that public intervention is unwarranted. Continuation of some state ownership seems to be an essential prerequisite, not only to avoid such a culture, but to maintain and legitimise public debate about the direction of economic and social development.

Certainly the degree of real social control over enterprises need not be less than existed under the previous system in Vietnam. Some Western critics have complained that the introduction of market reforms in Vietnam and elsewhere has led to the abandonment of social welfare programmes. What is abundantly clear, however, is that it is not the market reforms that are responsible, but the severe fiscal crisis of the Vietnamese state, brought about by the massive budget deficits required to maintain an inefficient public sector. Maintenance of health, education and welfare systems, the past achievements of which the Vietnamese are justifiably proud, will therefore be dependent upon continued reform of the state sector enterprises.

State and civil society

Whatever the intentions of the Vietnamese Communist Party leaders, it is clear that the economic reforms they began introducing in the late 1970s have achieved not only a momentum of their own, but some important transformations of the Vietnamese political economy. Probably the most significant of these derives from the attempt, only partially successful so far, to withdraw the Party from the day-to-day running of the society. This has involved not only a clearer distinction between Party and State, but the withdrawal of direct political authority (whether the Party or the State) from many areas of economic and social life.

An obstacle in the way of achieving this separation has been the way in which political authorities at provincial and local levels have been able to undermine reforms in such a way as to maintain the relative autarky of their districts, regions, enterprises or ministries. An illustration of this problem is provided by the numerous tax collection points—barriers to the free circulation of goods—which have been set up by local authorities. These were already recognised as a hindrance to the market economy of the South during the war, when efforts to blockade the RVN-controlled areas led to economic stagnation in the liberated zones due to their small market (Beresford 1989: 97–9). Orders were issued in the early seventies to lift these barriers to trade and, since 1979, several new orders have been issued to encourage direct trading within and between provinces. But the order against tax collection points was re-issued as recently as 1990 (BBC SWB, FE/0658 10 January 1990: B/4). Local authorities find them too attractive as a means to raise revenue and maintain control over resource allocation within their zone.

This type of local autonomy is a feature of the 'bureaucratic centralism and subsidy system'—its actual rather than its theoretical functioning. Fiscal autarky not only gives authorities an independent financial power in their region, but also protects local agriculture and industry from competition and sustains patterns of political and economic power. Moreover, local cadres and managers had to be quite resourceful under the administrative planning system in order to be able to obtain scarce resources and meet their targets. They became experts in hoarding materials, blackmarket trading, hiding production statistics and evading taxation demands from higher authorities (Fforde 1990: 18). Political control provided opportunities for private appropriation of resources, both illegally and through the 'perks' allowed to Party officials. The transition to a market economy enhances this, partly because more income is generated, enabling larger bribes, and partly because the opening up of previously illegal activities (hoarding of cash, free market operations) enables them to proceed on a larger scale.

While a primary goal of the reforms is to break this nexus between politics and production, it has not always been achieved. If the reform of state enterprises, is to succeed, for example, bankruptcy must be allowed. Otherwise there is no reason for enterprise managers to respond to the planners' economic signals. But in cases of state enterprises which cannot withstand the pressure of subsidy withdrawal and increasing competition from imported goods, no genuine bankruptcies have eventuated. In many cases, workers have been suspended or 'gone on holiday', but the enterprises, along with their management cadres, are still in existence. In October 1989 regulations providing for redundancy payments were promulgated, but the pace of layoffs under this scheme is limited by budgetary constraints (International Monetary Fund 1990: 22). In other cases, enterprises have continued to receive cheap loans from the State Bank which have enabled them to keep going. Late in 1990 this resulted in the introduction of some banking reforms, but genuine commercialisation of banking has yet to be achieved.

The struggle against this kind of political interference in economic decision-making is, therefore, by no means over. In the meantime, the existence of cadres with considerable control over resource allocation gives rise to the possibility that new bases of capital accumulation will be created. After all, the real basis for capital accumulation is not from the profits of petty commodity production by peasants and family firms, but from the concentration of large surpluses in the hands of those with control over major investment decisions. This need not be private accumulation, although in cases of corruption it often is. A danger, in my view, is that through the continuation of political control over resource allocation in the context of a highly decentralised economy, the material base for a sort of 'Balkanisation' can be created.

The operation of the state socialist economy has already created a number of semi-autarchic economic mini-'states' within the borders of a single nation (Vietnamese Communist Party 1991: 16).[12] A reflection of the strength of these can be seen in the case of the Party Secretary of Thanh Hoa province who, after having been exposed for corruption, was still promoted to the Central Committee and was able to shut up his critics for some time before a combination of central- and local-level reformers was able to break his stranglehold on the province. Given that the reforms threaten unemployment for both industrial workers and the large bureaucracies established under the old system, resistance to change has often been powerful. Instead, the local authorities have sought to protect themselves and their resource base by setting up barriers to competition from other provinces or from the private sector.

If the benefits of economic growth in the currently dynamic areas like Ho Chi Minh City are to flow through to the more backward parts of the country, the breakdown of local autarkies in which this type of capital accumulation is taking place seems essential (because it is a form of capital accumulation that reproduces the worst features of the old system). Otherwise the danger is that the southerners will end up doing business only with each other and with foreigners. The long-term potential for this type of development to lead to national division is well illustrated in the case of Yugoslavia where the Croats and Slovenes, with their more open economies, came to regard themselves as increasingly 'Western' compared with the more 'Eastern' Serbs (McFarlane 1988).

If, on the other hand, the reforms are successful in breaking the politics–production nexus, important implications for the Party's role in society emerge. The creation of a more diverse social base, as the economy grows and diversifies, inevitably leads to a diversity of political interests and seems likely to place strains on Vietnam's one-party system which are already reflected in calls by some intellectuals for a multi-party system. However, the Party has so far rejected the Eastern European pattern of creating a multi-party representative democracy. Party leaders are well aware of the potential of a 'technocratic' market-oriented approach to lead towards a new kind of dictatorship. In defending its political monopoly, the Party leadership at the Seventh Party Congress stated that 'if the party of the working class is deprived of its leadership role, power will no longer belong to the people and the social system will be subjected to change' (Nguyen Van Linh 1991: C1/5). This document expresses the sense that loosening the Party's grip on power would lead to the emergence of interest groups capable of pushing towards abandoning the mixed economy project altogether and establishing a full-fledged capitalist system in Vietnam. Apparently, the Vietnamese Communists consider that a one-party system can still adequately respond to the needs of a changing social base and maintain popular confidence.

Compared with Eastern Europe, they may have some justification for this view. As mentioned above, a feature of the VCP regime that has historically distinguished it from most other state socialist regimes has been its highly decentralised mode of operation and responsiveness to pressure from below. The degree of flexibility has varied, however. It emerges most vigorously during periods of national emergency (the majority of the past five decades) when the need for popular mobilisation for the achievement of common objectives has seen the Party rely heavily on the support of the masses. It has been less evident at times when 'socialist construction' has been high on the Party's agenda. The interests of important social groups may then be overridden.

Vietnamese leaders were perturbed by events in Eastern Europe and China in 1989 and some reacted in what can only be described as a panicky fashion. There was a spate of arrests of alleged 'CIA spies' and other 'reactionary forces of revenge within the country and from abroad', especially just prior to the April 1990 anniversary of the liberation of Saigon. However, a calmer response is also evident. Turley cites the speech by President Vo Chi Cong before the National Assembly in 1989, to the effect that Eastern European regimes had

> collapsed because they had adapted too slowly to the information explosion, growing popular political consciousness, and the scientific-technical explosion since the 1970s; they had violated the principles of 'socialist democracy', alienated the masses, and lost popular support; and they had clung too long to an outmoded economic model (Turley 1991: 8–9).

Vietnam, according to Cong, would not commit these errors. It is only the pace and scope of reform that is disputed, not the need for reform itself. As the Political Report of the Seventh Party Congress put it:

> Politics is an extremely complicated field of activities. Attempts to effect drastic political renovation without the necessary premises and without adequate steps will lead to political instability (Nguyen Van Linh 1991: C1/5).

The 'necessary premises' referred to are successful economic renovation, increased productive forces and availability of plentiful consumer goods.

A major aspect of the current phase of political reform has thus been the attempt to democratise the Party, to improve its responsiveness to social pressures and enhance popular confidence in it. This is seen in terms of applying democratic centralism which, 'on the one hand opposes arbitrariness and dictatorship, and on the other . . . anarchic liberalism' (Nguyen Van Linh 1991: C1/6). The way this will be achieved is not altogether clear. In general the Party has focused on improving the quality of personnel, especially through expulsions, campaigns of 'criticism and self-criticism' and attempts to recruit younger and more highly qualified personnel. The relationship between Party and the masses can then be strengthened via mobilisation of the mass organisations, the Vietnam Fatherland Front in particular, under the leadership of the renovated Party (Nguyen Van Linh 1991: C1/5–6). These campaigns have been less than efficacious in the past because they do not tackle the systemic problem, the built-in incentives to arbitrary use of power created by the politics–production nexus. However the methods employed do demonstrate that the Vietnamese are sticking to a traditional socialist notion of democracy, that is one of *popular mobilisation*, to achieve goals essentially set by the Party.

Conclusion

There seem to be a number of contradictory tendencies in operation. One is towards marketisation combined with corporatisation of the state and collective sectors and growth of the private sector and is promoted by the policies of the dominant group within the Communist Party. A goal of these policies is to break down the autarky of the old system and create a genuinely national market as well as to promote growth and efficiency which the old system could not. In other words, it is a tendency towards national economic integration. This tendency has clearly become stronger since the Sixth Party Congress in 1986 than it was before. But it is encountering resistance from a tendency to reproduce many of the worst aspects of the state socialist system. In the new decentralised economic environment, however, this does not simply reproduce the old system, but enhances centrifugal forces in the economic base.

Both of these tendencies have created new political constituencies. On the one hand, the success of economic reforms, most notably in the southern part of the country, has created pressure for their extension. Given the relative weakness of the state socialist system in the South anyway, the reforms would seem to have created a permanent and growing interest in the mixed economy. Pressure arising from this for a 'more pluralist political system' may in fact be pressure for political supremacy of new interest groups, the main beneficiaries of the market system. On the other hand, the persistence of the nexus between political office and control over economic resources, and the ability of local leaders to control larger quantities of resources in the new environment, have also created a conservative political constituency among those dependent on the old system.

In these circumstances, it is not possible (if it ever was) to speak of a monolithic Communist Party, since the Party is the arena in which these battles are still fought out. While this does raise the possibility of schism in the Party, the trend over the past decade has been towards more, not less, openness. The momentum of the reforms may already have carried Vietnamese society beyond the point where the political constituency of conservatism has diminished too far for it to be able to mount a sustainable reaction. However, the fading out of this debate, if it is not accompanied by continued stimulation of democratic practices, could lead to a new authoritarian culture of the market economy.

Notes

1 The historical and political traditions of Vietnam are discussed in detail in Beresford (1988).
2 Reflected in the sacking of Nguyen Van Linh from his post as head of the Party Committee in charge of Transformation of the South during 1978.

3 The nature of bureaucratic centralism in relation to party structure, leadership structures, and the relationship to government are discussed in Beresford (1988: Ch. 6).

4 However, given the fiscal crisis of the Vietnamese state and the Western aid embargo, some decline in public health and education is already evident.

5 These replace the earlier three types for the DRV (state, collective, individual) and five for the South (state, joint state–private, collective, private (capitalist) and individual).

6 At the end of August 1990 this was set at US$50 per month for a simple labourer in foreign enterprises (BBC SWB FE/W0145, 12 September 1990: A/8). However, it is likely to be reduced in 1992.

7 In 1970 South Vietnam's exports covered less than 2 per cent of the region's import bill (Beresford 1989: 79).

8 Many of these reforms were first enunciated in Truong Chinh's Political Report to the Sixth Party Congress in December 1986 (Truong Chinh 1986).

9 What is actually meant by 'commanding heights' seems to vary. For many influential policy advisers it means simply that the state will be involved only in those areas necessary to economic development (infrastructure, development of new industrial sectors) which the private sector is unwilling or unable to undertake.

10 That this is already happening in the transitional phase is confirmed by Fforde (1990: 18).

11 The problem of managerial independence has already given rise to some debate within the Party about how to achieve greater responsibility to the legal owner.

12 The Party's draft political report referred to this phenomenon as 'partition of the markets according to administrative boundaries'.

References

Beresford, Melanie 1987, 'Vietnam: Northernizing the South or Southernizing the North?', *Contemporary Southeast Asia*, vol. 8, no. 4, pp. 261–75

—— 1988, *Vietnam: Politics, Economics and Society*, Frances Pinter, London

—— 1989, *National Unification and Economic Development in Vietnam*, Macmillan, London

—— 1990, 'Vietnam: Collective Agriculture in Transition', *Journal of Contemporary Asia*, vol. 20, no. 4, pp. 466–86

—— 1992, 'Industrial Reform in Vietnam', *Industrial Reform in the Socialist States*, ed. Ian Jeffries, Edward Elgar, London

BBC SWB, *Summary of World Broadcasts, Far East*, British Broadcasting Corporation, London

Bui Huy Khoat 1991, 'The Dilemma of Market Reform in Socialist Countries', Institute of World Economy, unpublished manuscript, Hanoi

Council of Ministers 1988, 'Regulations on Reorganising and Revamping the

Management of Agricultural and Forestry Cooperatives and Production Collectives', translated in JPRS–SEA–89–010, 2 March 1989

de Vroey, Michel 1974, 'Separation of Ownership and Control in Large Corporations—the Marxist View', Institut des Sciences economiques, Universite Catholique de Louvain, Working Paper no. 7419, September

FBIS, United States, *Foreign Broadcast Information Service*, Washington

Fforde, Adam 1982, 'Problems of Agricultural Development North Vietnam', PhD thesis, University of Cambridge

—— 1990, 'Some reflections on Vietnam's experience with the successful commercialisation of a neo-Stalinist economic system', paper presented to Conference on *Doi Moi*: Economic Renovation in Vietnam, Australian National University, September

Galbraith, J.K. 1969, *The New Industrial State*, Penguin, Harmondsworth

Government of Vietnam 1987, 'Law on Foreign Investment', mimeo, Hanoi

Ho Duc Hung 1984, *Cong Nghiep Phuc Vu Nong Nghiep*, NXB TP Ho Chi Minh, Ho Chi Minh City

International Monetary Fund 1990, 'Viet Nam—Staff Report for the 1990 Article IV Consultation', International Monetary Fund, 24 September

Le Manh Tuan 1988, 'Positive Results in Achieving Openness and Democracy in Settlement of Land Disputes in Provinces of Western Nam Bo', *Quan Doi Nhan Dan*, 27 December, translated in JPRS–SEA–89–010, 2 March 1989

McFarlane, Bruce 1988, *Yugoslavia: Politics, Economics and Society*, Frances Pinter, London

Miliband, Ralph 1968, 'Professor Galbraith and American Capitalism', *The Socialist Register 1968*, eds R. Miliband & J. Saville, Merlin, London

Nguyen Van Linh 1991, 'Seventh Party Congress: Political Report' translated in BBC, SWB FE/1109, 27 June

Tong Cuc Thong Ke 1989, *Nien Giam Thong Ke 1987* (Statistical Yearbook 1987), Hanoi

—— 1991, *Nien Giam Thong Ke 1989* (Statistical Yearbook 1989), Hanoi

Truong Chinh 1986, 'CPV Congress Political Report', in BBC SWB, FE/8447, 20 December

Turley, William S. 1991, 'Political Renovation in Vietnam: adaptation vs preservation in a post-communist era', presented at the Southeast Asia/Indochina Seminar Series, under the auspices of the Fairbank Centre and Harvard Institute for International Development, Harvard University, 28 January

Vietnamese Communist Party 1991, 'The draft political report to be presented at the Seventh Party Congress', Hanoi Radio, 4–6 April 1991, translated in FBIS–EAS–91–080–S, 25 April, pp. 1–24

Vo Nhan Tri 1990, *Vietnam's Economic Policy Since 1975*, Institute of Southeast Asian Studies, Singapore

White, Christine 1985, 'Agricultural Planning, Pricing Policy and Co-operatives in Vietnam', *World Development*, vol. 13, no. 1, pp. 97–114

Wood, Adrian 1990, 'Deceleration of Inflation with Acceleration of Price Reform—Vietnam's Remarkable Recent Experience', *Cambridge Journal of Economics*, vol. 13, no. 4, pp. 563–71

Index

248

Sudomo, General 69
Sudradjat, General 50, 52, 53
Sukarno, President 41, 42–3
Sukhumbhand Paribatra 167
Sulak Sivaraska 176
Sulun, General Saiful 67
Sunthorn Kongsompong, General 164, 179
Suparra Limsong 167
Supomo 42
Surein Pitsuwan 183
Surin Maisikrod 167
Suthikiat Chirathivat 186n
Sutowo family 56
Sutrisno, General Try 50, 53, 54
Suwanna Satha-Anand 181
Swainson, Nicola 19

Taiwan 10, 34
Tanjung, Akbar 66
Tapaples, P.D. 196
Taubert, A. 57
Taufik, Iman 56
taxation 31, 61, 116, 118
Taylor, J.L. 186n
Taylor, John G. 12
technicians, Singapore 85
technocrats, Indonesian 62
television: Indonesia 57, 58; Malaysia 138
Thailand 2, 5, 7, 9, 10, 11, 14, 17, 18–19, 20, 23, Chapter 7; constitution, 1991 162, 185n; coups, military (1976) 162, 164, (1990) 164, (1991) 180, 164, 171, 180, 182; uprisings (1973) 164, 185n, (1992) 164, 177, 183–4; system of government 161ff; state and civil society 168ff; changes 168–9
Thambipillai, Pushpa 123
Thammasat University, Thailand 185
Thanin Kraivixien 162
Thanom Kittikachorn, General 163
Thompson, E.P. 27
Thynne, Ian 95
Toh Mun Heng 88
Tolleng, Rachman 67
Tong Cuc Thong Ke 221, 222, 225

Town Councils, Singapore 87–8, 105n
trade (exports/imports): Brunei 110, 114, 117; Indonesia 40; Malaysia 134, 140–1; Philippines 192; Singapore 76; Vietnam 214, 223, 235n
trade unions 81, 86, 147, 148, 150, 169, 173, 174, 185n, 198, 203–04, 205
transition to democratic forms 3, 13–14, 21–4
Transitions theory 3, 20–4, 29, 34
Trimberger, Ellen Kay 17, 30
Truong Chinh 235n
Turley, William S. 232–3
Turnbull, C.M. 80
Turner, Bryan 17
Turton, Andrew 168–9, 178–9

United Malays National Organisation (UMNO) 136, 137, 138, 139, 145, 146, 152, 153, 154, 155
United Nations 111
Uruguay 33

values, national, *see* cultural values; ideology
Ver, General 23
Vietnam Chapter 9; economic reforms 216–18; foreign investment 221–5; industrial development 223; land reforms 215, 224; private sector 221–5; provincial/local autonomy 230–2; state and civil society 229–33; state-owned enterprises 226–9
Vietnam Fatherland Front 233
Villegas, Edberto M. 197, 204, 205, 206–07, 207
Vo Chi Cong, President 232–3
Vo Nhan Tri 222
Vogel, Ezra 90

wages legislation, Philippines 205–06, 208
Wahid, Abdurahman 63, 66
Wahono, General 66
Wanandi, Jusuf 66
Ward, Ken 44

Recent books on Asia

Challenges of Economic Reform and Industrial Growth
Christopher Findlay (ed.)

Japanese Financial Markets and the Role of the Yen
Colin McKenzie and Michael Stutchbury (eds)

Understanding the Asian Manager
Hari Bedi

South Pacific Foreign Affairs Handbook
Steve Hoadley

Indonesia: Rise of Capital
Richard Robison

Barefoot in the Boardroom
Bill Purves

Southeast Asia
Milton Osborne